HERB & SPICE COMPANION

Quarto is the authority on a wide range of topics.

Quarto educates, entertains and enriches the lives of our readers—enthusiasts and lovers of hands-on living.

www.quartoknows.com

© 2015 Quarto Publishing Group USA Inc.

First published in the United States of America in 2015 by
Wellfleet Press, a member of
Quarto Publishing Group USA Inc.
142 West 36th Street, 4th Floor
New York, New York 10018
quartoknows.com
Visit our blogs at quartoknows.com

10 9 8 7 6 5 4 3 2 1

ISBN: 978-1-57715-114-2

Design and Page Layout: Ashley Prine, Tandem Books
Editor: Katherine Furman, Tandem Books
Cover Image: © Andrelix/Shutterstock; cover drawing © Ksenia Lokko/Shutterstock

Printed in China

HERB & SPICE COMPANION

COMPANION

The Complete Guide to
Over 100 Herbs & Spices

Lindsay Herman

WELLFLEET
PRESS

CONTENTS

AN INTRODUCTION

JUST A COUPLE OF DECADES AGO, THE WORLD OF HERBS AND SPICES WAS ONLY as varied as the typical supermarket shelf. How times and meals have changed! Thanks to a booming agriculture industry and wide-reaching international trade, it's now possible for tasty, exciting flavors from the other side of the globe to wind up on your dinner plate.

Specialty food stores and well-stocked supermarkets today offer herbs and spices from Latin America, Europe, the Middle East, and Asia, while farmers markets sell top-notch produce, sourced from around the world but grown on local farms. If your town doesn't have a fancy specialty store or farmers market, don't worry. Online garden centers, nurseries, and spice merchants have made it easier than ever to purchase exotic herbs and seeds grown anywhere from Argentina to Zanzibar.

Whether you're a newbie in the kitchen or an herb-growing pro, the sheer variety of flavors available can be exciting and a bit overwhelming. For culinary beginners, Western classics are a great place to start: basil, dill, garlic, oregano, parsley, rosemary, sage, and thyme. They are easy to find, and their complementary ingredients will be, too. They're also some of the easiest herbs to grow at home. Once you've gotten the swing of these staples, feel free to experiment with your cooking and add new flavors to the mix.

But before you run out and buy up all the seasonings in your grocery store, read through these introductory chapters for a primer on herbs and spices.

Herbs & Spices 101

Although it's easy to use the words "herb" and "spice" interchangeably, there's actually a major difference between the two.

Herbs are generally the leafy green foliage and tender stems of a plant, used either fresh or dried in cooking. Most herbs grow wild in temperate climates, where their growing cycles sync with the changing seasons. Spices, on the other hand, are almost exclusively native to the tropics and subtropics, and they come from various other plant parts, including the bark, berries, fruits, seeds, roots, and rhizomes. For example, allspice and peppercorns are technically berries, while cloves and capers are flower buds. Nutmeg is a seed; ginger is a rhizome; and cinnamon is made from tree bark. All spices are typically dried after they're harvested, and some require further processing in order to develop their signature flavors. There are also several plants that offer up both herb and spice: coriander (cilantro), dill, and fennel all produce edible leaves as well as seeds.

One interesting similarity between herbs and spices is their role in early medicine. Virtually all have been used as curatives at some point in history. In fact, before herbs and spices were widely used in the kitchen, they were prized for their medicinal and mystical powers in ancient Egypt, Greece, Rome, India, and China. Dating back to 1500 BC, the oldest known medicinal text, the *Ebers Papyrus*, contains more than 800 ancient Egyptian remedies featuring plants such as chamomile, cinnamon, coriander, cardamom, fennel, garlic, mint, sesame, sage, and thyme. Egyptians also used herbs for embalming, cosmetics, and perfumes.

Herbs and spices also held symbolic meaning in ancient cultures, and some have even carried through to the modern day. In Greece and Rome, for example, poets, athletes, and war heroes wore wreathed crowns of bay (laurel) leaves, a symbol of honor. Today, poet "laureates" are wordsmiths of the highest order, and a "baccalaureate" degree is offered to university students upon graduation.

While some herbs and spices are still used for their medicinal properties, this book covers only those with value in the kitchen. Luckily, most tasty seasonings grown from the earth also have great health benefits: They are natural digestive aids, and many offer antibacterial, antioxidant, and anti-inflammatory properties. They're also low in calories and high in vitamins and minerals, making these flavor boosters an all-around healthy addition to any meal.

How to Use This Book

Herb & Spice Companion is divided into an Herb Guide and a Spice Guide, together containing one hundred profiles of the world's most commonly used seasonings. Each guide is organized by availability in the marketplace: First up are the seasonings that are widely sold at well-stocked supermarkets, specialty markets like Whole Foods and Fairway, and local farmers markets. The more exotic seasonings come next. These will take a little exploring to get your hands on, but many can be found in ethnic markets or via online herb and spice merchants.

For those interested in starting an herb garden at home, each profile features growing instructions that detail the plants' basic needs, including light, water, and soil requirements. See the following chapter, Growing Herbs & Spices at Home, for more information. To learn how to store your seasonings for optimal freshness, flip to Drying, Freezing, and Storing Herbs & Spices on page 17. And finally, when you're ready to savor their flavors, each profile offers preparation tips and cooking suggestions.

GROWING HERBS & SPICES AT HOME

There is no question that herbs are at their best when picked fresh from the ground: They're at peak flavor and peak nutritional value. Unfortunately, some of the most delicious herbs and spices can be impossible to find fresh at your local supermarket. Their seeds, however, are likely available at nurseries, gardening centers, or via online shops, making it possible to grow fresh herbs from anywhere in the world right in your home. It's a worthwhile investment: You'll cut the cost of herbs from your shopping lists, and when it's time to whip up a meal, you've already got the freshest seasonings on hand. Growing your own herbs and spices also opens up a world of culinary options, thanks to the incredible variety of flavor combinations on offer, from fresh lavender to cinnamon basil to pineapple sage to chocolate mint.

Worried about your lack of garden space? No problem. Herbs are some of the simplest plants to grow in tight quarters. Most common herbs can thrive in small containers indoors, as long as they're stationed in a sunny window and treated to an adequate water supply and great drainage. Plus, you'll get the added pleasure of fresh herbal aromas filling your home all day long.

The following are easy to find at local nurseries or garden centers in the United States:

- Basil
- Chives
- Cilantro
- Dill
- Fennel
- Mint
- Oregano
- Marjoram
- Parsley
- Rosemary
- Sage
- Tarragon
- Thyme

Spices, on the other hand, *do* often require a bit more work than herbs. Because spices are generally made from other parts of the plant—the seeds, roots, or rhizomes, for example—they frequently need to be dried or processed before they're ready for the kitchen. Vanilla beans, for example, go through a complicated curing process in order to develop their flavor. Likewise, cinnamon is scraped from the bark of the cinnamon tree and rolled into tight quills, or "cinnamon sticks," as it dries, a labor-intensive process carried out by hand in Sri Lanka.

The most practical spices to grow at home are the seeds or berries of plants that also offer useful leafy greens. Cilantro, for instance, grows on the coriander plant, which produces flavorful coriander seeds at the end of its short lifespan. Snip the tasty leaves all through the summer, then harvest the seeds for their spice at the end of the season. Fennel, dill, and fenugreek are all easy-to-grow plants that serve double-duty as herb and spice.

Seeds and fresh plants from a nursery will come with detailed growing instructions, and you can check the individual profiles throughout this book for general growing tips.

Gardening 101

Herbs are generally low-maintenance plants with very few basic requirements: sunlight, air, soil, and water. Three general categories of plants are distinguished by their life cycles. Annuals live for one season, then flower, produce seeds, and die; common annuals in the herb garden are basil, fennel, coriander, and dill. Biennials grow back for a second season before they seed, while perennials like thyme and oregano live through several seasons or longer.

COMMON PLANTS BY LIFE CYCLE

ANNUALS	BIENNIALS	PERENNIALS
• Basil	• Angelica	• Bay Leaf
• Borage	• Caraway	• Chives
• Chervil	• Celery	• Fennel
• Cilantro	• Parsley	• Lavender
• Dill		• Lemon Balm
• German		• Lovage
Chamomile		• Oregano
• Marjoram		• Mint
• Nasturtium		• Roman Chamomile
• Summer Savory		• Rosemary
		• Sage
		• Salad Burnet
		• Sweet Woodruff
		• Tarragon

Annuals generally die off with the arrival of cooler weather. However, in temperate or cold climates, if you can provide warm conditions indoors, plants like basil and dill can spend the winter inside and continue producing leaves for longer. Pinch or snip off any flowers as they appear to prevent the plants from seeding and dying. Regular harvesting will help keep the plants thriving for a longer growing season.

Growing Essentials

Throughout this book, you'll see basic growing specifications for each plant. These include container size, sunlight, soil type, starting method (seeds, cuttings, or young plants), watering needs, harvest technique, and tips for general plant care. But the first step in starting an herb-and-spice garden is to know what plants need and whether you can accommodate them.

Climate Considerations

Many herbs will grow healthily in an outdoor garden, but know that climate is the determining factor of a plant's productivity. Climates vary widely around the world, so it's helpful to learn what the growing season entails in each plant's native region; these are the conditions it needs to thrive. Pay close attention to your plant's needs and arrange for similar conditions at home. Tarragon, for example, is native to temperate climates in Europe and Asia, and it isn't particularly tolerant of frost or extreme heat. When growing your own tarragon, make sure to protect the plant from frosts and super-hot temperatures. To do this, you can add mulch to the soil in winter to protect it from the cold; you can then provide shade for the plant on summer afternoons, when the sun is at its peak strength.

Timing is also crucial. Plant your herbs at the right time of year, and they'll offer up delicious flavor all season long. Herbs that love summer weather—such as basil, dill, and cilantro—should generally be planted in spring, after the last frost of the season. In hot climates, however, these herbs can be planted in fall to yield harvests throughout the winter.

Luckily, growing plants in containers makes gardening a little more flexible. Plants can live outdoors during their preferred seasons and then be moved indoors when the weather changes. This can lengthen a plant's life and lead to additional harvests well past its usual expiration date. The only hiccup: container gardening requires more attention on the part of the gardener.

Containers

Most herbs will grow in a variety of containers, including pots, barrels, window boxes, hanging baskets, and even repurposed household staples like colanders or tin cans. Containers not only allow you to grow plants indoors, but they also make it easy to give your plants the best hours of sunlight—a necessity for many herbs. If your scallions need six to eight hours of sunlight per day, you can move their pot from the kitchen windowsill to the patio to the driveway so they're in the sun all day.

The key factors to consider when choosing a container are size, material, and drainage.

Size: Know the expected full-grown size of each plant, along with the growing habit of its roots, and choose the appropriate container size. A too-small container might stifle large or sprawling roots, limiting the amount of moisture, nutrients, and air circulation needed for the plant to thrive. A too-large container calls for more soil, which will retain water for longer and possibly drown the roots, causing them to rot.

Material: Unglazed terra-cotta pots are the top choice for most herbs. Their porous walls encourage air circulation and allow moisture to evaporate freely, which is absolutely crucial for plants that need quick-draining soil or dry conditions.

Clay also offers protection from extreme and sudden temperature changes, and its sturdy, heavy build holds up against strong winds. Plastic containers, on the other hand, are lightweight and impermeable. They're more suited to plants that don't mind moisture lingering in the soil.

Drainage: A well-draining container is perhaps the most important necessity for growing healthy herbs. Drainage holes should be at the base of the container, and there should be enough of them so water can freely drain out the bottom. Not enough holes in the pot you love? Drill your own. Contrary to popular belief, adding a layer of gravel beneath the soil in a container does *not* improve drainage—in fact, it does the opposite. Water will collect in the soil and smother your roots. Instead, for optimal drainage, choose good-quality soil that drains readily and mix in compost or perlite for extra help.

Light

Most herbs require plenty of direct sunlight in order to thrive and develop the best fragrance and flavor. The absolute minimum is usually four hours per day. To maximize your herbs' sunbathing time, position them in the garden so they're facing south, east, or west; if indoors, choose a south-facing windowsill. Container-grown herbs are obviously easy to maneuver throughout the day in order to catch the optimal amount of light (or shade, depending on the plant). If your home gets too little sunlight for herbs, consider investing in artificial grow lights.

The general light requirements vary from full sun to partial shade to full shade.

Full sun = more than six hours
Partial shade = four to six hours
Full shade = four hours

Soil

Soil-testing kits are available at many nurseries, and these will help determine your soil's drainage abilities, pH levels, and mineral content—all important factors to consider when preparing soil for an herb garden. Herbs generally need soil that's moist (but not wet), freely draining, and rich with nutrients. Drainage is of utmost importance; roots should never sit in wet soil. Heavy soil, or clay, drains poorly and retains water around the plants' roots, which can cut off oxygen and lead to root rot. However, if the soil drains too *quickly*, the roots will dry out. This is the opposite end of the soil spectrum—sandy soil. The best soil for growing herbs is generally a mixture of clay and sand, called a *loam*; but of course, it depends on the specific plant's needs.

You can test your soil's drainage yourself by digging a hole twelve inches deep and filling it with water; watch how quickly the water drains. It should start draining within ten seconds. After a half hour, if there's still a hole filled with water, you've got drainage problems. If the water's completely drained in less time, your soil might not retain enough moisture to nourish the herbs.

Whether too heavy or too sandy, to improve drainage mix in an appropriate compost or other organic matter depending on the soil's needs. Sandy soils should be amended to improve water retention, while clay soils should be amended to increase porousness. Another way to improve drainage is to plant herbs in a raised bed or small hill in the garden.

One more benefit of container gardening is the use of potting soil rather than garden soil. Containers don't offer the natural drainage found in the garden, so potted plants need to be accommodated with a healthy water supply as well as extremely well-draining soil. Potting soil is specifically created to be the perfect medium for growing plants in containers, and there's no ground soil included. An ideal potting mix will be soft, light, and loose, so it drains freely while still nourishing the roots. It will include nutritious ingredients like bark, peat moss, lime, humus, compost, perlite, or vermiculite. Container-grown herbs will likely also need fertilizer; while garden herbs send their roots through the ground to collect nutrients and water, the roots of container herbs are confined behind walls. Check the requirements on your herb plants to know what fertilizers are best.

Starting from Seeds

The easiest way to start growing herbs at home is to purchase young plants from a nursery or garden center. You'll usually find great variety, including some spice plants, and you can sample them before you buy. But, of course, this can get costly. The more economical (and adventurous!) method is to start from seeds. Most seed packets sold at reliable garden centers will come with specific instructions for your chosen plant. These will cover light requirements, soil or potting mixes, and sowing tips.

It's often advised to sow seeds indoors up to three months before planting outside in the garden; this will allow the seeds time to germinate, or sprout into seedlings, and give your growing season a head start. Germination time is usually two to three weeks, but it can be different for every plant. For example, many plants (mostly perennials) experience a dormant season every year, usually during winter; they need this dormancy in order to complete their seasonal cycles and sprout new growth in spring. If your seeds are dormant, their outer coating is hard and impermeable until the dormancy ends.

In many cases, they'll need special treatment in order to break out and germinate. These treatments are called *stratification* and *scarification*. The stratification process simulates weather conditions that the seeds experience in their native climates. They'll remain dormant until this season runs its course; only then are they finally ready to sprout. Stratification usually involves creating a cold and moist environment to simulate a winter spent in the ground: for example, two to three months of chilling in the refrigerator in moistened sand, peat, or even a paper towel. (If stratifying can be done in the ground during the actual winter season, all the better!) This process softens the seeds' hard coating and readies them for germination.

Scarification involves scratching or sanding dormant seeds in order to penetrate their outer coating. Soaking seeds is another easy method for triggering germination; many seeds require soaking in water overnight before they're sown in soil.

Once seeds have successfully germinated, they can be sown in starter pots to encourage seedling development. These should contain a healthy potting mix and be treated to plenty of moisture and optimal temperatures for growth. Conditions will vary depending on the herb, so follow your seeds' instructions carefully. When the seedlings are thriving and healthy, they're ready to be transplanted to their permanent spot in the ground or in a designated container. Some seedlings grow deep roots that don't take kindly to transplanting; these should be transplanted sooner rather than later, before their roots fully develop. A good rule of thumb is to wait until two sets of leaves appear before transplanting. Make sure the last frost has passed and the garden soil is warm enough for your young plants.

Starting from Cuttings and Root Divisions

Some herbs can also be propagated using parts of already thriving plants: divided roots and stem cuttings. The divided-root method works best for perennials that grow in clumps, such as chives, mint, lemon balm, oregano, and tarragon. They should be several years old—from three to five years—and almost nearing the end of their life. Simply dig up a plant with a developed clump of roots (about eight inches big). Use a garden fork, shovel, or very sharp knife to split the roots into clumps of about two inches each. Plant them back in the ground or in a nutritious potting mix in containers.

To grow from cuttings, a branch is snipped from a healthy plant and then sown in soil or potting mix to develop its own roots. This method is ideal for shrubs and woody plants like sage, thyme, and rosemary. With garden shears or a sharp knife, cut a healthy, firm stem from just below a growth of leaves; the cutting should be between two and six inches long. Remove leaves from the lower third of the cutting, as this portion will be planted in sand or potting mix to begin developing roots. The plant might need rooting hormone to support this process, and it definitely needs plenty of water after the cutting is sown.

Watering

When garden plants don't get enough water, they'll send their roots deeper into the ground to find it. Container-grown plants don't have that opportunity, so a steady watering schedule is crucial. Keep in mind that warmer seasons will require more frequent watering than in wintertime. Know what your herbs need in terms of moisture and make sure your potting mix drains at a rate that's healthy for your particular plants. Some plants need their soil to be consistently moist (but never wet); others need the surface soil to dry out a bit between waterings; and still others need their soil to dry out completely before being watered again. Most herbs are somewhat tolerant of a little drought, but their needs vary depending on species, climate, humidity, and soil.

A great way to test whether your herbs need watering is by simply sticking your finger into the soil. If it feels dry down to two inches deep, it might be time to water. Follow instructions carefully. To ensure your container plants get enough hydration, water them until it starts leaking out of the drainage holes.

Harvesting Herbs

Herbs are harvested for their leaves either by hand, scissors, garden shears, or a sharp knife. The tool depends on the toughness of the stems and the method of harvesting. Basil leaves, for example, can be pinched off easily by hand, while fennel stalks and lavender stems should be cut with shears or a knife.

Many herbs can be harvested throughout the growing season, and this is a great way to encourage fuller fresh growth as the season wears on. Snip up to one-third of the plant's foliage or stems at a time, and regularly remove flowers to prevent the plant from going to seed.

Leaves usually reach their peak flavor just before the plant flowers, and this is a great time to collect a full herb harvest that can serve you in the kitchen throughout the winter. When you're collecting all foliage at the end of the season, cut down or dig up the whole plant. Annuals should be dug up, while perennials should be cut down and left in the ground to grow back healthily next season.

Harvesting Spices

Seed spices are harvested very differently: The plants are allowed to flower and develop seeds over the course of a full season. They're then collected carefully before they drop to the ground and start the growing cycle all over again. To collect seed heads (seedpods or flower heads), place a paper bag over the top of the stem and snip from the base, turning the bag upside down and making sure all seeds are contained.

Spices, however, come in many forms other than seeds, including rhizomes, bark, and berries. All are harvested in distinct ways: Rhizomes like ginger, for example, are dug up and either removed whole or separated into chunks, with some sections replanted and the rest harvested. Follow the specific instructions for each plant in your herb and spice garden.

DRYING, FREEZING, AND STORING HERBS & SPICES

Whether growing your own or buying them from a supermarket or spice shop, you should know how to store your herbs and spices to prolong their freshness and maximize their flavors in cooking.

Spices are generally dried immediately after they're harvested. The process can be complicated and sometimes requires special conditions for the best quality; commercial spice producers may use machinery or facilities that are designed for this purpose. The drying technique varies by spice, as rhizomes, fresh peppers, berries, and vanilla beans all have unique requirements to properly dry the spices and activate their crucial flavor compounds. Most fresh seeds, however, can be dried in the sun or hung from their stems in paper bags to dry naturally over the course of several weeks. This is especially easy for seeds like dill, coriander, and fennel. All spices should be stored in airtight containers and shielded from direct sunlight, preferably in a dark, dry cabinet.

Herbs, on the other hand, are enjoyed either fresh or dried, depending on their use in cooking. Luckily, the drying process for herbs is straightforward and relatively simple.

Fresh vs. Dried Herbs

Debating whether to use fresh herbs or dried? Fresh is often best, both in terms of flavor and nutritional value. But it's not the *only* option. Many long-cooked dishes call specifically for pungent dried herbs like oregano, rosemary, sage, and thyme. In these recipes, fresh herbs simply can't withstand the heat and lengthy cook times, and the dried herbs offer more robust flavors that permeate through the entire dish.

Additionally, dried herbs come in handy when you're short on fresh ingredients and need a substitute in a pinch. And they do the trick using much smaller quantities. In fact, dried herbs are especially useful in the winter months, when warm-weather herbs are no longer in season and at their most expensive.

In the end, though, choosing between fresh and dried herbs is mostly a matter of how often you'll use them. Do you love cooking Italian food? Opt for fresh basil, parsley, and oregano, since you'll get great use out of those herbs in your kitchen. If you only rarely use rosemary or dill, settle for the dried stuff: You'll have some on hand if you need it, but it won't be a costly (and wasteful) kitchen staple.

Here are some other general rules for choosing herbs in the kitchen.

When to Go Fresh

In a perfect world, where delicious fresh herbs are available for free in every home, the answer would be easy. But in reality, factors such as growing seasons, affordability, and marketplace accessibility can make the decision difficult.

There are some herbs, however, whose freshness is essential to any meal. Tender, moist herbs with delicate flavors—like basil, chervil, cilantro, and parsley—should be used fresh as often as possible. They lose their flavor and texture when dried (just as they will when overcooked), and will therefore be mostly useless. To get the most out of fresh herbs, especially when they're out of season and harder to come by, add them at the end of cooking or just before serving for optimal flavor.

Storing Fresh Herbs

As wonderful as fresh herbs can be, if you buy them cut from a grocery store or farmers market, you've got about two days until they start to wilt and lose their color. The most common storing method is to wrap herbs in a damp paper towel, place them in a zip-tight plastic bag, and stow them in the refrigerator door, the warmest part of the fridge.

While this will get you a few days of freshness, most herbs can do better than that. Try this easy method for keeping them fresh for up to two weeks. It's ideal for herbs with strong stems, like parsley, basil, mint, rosemary, and cilantro.

Trim the stems as you would with flowers.

Place the herbs in a jar or vase of cold water, making sure the leaves sit above the top of the vase.

Cover loosely with a plastic bag.

Keep basil at room temperature on the kitchen counter, and mint on the windowsill; store all other herbs in the refrigerator door.

Refresh the water every day or two, and trim off any decaying stems and leaves.

Freezing Fresh Herbs

Hoping to save your fresh herbs for future use? If they're not suitable for drying—like the tender herbs basil, chervil, parsley, and cilantro—you can freeze them! Freezing will keep them flavorful for up to four months. You can freeze them whole, chopped, or pureed, depending on freezer space and your preferred preparation in cooking.

- **Whole leaves**: Coat leaves with olive oil and freeze in a single layer on waxed paper in an airtight container.
- **Chopped or pureed:** Chop or puree herbs with a bit of olive oil or water, and store in ice-cube trays, plastic bags, or small containers. (This is ideal storage for a future pesto!).

When to Go Dried

Yes, many herbs lose their flavor when dried. But there *are* several that hold up well: bay leaves, oregano, rosemary, savory, sage, and thyme. These have thicker, sturdier leaves and stems than their tender, soft-leaf counterparts like basil and parsley.

During the drying process, the robust flavors in these herbs become concentrated

and more intense, so you'll get a stronger punch with smaller amounts than you'd get with fresh herbs. When swapping dried herbs in place of fresh, use only one-third the amount called for in the recipe. So, if the recipe says 1 tablespoon fresh thyme leaves, use 1 teaspoon dried thyme (3 teaspoons equals 1 tablespoon). Likewise, if using fresh herbs instead of dried, multiply the amount by three: 1 tablespoon dried oregano calls for a substitution of 3 tablespoons fresh.

Drying Fresh Herbs

Rather than paying for pricey dried herb packets at the supermarket, it's simple to dry herbs on your own. If you have an herb garden, harvest your herbs when they reach peak flavor and aroma—as the buds appear but before the flowers open. If you don't grow your own, stock up on fresh herbs when they're readily available at your local market.

Two effective methods are air-drying and oven-drying. Air-drying is ideal for herbs with lower moisture content, like oregano, rosemary, sage, and thyme. Tender, moist herbs like dill, basil, mint, and chives need a quicker drying method, or they're likely to grow mold. Heating in an oven or microwave is an option for quicker drying, but take care not to overheat or your herbs will lose their oils, colors, and flavors.

First, rinse herbs clean in cold water, if necessary, then pat dry with a paper towel and spread over towels to dry completely. Next, follow these easy steps, and your herbs will be dried within two to four hours (oven-drying) to a couple weeks (air-drying).

Air-dry:

1. Trim and discard any damaged or discolored leaves or stems.
2. Collect five to ten sprigs or branches per bundle, and tie the bouquets with a twist-tie or rubber band at the stems.
3. Hang bouquets upside down in a dark, warm, airy room. (Don't dry them outside, as sunlight and moisture in the air can diminish the herbs' color and flavor.) Hanging plants upside down will allow the oils to pool into the leaves, resulting in better flavors and brighter colors.
4. To test if your herbs are completely dried, after a week touch the leaves with your fingertips—they should feel brittle and crumble when you press or rub them in your hands.

Oven or Microwave:

1. If drying in the oven, preheat to 180°F.
2. Arrange the sprigs or individual leaves on a shallow baking sheet and heat for 2 to 4 hours with the door open.
3. If drying in the microwave, arrange leaves or sprigs in one layer between two sheets of dry paper towel.
4. Heat on high power for 1 to 2 minutes, and check for brittleness. If needed, heat for an additional 30 seconds and test again.

When your herbs are completely dried, pull the leaves from the stems and store in a sealed, airtight jar. Check your herbs regularly for a few days to make sure there's no remaining moisture. If you *do* notice any moisture, your herbs are at risk for mold. Follow the previous steps to dry them thoroughly again.

Note that dried herbs *do* lose their flavor and "expire" eventually, generally after eight months to a year. Some, like dried bay leaves, can last for up to two years. To test them, crumble a bit in your hand and take a whiff: If the color and aroma are still potent, they're good to use. If the aroma is a little weak, try using more than usual to get the flavor you like. If the aroma is very weak or nonexistent, toss them in the trash.

Or, nix the guessing game and simply refresh your dried herbs and spices every six months to a year. Your tasty meals will be well worth it!

HERB GUIDE

From common to exotic, robust to tender, this
section covers all the herbs you'll ever need.

COOKING WITH HERBS

Culinary herbs can be divided into two general categories that will help you determine how to cook them: robust herbs and tender herbs.

Herbs with robust, deep flavors—such as thyme, rosemary, curry leaves, garlic, and sage—will hold up well to heat. These herbs can cook for long periods of time and are often added at the beginning of a recipe, so the rich flavors have time to simmer and emanate thoroughly into a dish while cooking. Robust herbs are great for stews, soups, roasts, and dishes that are braised or grilled. Of course, if a slow-cooked dish needs more flavor after cooking, you can add chopped herbs to taste before serving (But use caution: a little goes a long way!).

At the other end of the spectrum are tender herbs, such as cilantro, basil, dill, parsley, and chives. The leaves and stems of tender herbs should be added at the end of cooking or just before serving, as they can't withstand much heat and will lose their flavor if cooked for too long. These herbs are delicious additions to fresh salads, soups, eggs, fish, vegetable dishes, and potatoes.

ROBUST HERBS		vs.	TENDER HERBS	
• Bay leaf	• Thyme		• Basil	• Horseradish
• Culantro	• Winter		• Catnip	• Marjoram
• Curry leaf	Savory		• Chervil	• Mint
• Lavender			• Chives	• Parsley
• Lemongrass			• Cilantro	• Scallions
• Myrtle			• Dill	• Summer
• Oregano			• Fennel	Savory
• Rosemary			• Fenugreek	• Tarragon
• Sage			• Garlic	• Watercress

Preparing Fresh Herbs

Herbs can be prepared in a variety of ways depending on their uses in a dish. There are several delicious herbs that require special preparations: garlic, horseradish, lemongrass, and wasabi. See their specific prep instructions to handle them properly for cooking.

The majority of herbs in this chapter are leafy greens and (sometimes) flowers. The first step is to wash and dry them thoroughly. Leafy herbs must be completely dry before chopping; even a little moisture can leave them soggy and mushy when they're cut with a knife. Use a salad spinner or shake them dry over the sink, then lay them out over paper towels to dry completely.

Then they're ready for prepping!

Removing Leaves from Stems

Whole sprigs are used to flavor soups, stews, marinades, and sauces; these are removed from dishes before serving because the stems are usually inedible. To prepare herbs that will be chopped and eaten, you must first separate the edible leafy parts from the tough stems. Methods vary by the type of herb: Some leaves can be plucked one by one, while others call for more efficient techniques. Use the following tips for quick and easy herb prep.

Large-leaf herbs: basil, mint, sage

Pluck leaves from their stems, and use them whole or tear them into pieces—no chopping necessary.

Herbs with woody stems: rosemary, thyme, tarragon, marjoram, oregano

Hold the top of the stem in one hand. Grasp it with the fingers of your opposite hand and slide them down the stem to knock off the leaves.

Herbs with delicate stems: dill, fennel

Dill and fennel leaves can be plucked upward from their thick stems, branch by branch.

Herbs with thick bottom stems: cilantro, parsley

Cilantro and parsley have thick bottom stems, but their slender branches are edible. Simply slice off the bottoms. Or, try this easy trick: Hold a bunch upside down by the stems, and shave downward with a knife to slice off the leaves and their delicate branches. (Cilantro and parsley stems can be used to flavor broths and sauces.)

Chopping and Crushing

When slicing or chopping herbs, use a sharp chef's knife with a broad blade. And, of course, you'll also need a cutting board. Here are the basic prep techniques for herbs.

Chop coarsely to cut herb pieces that are roughly ¼- to ½-inch big; they don't have to be uniform in size. Coarsely chopped herbs will retain their flavor for longer than those chopped finely.

- Collect the leaves into a pile.
- With the knife in your cutting hand, rest the tip on the cutting board and hold it in place with the fingers on your opposite hand.
- Slice through the pile of herbs using the back of the blade, rocking the knife back and forth along its cutting edge (rather than lifting the whole blade up and down).

Chop finely to immediately release as much of their flavorful oils as possible. Finely chopped herbs generally don't withstand much cooking, since their oils escape quickly and their flavors soon dissipate. Add to dishes immediately after chopping and just before serving.

- Chop herbs once (as above), then gather them into another tight pile and chop through them again.
- Repeat a third time—and a fourth— to get a finer chop.

Chiffonade are finely sliced leaves that are used as either garnish or seasoning.

- Remove thick stems or veins from the leaves, then stack several leaves on top of one another.
- Roll the stack of leaves tightly into a thin tube.
- Holding it in place with one hand, slice through the rolled leaves to create slender strips about ⅛- to 1/16-inch wide.

HERB BUTTER

This is a delicious and clever way to use herbs in an everyday condiment. Combine ½ to 1 cup of finely chopped herbs with 1 cup unsalted butter in a food processor. If you like, add up to 2 tablespoons of lemon juice for a touch of acidity, and blend. Store in an airtight container in the fridge. Any of the following herbs, or a combination of them, will make a delicious herb butter.

- Basil
- Chives
- Dill
- Garlic
- Lemon Verbena
- Oregano
- Parsley
- Rosemary
- Sage
- Tarragon
- Thyme

Crush herbs using a mortar and pestle to release their oils and soften them for sauces like pesto and aioli. Garlic is especially flavorful when crushed using a mortar and pestle.

- Place leaves in the mortar (or bowl) and pound them with the pestle. Their oils will gradually seep out during the pounding and create a paste.
- Add oil, vinegar, yogurt, or mayonnaise to make any variety of sauces, dips, dressings, or marinades.

FLAVOR CHEAT SHEET

Looking for a particular flavor? Use this list to find an herb that fits the bill.

- **Anise:** chervil, dill, fennel, tarragon, anise hyssop
- **Bitter:** chicory, fenugreek, hyssop, lovage, myrtle
- **Tart or Citrus:** bergamot, hottuynia cordata, lemon balm, lemon verbena, lemongrass, sorrel
- **Fresh:** borage, parsley, perilla, salad burnet
- **Minty:** catnip, mint, nepitella (or lesser calamint)
- **Onion:** chives, garlic, scallions
- **Pungent, earthy, or spicy:** arugula, cilantro, culantro, curry leaf, epazote, horseradish, marjoram, oregano, rau răm, rosemary, sage, savory, thyme, wasabi, watercress
- **Sweet:** angelica, basil, bay leaf, chamomile, elderflower, lavender, marigold, myrtle, pandan, rose, scented geranium, sweet cicely, woodruff

COMMON KITCHEN HERBS

These herbs are easy to find at the grocery store or farmers market, or they may already be in your kitchen.

ARUGULA

Eruca sativa

Flavors: peppery, nutty, increasingly bitter with age, with mustard

Also called rocket, roquette, rucola, and Italian cress, this tangy herb has been a staple in the Mediterranean diet since the ancient Romans, who also considered it an aphrodisiac. Due to its strong, peppery flavor, arugula was mostly ignored in the United States until the 1990s; but it's now a certifiable "It" food, used as an herb, a salad green, and a vegetable in its own right.

Arugula's robust flavor adds oomph to mixed green salads, spicing up mild greens like romaine, spinach, and butter lettuce. When cooked, arugula loses some of its pungent flavor and tastes more like a mild green. Add only at the end of cooking for optimal flavor.

HEALTH BENEFITS
Arugula is an ultra-nutritious cruciferous vegetable—a relative of cabbage, broccoli, cauliflower, horseradish, and mustard greens. Packed with vitamins A, C, E, and K, as well as minerals like calcium, iron, and potassium, it's also thought to play a role in cancer prevention.

In the Garden
Arugula is an annual that likes the cool weather of late spring and early fall. Leaves harvested at the height of summer will have a spicier bite, as the flavor gets stronger when the plants start to flower.
Size: 6 to 12 inches tall
Container: 6 inches
Light: Partial shade
Soil: Rich, fertile, well drained
Plant: Seeds or young plants

Water: Regularly, when soil feels dry to the touch

Harvest: Take the outermost leaves first, and the interior will generate new leaves throughout the season. Harvest frequently to promote new growth.

Care: If the sun gets strong and hot, provide arugula plants some shade, especially in the afternoon. Mix compost into the soil for added nutrients and to retain moisture.

SUBSTITUTIONS

- Baby spinach + pinch of pepper
- Dandelion greens
- Endive
- Escarole
- Radicchio
- Watercress

PAIRINGS

Fruits and Vegetables: avocado, beets, berries, citrus, corn, lettuces, mushrooms, onions, oranges, pears, potatoes, tomatoes

Proteins: beef, chicken, cheeses, eggs, fish and seafood, nuts, prosciutto, veal

Seasonings: balsamic vinegar, chervil, garlic, lemon juice, olive oil, parsley, pepper, red pepper flakes

Keep It Fresh

If purchased in a bunch with roots, wrap the roots in a damp paper towel, place in a plastic bag, and store in the refrigerator crisper. For just the leaves, layer in paper towels to keep them as dry as possible, place in a zip-tight plastic bag, and store in the crisper. Arugula should not be frozen or dried.

In the Kitchen

Dishes: Salads, sandwiches, soups, pastas, pizza, sauces

Prep: Use whole leaves in any dish you like.

Serve: Arugula offers a tangy counterpoint to big-flavored cheeses like Parmesan and Gorgonzola, to fresh fruit like oranges and pears, and to omelets and potato dishes. Sauté the leaves with garlic, or steam them, then serve alongside fish, poultry, or meat for an easy side dish.

BASIL

Ocimum basilicum

Flavors: sweet, spicy, and peppery, with hints of clove, anise, and mint

An ever-popular summertime herb, basil originated in India but is now grown in warm climates throughout Europe, Asia, and the Americas. There are dozens of varieties to try and countless ways to prepare them in cuisines from across the globe.

Sweet basil is most common in Western cuisines, especially in Mediterranean food, and other popular basils in Western cooking include purple basil, purple ruffles, cinnamon, lettuce, and African Blue. Basil is a tender herb, so its flavor won't withstand high heats or long cook times. If adding to a cooked dish, do so at the very end of cooking or just before serving.

HEALTH BENEFITS

Fresh basil is a nutritional dynamo, with anti-inflammatory, antibacterial, and antioxidant powers that boost the immune system, improve the health of your heart and arteries, and soothe stomach upset. The tasty herb has also been shown to reduce stress and symptoms of anxiety disorders.

BASIL VARIETIES

- African blue
- Bush basil
- Cinnamon basil
- Lemon basil
- Lettuce basil
- Licorice basil
- Purple ruffles basil

In the Garden

Basil is an annual that makes a great indoor plant all year-round, as long as the container has suitable drainage and is positioned in a sun-soaked windowsill.

Size: 1 to 2 feet tall
Container: 10 inches in diameter
Light: Full sun
Soil: Moist, rich, well drained
Plant: Seeds, seedlings, or transplants

Water: Regularly, when soil feels dry to the touch; do not overwater. Water only around the base of the plant and not over the leaves; wet leaves will yellow in the sun. For seedlings, mist with water from a spray bottle to avoid oversaturating the soil.

Harvest: Snip or gently pinch off leaves as they ripen throughout the season; start with the top-most outer leaves, and new ones will regenerate. Harvest completely before the first fall frost.

SUBSTITUTIONS
- Arugula
- Baby spinach
- Cilantro
- Oregano
- Thyme

PAIRINGS

Vegetables: artichokes, eggplant, mushrooms, olives, potatoes, tomatoes, zucchini
Proteins: beans, beef, cheeses, chicken, eggs, fish and seafood, pork
Seasonings: balsamic vinegar, capers, chives, cilantro, garlic, mint, oregano, parsley, rosemary, thyme, savory

Care: Snip any flowers as you notice them to promote new growth and prevent seeding. In cool climates, bring plants indoors before the first frost in the fall or winter.

Keep It Fresh

Freeze basil according to directions on page 19. Basil should not be dried, as the flavor is significantly diminished.

In the Kitchen

Dishes: Salads, sauces, dressings, marinades, soups, pastas, pizzas
Prep: Use whole basil leaves or tear them into smaller pieces before adding to a dish.
Serve: Basil adds fresh flavor to virtually any dish, especially when added fresh before serving. In Italian cooking, it's essential in pesto sauces, layered on caprese salads, sprinkled over pizzas, and stirred into pasta sauces, marinades, and dressings. If it will be cooked slightly, consider adding extra after cooking to revive any flavor lost to the heat.

THAI BASIL

Ocimum basilicum horapha

Other common name: Bai Horapa

Flavors: anise-licorice plus sweet, spicy, peppery, and clove

Despite its name, Thai basil is essential in various Southeast Asian cuisines beyond Thailand, including Cambodian, Laotian, and Vietnamese. It's an important component of Vietnamese pho, which is always accompanied by a garnish dish of lime wedges, bean sprouts, chopped chili peppers, and Thai basil leaves.

This basil-variant's anise flavor distinguishes it from its Mediterranean cousin—and earns it the nicknames anise basil or licorice basil. Its leaves are sturdier than those of sweet basil, making it more resilient to heat and therefore better suited for dishes with longer cook times, such as soups and curries. With its small, deep-green leaves emerging from purple stems, Thai basil also makes a pretty ornamental plant to grow at home.

HEALTH BENEFITS
Like sweet Mediterranean basil, Thai basil also works as an anti-inflammatory and can help relieve upset stomach and arthritis. Stocked with vitamins A, C, and K, as well as magnesium, calcium, and potassium, its antioxidant and antibacterial properties help promote cardiovascular health, alleviate asthma, and ward off symptoms of the common cold and flu.

In the Garden
Thai basil is a tropical perennial that grows successfully in indoor containers. Make sure it has adequate drainage and station it in a sun-filled window.

Size: 1 to 2 feet tall
Container: 2 gallons
Light: Full sun
Soil: Moist, well drained

Plant: Seeds, seedlings, or transplants
Water: Regularly, when soil feels dry to the touch; do not overwater. Water the plant around the base, and not over the leaves, which will cause them to yellow.
Harvest: Harvest regularly to promote regrowth: Gently pinch off outer leaves or snip with garden shears.
Care: Snip off any flowers as you notice them to promote new growth and prevent seeding. In cool climates, bring plants indoors before the first frost in the fall or winter.

SUBSTITUTIONS
- Basil + mint
- Cilantro
- Holy basil
- Mint
- Star anise

PAIRINGS

Fruits and Vegetables:
baby corn, bamboo shoots, bean sprouts, broccoli, cabbage, carrots, celery, eggplant, green beans, mango, mushrooms, pineapple, potatoes, radishes, scallions, snap peas, tomatoes, zucchini

Proteins: beef, cashews, chicken, duck, eggs, fish, peanuts, pork, tofu

Seasonings: anise seeds, chili peppers, cilantro, coriander seeds, cloves, cumin, curry powder and paste, fish sauce, galangal, garlic, ginger, lemongrass, lemon juice, lime juice, makrut lime, mints, red pepper flakes, soy sauce, tamarind, turmeric, vanilla

Keep It Fresh

Freeze according to directions on page 19. Thai basil should not be dried, as the flavor is significantly diminished.

In the Kitchen

Dishes: Curries, noodles, rice, salads, soups, and stir-fries
Prep: Use whole leaves or tear them into smaller pieces before adding to a dish.
Serve: Thai basil's intense anise flavor offers balance in spicy Asian stir-fries, rice, noodles, and curries. Raw, it makes a delicious addition to salads, spring rolls, and other cold dishes, and even adds an unexpected, herby dimension to ice cream and smoothies.

HOLY BASIL

Ocimum sanctum or Ocimum tenuiflorum

Other common names: Bai Gaprow or Tulasi

Flavors: spicy and peppery, with cloves, peppermint, and licorice

Called *bai gaprow* in Thai and *tulasi* in Sanskrit, holy basil is a spicy variant of the sweet basil plant. In India, the plant is indeed "holy": Devout Hindus use it in their daily worship practices and many homes have a tulasi plant on their property.

With a pungent, hot flavor, holy basil is a top choice for hearty, meaty curries. Raw leaves are not recommended for eating, as the flavor really comes out through cooking. And that flavor is intense: Use in smaller quantities than you would with Thai basil.

HEALTH BENEFITS
Holy basil is a prominent herb in Ayurveda, revered for millennia as a stress reliever and immune booster. Often sipped as a tea, it's believed to help the body manage physical and emotional stress. Holy basil has been used widely for its antioxidant, antibacterial, and anti-inflammatory properties, as treatment for colds, bronchitis, asthma, fever, stomach upset, arthritis, and headaches.

In the Garden
Holy basil is a tropical perennial that grows healthily indoors in a pot or container; place in a sun-filled window.

Size: 12 to 18 inches tall
Container: 2 gallons
Light: Full sun
Soil: Rich, fertile, well drained
Plant: Seeds, seedlings, or transplants
Water: Regularly, when soil feels dry to the touch; do not overwater. Water the plant around the base, and not over the leaves, which will cause them to yellow.

PAIRINGS

Fruits and Vegetables:
baby corn, bamboo shoots, bean sprouts, broccoli, cabbage, carrots, celery, coconut milk, eggplant, green beans, mango, mushrooms, onions, pineapple, potatoes, radishes, scallions, shallots, snap peas, tomatoes, zucchini

Proteins: beef, cashews, chicken, duck, eggs, fish and seafood, peanuts, pork, tofu

Seasonings: chili peppers, cilantro, cumin, curry powder and paste, fish sauce, galangal, garlic, ginger, lemongrass, lemon juice, lime juice, makrut lime, mint, red pepper flakes, soy sauce, tamarind, turmeric, vanilla

Harvest: Harvest regularly to promote regrowth: Gently pinch off outer leaves or snip with garden shears.

Care: Snip off any flowers as you notice them to promote new leaf growth and prevent seeding. In cool climates, bring plants inside before the first frost in fall or winter.

DRYING TIP

If fresh isn't available, dried holy basil can be an adequate (though not perfect) substitute, but you'll need to mix in some fresh Thai basil too. To soften the dried leaves, place them in a cold-water bath for ten to fifteen minutes and remove the stems. Combine with fresh Thai basil leaves to your desired taste.

Keep It Fresh

Freeze according to directions on page 19.

SUBSTITUTIONS

- Thai basil + mint
- Thai basil + black pepper
- Basil + mint
- Basil + black pepper
- Basil + red pepper flakes

In the Kitchen

Dishes: Stir-fries, curries, fried rice, drunken noodles

Prep: Use whole leaves or tear them into smaller pieces before adding to a dish.

Serve: Along with garlic, fish sauce, and fresh chili peppers, holy basil is one of the signature seasonings in Thai stir-fries. The intense herb also gives fire to meaty curries, as well as fish, tofu, and a variety of Asian veggies.

BAY LEAF

Laurus nobilis

Other common name: Bay Laurel Leaf

Flavors: subtly herbal and woody, intended as a background or base seasoning

Bay leaves are an integral aromatic ingredient in many cuisines, including French, Indian, and Mediterranean. They're used in classic French béchamel sauce and the bouquet garni herb mixture (see page 250). Perfect for recipes that undergo long cook times, they release their flavors gradually while cooking, creating a deep background flavor that imbues an entire dish. Bay leaves are always removed before serving, as they're hard and sharp even after cooking.

Grown on bay laurel trees, this is one of those rare herbs that's best consumed in dried form. In fact, finding fresh bay leaves at your local market might be a challenge—and if you *do* find them, they will probably be the variety grown in California, from a different tree and bearing a very different (minty) flavor.

> **HEALTH BENEFITS**
> Bay leaves contain eugenol, an antiseptic and anti-inflammatory compound that's used as a mild anesthetic at the dentist's office. The herb is also known to encourage healthy digestion and can prevent and help relieve gas, cramps, and general stomach upset. It's a natural diuretic, stimulating urination along with the body's detox processes, and it's believed to help regulate blood sugar.

In the Garden

The bay laurel tree can grow quite tall in the ground (like 60 feet!), but you can control its size by planting it in a container. This will also make it possible to move the tree indoors during the cold-weather months.

Size: 6 to 60 feet tall
Container: The largest size you like

Light: Full sun

Soil: Well drained, with plenty of compost

Plant: Seedlings or cuttings; seeds take up to six months germinate

Water: Thoroughly every few days, when the soil feels somewhat dry to the touch; do not overwater or let it dry out.

Harvest: After about two years, bay leaves should be ready for harvest. Snip ripe, full-grown leaves as needed.

Care: Prune regularly to keep the size in check. If you live in a hot or tropical climate, provide partial shade for the plant so it doesn't dry out. Protect it from strong winds and frosts. In cool climates, bring indoors before the first frost in fall or winter.

SUBSTITUTIONS
- 1 dried bay leaf = ¼ teaspoon dried thyme
- Indian bay or tejpat leaves (sweeter cinnamon-clove flavor)
- Juniper berries (for meat dishes)

PAIRINGS

Fruits and Vegetables: cabbage, carrots, celery, citrus, mushrooms, onions, peas, pickles, potatoes, tomatoes and tomato sauces

Proteins: beans, beef, chicken, fish, game, lamb, lentils, pork

Seasonings: allspice, basil, cayenne, chili powder, cloves, fennel, garlic, lemon juice, marjoram, oregano, paprika, parsley, pepper, red pepper flakes, rosemary, sage, savory, thyme

Keep It Fresh

Bay leaves should always be used dried (see directions page 20).

In the Kitchen

Dishes: Soups, stocks, sauces, stews, marinades, roasts, braises, rice

Prep: Simply place whole bay leaves in your pot or pan and cook; just remember to remove them before serving.

Serve: Bay leaves are known to bring out the flavors of other ingredients in a dish. Add a couple whole leaves to slow-cooked meats, lentils, stews, soups, and sauces, and remove before serving. But don't overdo it—a little bay leaf packs a lot of flavor.

INDIAN BAY LEAF

Cinnamomum tamala

Other common name: Tejpat Leaf

Flavors: clove-like, spicy, with cinnamon and cassia

Indian bay leaves are used much like bay leaves—in long-cooked dishes from which they're removed before eating. However, that's where the similarities end. Indian bay leaves have a completely distinct flavor closer to spicy clove and cinnamon than to the woodsy flavor of bay leaves. That's because they come from a species of cinnamon tree native to India; the dried bark from some *Cinnamomum* trees is used to make cassia and cinnamon (see pages 172, 174).

They're also larger than Western-style bay leaves, with three spines running vertically down the length of the leaf. In Indian markets, you might see both types of aromatic leaves labeled "bay leaf," so keep these differences in mind to choose the right one.

"BAY LEAF" VARIETIES

There are many other aromatic leaves used similarly to bay leaves, but with wonderful flavors all their own.

- Allspice leaf
- Avocado leaf
- Boldo leaf
- Curry leaf (page 98)
- Hoja santa (see page 199)
- Lá Lót (see page 199)
- Lemon verbena (page 112)
- Myrtle leaf (page 118)
- Pandan leaf (page 124)
- Perilla (page 126)
- Salam or Indonesian bay leaf
- West Indian bay leaf

In the Garden

Unfortunately, Indian bay leaves are not a practical herb to grow yourself: Not only are seedlings difficult to get ahold of, the trees (*Cinnamomum tamala*) need to grow for up to ten years before leaves are ready for harvest.

Native to the southern Himalayas, Northeast India, Myanmar, and Nepal, tejpat trees are planted permanently as seedlings when they're four or five years old.

Their leaves won't be harvested for another eight to ten years, but after that, they can grow for a century, reaching 60 feet tall. Leaves are harvested during the dry seasons, from October through December (and in some regions, through March), and then sun-dried for a few days before being sold commercially.

Keep It Fresh

To save Indian bay leaves for future use, freeze them in plastic bags (see page 19).

PAIRINGS

Fruits and Vegetables: cabbage, carrots, celery, coconut, onions, peas, potatoes, tomatoes

Proteins: almonds, cashews, chicken, eggs, fish, hazelnuts

Seasonings: cardamom, cayenne, chili powder, chili peppers, cilantro, cinnamon, cloves, coriander seeds, cumin, curry powder and paste, garlic, ginger, lemon juice, lime juice, mint, mustard seed, paprika, parsley, pepper, poppy seeds, red pepper flakes, scallions, soy sauce, tamarind, turmeric

In the Kitchen

Dishes: Rice, braises, curries, soups, sauces

Prep: Simply place whole Indian bay leaves in your pot or pan and cook; just remember to remove them before serving.

Serve: The sweet cinnamon flavor of Indian bay leaves is essential to many savory Indian dishes, including biryanis (rice dishes), kormas (braises), and meat, vegetable, and lentil curries. Ground leaves are a central ingredient in traditional garam masala spice blends (see page 250).

HEALTH BENEFITS

Long used in Ayurveda, Indian bay leaves offer anti-inflammatory, antibacterial, diuretic, and digestive properties. They've been used to treat coughs, flu, and asthma, and to prevent or ease digestive troubles like gas, nausea, and diarrhea. Like the bay laurel, Indian bay leaf also contains eugenol, a compound used as a mild pain-reliever and antiseptic.

CATNIP

Nepeta cataria

Flavors: minty and bitter

Although it doesn't have the same effect on humans as it does on cats, catnip is indeed edible and easy to incorporate into your herbal repertoire. A member of the mint family, catnip bears resemblance to that herb physically, aromatically, and in flavor. However, some find the fragrance and taste unpleasantly bitter (though probably not your cat). Often used in relaxing, stomach-soothing teas, fresh catnip can also be sprinkled into a variety of dishes for added minty seasoning.

If your yard hosts lots of bugs, take note: The substance that triggers a euphoric reaction in cats, called nepeta-lactone, is also an effective mosquito, termite, and cockroach repellant. So that catnip plant can serve triple-duty, as a culinary herb, cat toy, and insect repellant.

HEALTH BENEFITS
While catnip might drive your cat crazy, the herb actually has the opposite effect on humans: It's been known for centuries as a calming stress reliever for the body and mind. Catnip can help relieve stomach upset, including irritable bowel syndrome (IBS), indigestion, gas and menstrual cramps, and nausea. It's used to treat anxiety, headaches and migraines, and insomnia, as well as colds, cough, upper-respiratory infections, fever, and the flu. Thought to possess anti-inflammatory properties, catnip has also been used to relieve discomfort from arthritis, hemorrhoids, and hives.

In the Garden
Catnip is a perennial that will grow healthily in a container on a sunny windowsill. If your cat goes so cuckoo for catnip in the garden (i.e., she rolls all over it), protect the plant with a wire mesh screen, like chicken wire, or a wire cage.

Size: 2 to 3 feet tall
Container: 10 inches in diameter
Light: Full sun to partial shade
Soil: Rich, well drained
Plant: Seeds, cuttings, or divisions
Water: Regularly, when the soil feels almost dry
Harvest: Snip off full-grown stems at the base with garden shears.
Care: Protect the plant from strong winds but make sure it receives plenty of air circulation in its center to prevent mildew. If you live in a hot, sunny climate, treat catnip to some shade in the afternoon and keep the soil consistently moist. Catnip grows quickly and self-seeds, so snip flower buds when you see them to control spreading.

SUBSTITUTIONS
- Mint
- Lesser calamint

PAIRINGS

Fruits and Vegetables: carrots, cucumber, eggplant, lemon, lettuce, lime, mushrooms, onions, oranges, potatoes, tomatoes

Proteins: beans, cheeses, chicken, duck, eggs, fish and seafood, lamb, lentils, pork

Seasonings: basil, bay leaf, chili peppers, cilantro, garlic, honey, lemon juice and zest, oregano, parsley, pepper, sage, thyme

Keep It Fresh

If you plan to make catnip tea, dry the sprigs according to the directions on page 20.

In the Kitchen

Dishes: Teas, salads, sauces, soups, stews, marinades
Prep: Use whole or torn leaves in salads, and use dried, crushed leaves in teas.
Serve: Catnip has strong bitter-mint flavor, so use sparingly at first and add more to your liking. Toss leaves into salads, eggs, and potato dishes, or pair with rich meats like duck and pork.

CHERVIL

Anthriscus cerefolium

Flavors: sweet and subtle anise, with parsley

Chervil plants have lacy leaves that look much like parsley, only smaller and with intricately fringed edges. They're a relative of parsley, dill, and fennel—all of which are members of the carrot family—so you'll likely find it stocked near those similar herbs.

A signature herb of French cooking, chervil is essential to the traditional fine herbes blend (see recipe on page 250) and a common ingredient in creamy béarnaise sauce. It's a tender, subtle herb that's best served fresh or added at the end of cooking to keep the flavor intact. For this reason, chervil is ideal for salads, dressings, sauces, and eggs, or sprinkled over soups and cooked dishes just before serving. The herb's pretty leaves also make it a wonderful garnish.

HEALTH BENEFITS
Chervil is believed to soothe stomach upset, lower blood pressure, and aid circulation. It's also been used to relieve inflammation, including conditions such as gout as well as skin inflammation like eczema, acne, and topical allergic reactions.

In the Garden
Chervil is an annual that thrives in containers. Take care when choosing a pot, as it doesn't fare well when transplanted.

Size: 1 to 3 feet
Container: 8 to 12 inches deep
Light: High shade to partial shade
Soil: Moist, rich, well drained
Plant: Seeds; does not transplant well
Water: Regularly, so soil is consistently moist

Harvest: Snip or pinch the stems, starting with the ripe outer foliage first to let the young stems at the center grow.

Care: When the plants seed, sow again to start the next crop.

Keep It Fresh

Freeze chopped chervil for up to three months (see directions on page 19). Chervil should never be dried.

(see directions on page 19)

PAIRINGS

Vegetables: arugula, asparagus, beets, broccoli rabe, carrots, celery, endive, lettuce, green beans, kale, mushrooms, onions, peas, potatoes, shallots, spinach, tomatoes, watercress, zucchini

Proteins: beans, cheeses, chicken, cream, eggs, fish and seafood, turkey

Seasonings: balsamic vinegar, basil, capers, chicory, chives, dill, fennel, garlic, hyssop, lemon juice, mint, mustard greens and seeds, parsley, rosemary, tarragon, thyme

In the Kitchen

Dishes: Salads, dressings, marinades, sauces, soups

Prep: Use whole fresh leaves or chop them before adding to a dish.

Serve: Offering a somewhat subtle background flavor, chervil is known to enhance the flavors of other herbs and is often used alongside chives, parsley, and tarragon. The springtime herb adds a sweet balance to vinegars and bitter greens, and complements other spring-season foods.

CHIVES

Allium schoenoprasum

Flavors: mild onion, fresh, subtly spicy; milder than scallions

A member of the onion family and a relative of garlic, chives are used in many cuisines across the globe and enjoyed for their fresh, zesty crunch. They grow long, hollow green reeds from small bulb roots and sprout bright pink-purple flowers in summertime that are also edible and onion flavored. Garlic chives (*allium tuberosum*) are grown throughout Asia and have been used in Chinese cooking for close to five thousand years; true to their name, they have a stronger garlic flavor than standard chives.

A fundamental ingredient in the French herb blend fines herbes (see recipe on page 250), chives are always used fresh or added at the very end of cooking to retain optimal flavor.

HEALTH BENEFITS

Like onions and garlic, chives contain allicin, a compound believed to help lower cholesterol and blood sugar. They also offer several compounds with antioxidant powers, including vitamin K, carotenes, and quercetin, known to help stave off symptoms of aging and protect from degenerative conditions like heart disease and cancer.

In the Garden
For a steady supply of perennial chives in the kitchen, grow them in containers indoors in a sun-filled window.

Size: 1 to 2 feet tall
Container: 6 to 8 inches in diameter
Light: Full sun
Soil: Moist, rich, well drained; add compost
Plant: Seeds or clumps from a nursery
Water: Regularly, when soil feels dry to the touch

Harvest: Snip off whole stems rather than trimming just from the tips. Do *not* pull them out of the ground). Leave about one to two inches of stem at the base, and they'll grow back quickly.

Care: They tend to self-seed fairly aggressively, so keep them under control by snipping off flowers when they open and before they spread seeds. If growing in a garden, after a few years, divide clumps and replant in smaller batches. Simply separate into bunches of six bulbs each, then replant about one foot apart. Repeat every two or three years at the beginning of spring.

PAIRINGS

Vegetables: avocado, carrots, celery, cucumbers, lettuce, mushrooms, onions, parsnips, potatoes, shallots, tomatoes, turnips, zucchini

Proteins: bacon, cheddar cheese, cream cheese, eggs, fish and seafood (especially smoked salmon), goat cheese

Seasonings: balsamic vinegar, basil, chervil, cilantro, dill, fennel, garlic, lemon juice, mustard, paprika, parsley, red pepper flakes, sweet cicely, tarragon, thyme

Keep It Fresh

Chives freeze well, so for longer storage consider chopping and freezing in ice-cube trays (see freezing tips on page 19). Do not dry.

In the Kitchen

Dishes: Salads, soups, sauces, dips, dressings, marinades

Prep: Chop or mince and add to any savory dish. See chopping directions on page 26, or use scissors for easier, cleaner chopping.

Serve: Chives have a light oniony flavor that adds zip to salads, sauces, potatoes, eggs, soups, and mild spreadable cheeses. They're a favorite add-on for baked potatoes along with sour cream or butter, and they offer a fresh, crunchy texture to potato salads and yogurt dips.

CILANTRO

Coriandrum sativum

Flavors: pungent and complex, with spicy pepper, mint, and lemon

You'd be hard-pressed to find an herb more widely used than cilantro. You'd also be hard-pressed to find an herb that inspires as much controversy: Some people aggressively hate the flavor, finding it repulsive and claiming it tastes like soap. But those who love cilantro *really* love it, and they toss it freely into just about anything.

Used in many salsas, chutneys, relishes, and spice pastes in cuisines around the world, it's an integral seasoning in Mexican guacamole and the Yemeni hot sauces zhug and hilbeh (see recipes on page 251). Cilantro won't withstand much heat, so it's usually added at the very end of cooking or simply served fresh. Its seed, coriander (see page 178), is also a principal spice in Europe, western Asia, India, Central America, and the United States.

HEALTH BENEFITS

Cilantro is a fantastic herb for your health, as it's packed with fiber, iron, and magnesium as well as acids that promote healthy cholesterol while reducing bad cholesterol. It offers antibacterial, antiseptic, and antifungal benefits, too, and it helps fight inflammation caused by skin disorders like eczema. Cilantro also supports healthy digestion and can help prevent and relieve diarrhea, nausea, and vomiting.

In the Garden

Cilantro is the leafy foliage of the coriander plant, which is an annual that does best in mild climates between 60° and 80°F. Coriander will grow healthily in containers, but it's fussy if uprooted, so choose a suitable, permanent container.

Size: Up to 2 feet tall

Container: 18 inches in diameter

Light: Full sun
Soil: Moist, well drained
Plant: Seeds. To help germination, gently squeeze each seed until its halves split, then soak in water for two to three days and let dry completely before sowing.
Water: Regularly, to keep soil consistently moist
Harvest: Snip outer stems and leaves about once a week, taking only one small batch at a time to keep the plant healthy and growing. For the coriander, let the flowers develop and dry, then harvest the seeds (see page 179). You can wait for cilantro to self-seed, or sow fresh seeds every two to three weeks.
Care: Weed regularly or place mulch around plants to prevent weeds. In hot, sunny climates, plant in the fall and provide some shade; cilantro will quickly go to seed if overheated. Harvest often and snip off flowers as you see them so the plant can focus on growing foliage.

SUBSTITUTIONS
- Basil
- Culantro
- Parsley

PAIRINGS

Fruits and Vegetables: avocado, carrots, corn, jicama, lettuce, mango, onions, potatoes, tomatoes, tomatillos
Proteins: beans, beef, cheeses, chicken, eggs, fish and seafood, lamb, lentils, pork
Seasonings: basil, cayenne, chili peppers, chipotle peppers, chives, coriander seeds, cumin, curry powder, fennel, fish sauce, galangal, garlic, ginger, jalapeño, lemongrass, lemon juice and zest, lime juice and zest, makrut lime, marjoram, mint, oregano, paprika, parsley, red pepper flakes, saffron, scallions, soy sauce, turmeric

Keep It Fresh
Cilantro holds up well frozen in ice-cube trays (see tips on page 19). Do not dry.

In the Kitchen
Dishes: Salads, soups, dips, pastes, stir-fries
Prep: Use whole fresh leaves or chop before adding to a dish (see chopping tips on page 26).
Serve: If you love cilantro, you might find that its complex, refreshing flavor adds oomph to most any dish, including many from Latin American, Middle Eastern, and Asian cuisines. It pairs especially well with bright citrus, mild veggies, and bold seasonings like garlic, hot chili peppers, and mint.

DILL

Anethum graveolens

Flavors: mild anise, parsley, with lemon

Dill plants grow feathery, dainty leaves, and, if allowed to fully mature, clusters of yellow flowers sprout from the top, replicating the look and growth habit of their cousins parsley and caraway.

If you eat pickles, you're familiar with the distinct flavor of dill. It's a signature herb in many European and Asian cuisines, used for its fresh-tasting leaves and potent seeds that taste much like caraway and anise. The leaves are milder in flavor, subtly reminiscent of anise and parsley. Because they're tender, they aren't ideal for dishes with long cook times unless they're added at the very end.

HEALTH BENEFITS
This herb boasts antioxidant, anti-inflammatory, antispasmodic, and antiviral powers that make it a fantastic addition to a regular diet. Among its many benefits, dill aids digestion, helps clear up coughs and congestion, and has been used to sanitize and disinfect the mouth and injuries to the skin. (For example: Hippocrates allegedly tended to Greek soldiers' burn wounds with dill.)

In the Garden
Dill plants are annuals that grow a long taproot that makes transplanting difficult, so choose a location that will be adequate for a full-grown plant.

Size: 3 feet tall

Container: At least 12 inches deep

Light: Full sun

Soil: Light, rich, well drained

Plant: Seeds or young plants. Dill forms thick, sturdy roots, so transplant only young potted plants with roots and soil together.

Water: Frequently at first, but less often when established; when the soil feels dry.

Harvest: Snip or pinch off individual stems from the base, only a few at a time, leaving the rest of the plant intact. Or, you can let the older dill plants flower and develop their tasty dill seeds (see page 182).

Care: Protect from winds or support with stakes in the ground. Harvest regularly to keep your dill plant producing more leaves. Snip off any flowers you see so the plant can focus on its foliage. Sow new seeds every two or three weeks to maintain a steady supply in your kitchen.

PAIRINGS

Vegetables: asparagus, beets, carrots, celery, cucumber, onions, potatoes, spinach, tomatoes, zucchini

Proteins: cheeses, chicken, eggs, beans, fish and seafood, lamb

Seasonings: balsamic vinegar, basil, capers, garlic, horseradish, lemon juice, mustard, paprika, parsley, scallions

SUBSTITUTIONS
- Tarragon
- Fennel leaves

Keep It Fresh

For longer freshness, freeze in ice-cube trays (see page 19).

In the Kitchen

Dishes: Salads, sauces, dips, dressings, marinades, soups, breads, rice

Prep: Use whole fresh leaves or chop before adding to any dish. If you're chopping dill, make sure it's completely dry. Remove the thick stems below the fronds, then follow the chopping tips on page 26.

Serve: Dill is an ever-popular counterpart to seafood, particularly salmon, shrimp, and scallops. It adds a garden flavor to savory breads, and makes a delicious herby dip when combined with soft, spreadable cheeses, yogurt, or sour cream.

FENNEL

Foeniculum vulgare

Flavors: sweet, mild, lightly spicy, anise

Fennel is used in the kitchen for its stems, its elegant feathery leaves, and its anise-flavored dried "seeds," which are actually fruits (see page 184). Native to the Mediterranean, it's a beloved staple in Italian cooking. Note that there are two main varieties of fennel: Herb fennel and Florence fennel, which has a large, firm bulb and is widely consumed as a vegetable for its crunchy bulb rather than as an herb.

Fennel's delicate, feathered leaves are more than just a pretty garnish. While they look like dill, but they have a much softer, sweeter anise flavor.

HEALTH BENEFITS
Known throughout history as an effective digestive aid, fennel can be eaten, prepared as a tea, and chewed in seed form to work its magic on the gut. Fennel is rich in potassium and fiber, and its vitamin C content makes it a great immunity booster.

In the Garden
Fennel, a perennial, doesn't transplant easily, so find a suitable spot and stick with it.

Size: Herb fennel, 4 to 6 feet; Florence fennel, up to 2 feet
Container: 12 inches deep
Light: Full sun or partial shade
Soil: Rich, moist, well drained
Plant: Seeds (soaked in water for five days before planting), or divided roots
Water: Regularly until the plant is established, when cutting it for harvest or replanting, and during drought. Drought tolerant; don't overwater or your roots may rot.
Harvest: Cut down stalks and water the plant so it regrows. For the seeds, let the fennel grow until the flowers turn brown and the seeds are green-yellow (see page 184).

Care: Keep fennel far from any dill plants in the garden, as they can interfere with one another and produce unpleasant flavors. Fennel self-seeds readily; snip off flowers to keep seeding under control.

Keep It Fresh

Store fennel in the warmer sections of the refrigerator, like in the door, to prevent freezing. Fennel will lose flavor whether frozen or dried. To use it in future soups, freezing is the better option (see page 19).

PAIRINGS

Fruits and Vegetables: asparagus, beets, Brussels sprouts, cabbage, carrots, celery, citrus, cucumbers, onions, mushrooms, potatoes, tomatoes, zucchini

Proteins: beans, cheeses, chicken, duck, eggs, fish and seafood, lamb, lentils, pork

Seasonings: basil, cardamom, cayenne, chervil, chives, cinnamon, cloves, coriander seeds, cumin, fenugreek, garlic, ginger, lemon juice, mint, mustard nigella, oregano, parsley, peppercorns, thyme, turmeric

see page 19

SUBSTITUTIONS

Stalks:
- Celery (raw or quickly cooked)
- Bok choy
- Onions (cooked)

Leaves:
- Dill (grassy, less sweet)
- Parsley
- Cilantro

In the Kitchen

Dishes: Salads, sauces, soups, roasts

Prep: Use whole fennel leaves or, if using stems, chop the segments you need.

Serve: Sprinkle fennel leaves over soups, salads, pastas, grilled fish, and meat dishes, or stir into sauces. They add an interesting twist to pesto when swapped in for basil, and their mild anise flavor pairs nicely with citrus and other fruits, making them a delicious addition to smoothies and juices. Stems can be cooked alongside pork and lamb roasts.

GARLIC

Allium sativum

Flavors: pungent, spicy

Lovingly dubbed "the stinking rose," garlic is one of the most recognizable flavors in the world, essential to Mediterranean and Asian cuisines. It's a member of the lily family, along with its similarly pungent relatives, chives, leeks, and onions.

Most commonly found in raw bulb form, garlic can be cooked whole for a sweet and mellow effect, or chopped up to release stronger flavor. However, it shouldn't be cooked for very long because it loses flavor and nutritional value during cooking; it also burns easily, which radically affects the taste (read: it's icky). Add at the end of cooking to avoid ruining your dish.

In addition to fresh garlic, you'll also find it sold as powder, flakes, granules, paste, juice, and extract.

HEALTH BENEFITS

Garlic is one of the best herbs for all-around health: It helps fight infections caused by bacteria, viruses, and fungi, and is thought to be a powerful weapon against the common cold and flu. It's also a well-known anti-inflammatory, great for people who suffer from chronic inflammatory conditions like Crohn's disease, psoriasis, and arthritis. The stinking rose also offers antioxidant properties, which can boost the immune system and postpone or prevent degenerative conditions related to aging. On top of all that, garlic is good for the heart. It can help lower blood pressure and cholesterol, and prevent or eliminate plaque buildup in the arteries.

In the Garden

The best time to plant garlic, which is a perennial, is in mid-autumn, after the first frost. In wintry climates, plant garlic about six weeks before the ground freezes. This crop will be harvested the following summer. In hot climates, plant in late winter or early spring. Don't buy garlic for planting from the supermarket, since they often sell varieties that aren't locally grown; visit a local nursery instead.

Size: 1 to 4 feet tall

Container: at least 8 inches deep and 8 inches wide for one bulb; larger for multiple bulbs spaced about 4 inches apart

Light: Full sun

Soil: Rich, loose, well drained

Plant: Cloves with husks: one clove will yield one garlic bulb. Plant each clove, tip pointing up and root end down, about 2 to 3 inches deep and separated from the next by up to 6 inches. Cover with soil.

Water: Thoroughly after planting, then again after removing mulch in spring. After that, water every few days during the spring or whenever the soil feels dry.

Harvest: As the garlic grows in springtime, you'll notice long curled stalks, or "scapes," growing out the top of your garlic bed. Cut these off as you see them (and eat them, if you like) to keep the garlic focused on nourishing the bulb. When most of the tops turn yellow or begin to droop over, harvest by loosening the soil around each bulb and carefully lifting (not pulling) out of the ground.

SUBSTITUTIONS
- Leeks
- Onions

KEEP IT FRESH: DRYING AND STORING GARLIC

Enjoy juicy fresh garlic whenever you want and store the remaining cloves in a zip-tight plastic bag in the fridge. Or, dry the entire harvest—a process called "curing," which helps the flavor fully develop and extends its shelf life.

Place homegrown garlic in a shady, dry location with good air circulation, such as beneath a large tree or on a roofed porch, for a few weeks or until completely dried. Make sure the garlic is protected from rain and sun. The skin should feel brittle, and the whole bulb should be dry and hard.

Store garlic bulbs at cool room temperature in a dark spot with good air circulation, either uncovered in a container or inside a mesh bag on the counter. Bulbs can keep for up to two months if stored properly; cloves separated from the bulb will stay fresh for up to ten days. Place chopped or minced garlic in an airtight container in the refrigerator and use it soon.

Freeze whole or chopped garlic in zip-tight freezer bags, but know that flavor and texture can be different from fresh garlic. You can also dry minced garlic in the oven to make garlic flakes or garlic powder: Spread minced garlic on a baking sheet and heat at 115°F for up to forty-eight hours. Store dried garlic flakes in an airtight container on the kitchen counter for a few months, or freeze for up to a year. To make garlic powder, grind the flakes using a clean coffee grinder, blender, or food processor.

Care: Place a thick layer of mulch over the soil to protect the garlic during the winter. Cold climates call for more mulch, hot climates less. Remove the mulch after the last frost in spring, then water thoroughly. Snip off any flowers to promote bulb growth. Weed regularly.

In the Kitchen

Dishes: salads, soups, sauces, dressings, marinades, stir-fries, pastas, pizzas, roasts (just about anything)

Prep: Simply pull apart the garlic bulb to separate the number of cloves you'll need for a recipe. If your recipe calls for crushed garlic, use a garlic press or the flat side of a kitchen knife against the side of one clove. Place the blade flat over the clove, then press down firmly with the palm of your hand, using your weight to thoroughly flatten the garlic. Peel off the skin, then chop or mince (see chopping tips on page 26).

Serve: Garlic goes well with just about any savory dish. Raw garlic is hard, pungent, and spicy; finely minced, it's sprinkled into salads, soups, dressings, salsas, guacamole, and sauces like pesto and aioli. When cooked, the flavor is smoother and relatively mild. Roast whole garlic alongside beef, pork, lamb, or chicken; chop or mince garlic, and add to stir-fries, curries, pasta sauces, cooked veggies, and rice. Use these pairing suggestions as a starting point, then go wild and add garlic to whatever you like!

PAIRINGS

Vegetables: artichoke, asparagus, avocado, carrots, celery, eggplant, mushrooms, onions, peas, peppers, potatoes, tomatoes, zucchini

Proteins: beans, beef, chicken, cheeses, eggs, fish and seafood, pork, sausage

Seasonings: basil, bay leaf, cayenne, cumin, ginger, honey, lemon juice, oregano, parsley, red pepper flakes, rosemary, soy sauce, thyme, Worcestershire sauce

GARLIC PREP

The method you use to prepare garlic can have a real impact on flavor. For example, crushing garlic will squeeze out its sticky, pungent juices, while a standard mince with a knife is typically somewhat dry and mild.

No matter what method you're using, first separate the individual cloves of the bulb. Then follow these simple steps to prepare garlic for cooking:

- Slice off the root end of each clove.
- Place the flat side of a chef's knife over the clove, and press down firmly with the palm of your hand, using your weight to flatten the garlic. This will separate the flakey skin from the flesh.
- Peel away the skin.

Then prepare as needed:

- **To slice:** Hold a clove lengthwise between thumb and forefinger then slice thinly along its length from one end to the other.
- **To chop:** Slice thinly then hold the slices together in a tight pile. Chop crosswise down the length of the clove. The finer the chop, the juicier (and more flavorful) the garlic.
- **To mince:** Slice thinly, chop crosswise, then gather the garlic into a tight pile and chop finely or "mince." Gather the minced garlic into another tight pile and repeat for a finer, juicier mince.
- **To crush:** After chopping garlic, sprinkle salt over it to absorb some of the juices. Place the flat side of your knife over the chopped garlic and press down firmly with the palm of your hand, just as you did before. This time, use your weight to crush the garlic to a thick paste; repeat over the entire pile. Alternatively, crush garlic in a press or using a mortar and pestle.

HORSERADISH

Armoracia rusticana

Flavors: pungent, spicy, zesty, mustard-like

This long, beige-brown root is a staple in German, Austrian, Scandinavian, and French regional cuisines. Traditionally, the root was chopped or sliced, mixed with vinegar, and served as a condiment for roast beef and other rich meats and fish. The shredded root is now often combined with may-onnaise, sour cream, or yogurt to make zesty sauces and dips. Horseradish should not be cooked, as its flavor dissipates quickly and completely when exposed to too much heat.

HEALTH BENEFITS
Known for its antibacterial, antiviral, and antifungal properties, horseradish can help treat infections in the respiratory system and urinary tract. Its pungent heat can help kick colds and congestion; just one whiff or taste clears the sinuses and breaks up mucus.

In the Garden
Find a spot in your garden exclusively for the horseradish, a perennial, since it can grow very large and spread out quite a bit if not given boundaries. Even better, you can control growth by planting in a container; go for one that holds more than 15 gallons, or use a half-barrel or whiskey barrel planter.

Size: 3 to 5 feet tall

Container: At least 15 gallons

Light: Full sun or partial shade

Soil: Moist, rich, well drained

Plant: Crowns or roots. A few weeks before the last winter frost, plant one root about five inches deep at a 45-degree angle, so the top sits about 2 inches beneath the surface of the soil and the slanted end faces downward. This will ensure that your new roots grow downward into the ground without getting snarled. Separate multiple roots by 2 feet.

Water: Regularly after planting and during droughts, but less once established

Harvest: Harvest the roots after several frosts in the fall, or after a full year. Dig up the soil, gently pull out your roots, and cut off the leafy tops; if you'd like, replant leftover pieces of root for the following year.

Care: Weed regularly. Carefully keep track of all root bits in the garden while you harvest, as any strays will likely lead to new plants and an ever-growing horseradish patch. It will continue to grow every year until you completely pull up and dispose of the roots.

Keep It Fresh

Fresh-cut horseradish root will stay edible for about one to two weeks in a zip-tight plastic bag in the refrigerator. If you're growing horseradish in your garden, you can store a whole uncut root in dry sand to maintain a supply through the winter; keep it in a cool, dark spot in your house. For longer freshness, freeze grated horseradish in ice-cube trays or small containers for up to six months (see instructions on page 19).

Homemade horseradish sauce will keep in a sealed jar in the refrigerator for about four to six weeks. Check for color and odor to make sure it's still fresh.

In the Kitchen

Dishes: Sauces, dips, dressings, marinades, soups, salads

Prep: If you're peeling and preparing your own horseradish, be aware that the odor is intense and gets even more so as it's grated. Open up your kitchen windows to provide some ventilation. Scrub your horseradish root completely clean, then peel and cut into chunks. To protect your eyes and nostrils, opt for a food processor rather than grating the root on your own—the task will be less arduous and your senses will thank you (no tears or sniffles!). Combine with distilled vinegar or lemon juice to preserve the flavor then stir into any dish, or prepare a sauce with sour cream, mayonnaise, or spreadable cheeses.

Serve: A perfect winter herb, horseradish will turn up the heat on any dish and complement most meats and cold-weather vegetables. It's also used as a zesty sandwich spread, as a frequent addition to Ukrainian and Polish borscht (beet soup), and as a spicy kicker in Bloody Marys. Try it with the food pairings to the left for a germ-fighting, cold-kicking meal.

PAIRINGS

Fruits and Vegetables: beets, broccoli, cabbage, carrots, cauliflower, celery, endive, lemon, lettuce, onions, parsnips, potatoes, tomatoes, turnips

Proteins: beef, cheeses, chicken, eggs, fish and seafood, ham, sausages

Seasonings: cayenne, celery seed, dill, fennel, garlic, lemon juice, mustard, paprika, parsley, Worcestershire sauce

LAVENDER

Lavandula angustifolia

Flavors: sweet, floral, slightly bitter, subtle citrus and mint

With a calming, lightly floral fragrance long treasured in perfumes and cosmetics, lavender has been gaining culinary ground over the last half century. In addition to the lovely aromatics, it adds a beautiful burst of color to any home garden, with bright purple or blue-purple flowers and grayish-green stems.

Lavender is an essential herb in traditional Provençal cuisine, used in herbes de Provence blends (see page 250). Both the flowers and leaves of English lavender can be used in cooking. Leaves can substitute for rosemary in savory dishes, while vibrant purple flowers make beautiful garnish for salads and decoration on cakes, pastries, and in champagne flutes.

> **HEALTH BENEFITS**
> Lavender has been used over the centuries to soothe headaches, digestive troubles, and inflamed skin conditions. Today, lavender oil is used in aromatherapy to relieve symptoms of anxiety, including insomnia, depression, irritability, and stress-induced digestive issues.

In the Garden

Lavender, a perennial, does best in drought-prone climates with low (or no) humidity and moisture, or else it's susceptible to root rot and fungus. Good drainage and air circulation are crucial. Consider planting on a mound or raised bed, and spread out plants so they're 3 feet apart. In rainy or humid regions, opt for containers with drainage holes instead of the garden bed; this will protect lavender from excessive moisture and provide plenty of circulation.

Size: 1 to 3 feet tall

Container: 12 to 16 inches in diameter

Light: Full sun

Soil: Dry, sandy, well drained. Add sand, gravel, or compost to improve drainage, protect against frosts, and prevent weeds.

Plant: Young plants

Water: Regularly at first, until the plants are established; then only occasionally when needed, in drought conditions or when the soil is dry.

Harvest: Wait one year to harvest. Lavender hits its peak after three years. Harvest leaves when needed; for best fragrance and flavor, harvest flowers in the spring or summer just before they open completely. Snip from the base of the stems until you have a bouquet.

Care: Don't prune until after the first year, and then prune every spring to make room for new, healthy growth and to give your lavender a more manicured look. Protect lavender from cool winds.

Keep It Fresh

To enjoy the fragrance and flavor for longer, dry your lavender sprigs according to the directions on page 20.

PAIRINGS

Fruits and Vegetables: apple, apricots, berries, cherries, figs, lemon, onions, oranges, peaches, pears, potatoes, plums, rhubarb, shallots

Proteins: chicken, cream cheese, eggs, goat cheese, lamb, mascarpone, nuts, rabbit, salmon

Seasonings: basil, cinnamon, cloves, fennel, fennel seeds, garlic, ginger, honey, lemon juice, lemon zest, marjoram, mint, oregano, parsley, pepper, perilla, rose, rosemary, sage, savory, thyme, vanilla

In the Kitchen

Dishes: Salads, roasts, stews, sauces, rice, dressings and marinades, ice cream, custard, cakes, jams, teas

Prep: Chop or use leaves and flowers whole in your recipes. A common way to prepare lavender for baking is to grind flowers into a lavender sugar. You can also infuse the flowers into cream or milk; or simply chop fresh flowers or grind dried flowers, then stir into butter, dough, or batter before baking. Note that a little bit of lavender packs a *lot* of flavor, so use scant amounts at first and gradually add more to taste.

Serve: Lavender adds an elegant floral dimension to both sweet and savory meals, from fruity desserts to rich roasts to sweet-savory combo dishes. Try it with roasted lamb, pork, and chicken, and in stews, rice, sauces, and marinades. Fresh or dried flowers can be used in baked desserts, custards, ice creams and sorbets, fruit compotes and jams, lemonades and ice teas, and honey, chocolate, or syrup infusions.

LEMONGRASS

Cymbopogon citratus

Flavors: tangy, tart lemon with hints of floral, mint, ginger, and pepper

Cool, fresh lemongrass is a favorite flavoring in Indonesian, Malay, Thai, and Vietnamese cuisines. It features prominently in intricately flavored Malaysian dishes that crisscross between sweet and sour, salty and spicy, and citrus and fish. Lemongrass flavor deepens as it cooks, so add early during cooking for an intense effect, or wait until later for a lighter seasoning. Stalks can be bruised or crushed to release flavor during cooking (then removed before serving), or finely chopped, minced, or pounded to a soft pulp.

Lemongrass is also available in dried powder form, called sereh powder; one teaspoon of sereh powder provides a comparable flavor to one fresh stalk.

HEALTH BENEFITS

Lemongrass can promote healthy digestion and is often consumed as a tea for its stomach-calming effects, including relief from cramps, vomiting, and diarrhea. Its relaxing aroma makes it one of the top-selling essential oils in the world, believed to reduce anxiety and ease muscle pain, joint pain, headaches, and stomachaches.

In the Garden

Lemongrass, a perennial, grows naturally in tropical, sunny climates. In cold climates, lemongrass will grow well indoors in a container when treated to lots of direct sunlight. Just move your lemongrass outside in spring after the last frost and back inside for the winter.

Size: Up to 6 feet

Container: 16 inches in diameter or 5 gallons

Light: Full sun

Soil: Moist, rich, well drained

Plant: Stalks, with tops and decaying layers removed. Place in a glass of water in a sunny window for a few weeks (changing the water every day), until it grows roots that are 1 to 2 inches long.

Water: Regularly, to keep soil moist
Harvest: Harvest when stalks hit 1 foot tall and about ½ inch thick at the base. Pull stalks up using your hands, or cut from the base with a sharp knife.
Care: After a few years, divide and replant to prevent crowding.

Keep It Fresh

For longer freshness, store stalks in a plastic bag in the freezer. (see page 19).

In the Kitchen

Dishes: Curries, soups, stews, salads, marinades, teas
Prep: The best lemongrass flavor comes from the inner layers of its bulbous lower half, about 5 inches of the stalk. However, you can also use the upper stems for flavoring in teas, soups, and marinades. Slice off the bottom root end and the green top, and remove the thick green outer layers to reveal the softer white or yellow core—this is the aromatic, flavorful flesh of lemongrass.

Serve: To suffuse lemongrass flavor into stews, marinades, curries, or other hot dishes, slice the inner stalk into long-ish sections (about 2 or 3 inches each), and bruise each section by either bending it or crushing it with the side of a large kitchen knife. This will release the stalk's aromatics so it permeates into your dish while cooking. Remove the lemongrass stalks before serving.

For an edible lemongrass seasoning, use only the bottom few inches of the stalk that are the most tender and flavorful. Chop finely or mince (see tips on page 26), then toss into stir-fries, soups, or salads. You can also crush the chopped lemongrass with a mortar and pestle to form a paste (see tips on page 27), which can be added to cooked dishes like curries and stir-fries.

PAIRINGS
Fruits and Vegetables: cabbage, carrot, coconut, mushrooms, onions, peaches, peas, pears, peppers, shallots, tomatoes
Proteins: beef, chicken, fish and seafood, peanuts, pork, tofu
Seasonings: anise seeds, basil, chili peppers, chili paste, cilantro, cinnamon, cloves, coriander seeds, cumin, curry powder, fennel, fish sauce, galangal, garlic, ginger, jalapeño, lemon juice and zest, lime juice and zest, makrut lime, mint, shrimp paste, soy sauce, tamarind, Thai basil, turmeric

MARJORAM

Origanum majorana

Flavors: Oregano-like but sweeter, lightly spicy, with hints of floral, clove, and citrus

Often associated with the more robust oregano (*Origanum vulgare*), marjoram deserves its own spotlight as an herb with distinct flavor and uses. Bees, butterflies, and birds tend to swarm around marjoram plants in the garden, making them an appealing plant to grow every summer.

Essential to French herb blends bouquet garni and herbes de Provence (see page 250), marjoram flavors anything from roasts and stuffing to lighter fare like fresh salads and egg dishes. The herb's sweetness also complements fruity and creamy desserts. Its delicate composition makes it unsuitable for long-cooked dishes, where its charms will dissipate in the heat. Instead, it is best used fresh or at the very end of cooking.

HEALTH BENEFITS
Like most herbs, marjoram is great for healthy digestion and also offers antibacterial, antiviral, and anti-inflammatory properties. It's high in vitamin C and carotenes, both known for their antioxidant activity, which helps protect against age-related decline in health.

In the Garden
Marjoram, an annual, grows successfully in containers positioned in a sun-filled window. In cold climates, plant in a container and bring indoors in winter.

Size: 1 to 2 feet tall
Container: At least 6 inches deep
Light: Full sun
Soil: Rich, well drained
Plant: Seeds, cuttings, or young plants
Water: Regularly, when soil feels somewhat dry to the touch; do not overwater.

Harvest: Snip leaves as you need them. If you're drying marjoram, wait until the blooms appear and snip off whole sprigs before they flower, leaving at least two-thirds of the plant intact so it regrows.

Care: Trim regularly and snip off flower buds to promote new growth. In temperate climates, place mulch around the plants during the winter.

Keep It Fresh

Marjoram is very often used dried and can be frozen in ice-cube trays if you want to save the fresh stuff for later (see directions on page 19).

SUBSTITUTIONS
• Basil
• Sage
• Savory
• Thyme
• Oregano (only in hearty dishes; use sparingly)

PAIRINGS

Fruits and Vegetables:
apples, apricots, asparagus, beets, cabbage, carrots, cauliflower, celery, cherries, eggplant, mushrooms, oranges, peas, peppers, pomegranate, potatoes, spinach, squash, tomatoes

Proteins: beans, cheeses, chicken, eggs, fish and seafood, sausages, turkey

Seasonings: bay leaf, chives, garlic, horseradish, juniper, nutmeg, oregano, parsley, pepper, savory, thyme

In the Kitchen

Dishes: Salads, soups, stews, casseroles, stuffings, sauces, dressings and marinades, liquors, teas, desserts

Prep: Add leaves and flowers, whole or chopped, to any dish at the end of cooking or just before serving.

Serve: Dried marjoram is more potent than fresh, so may be better suited for dishes containing heartier foods like potatoes, beans, and cabbage. Both fresh and dried marjoram will flavor cooked dishes like roasts and lamb stews. Fresh leaves and flowers are tossed into green salads, eggs, soups, and veggie dishes. Stir fresh marjoram into soft, spreadable cheeses and herb butters, and infuse into vinegars, syrups, and liqueurs. It also adds complex sweet-floral flavor to custards, ice creams and sorbets, and fruit-pie fillings.

MINT

Mentha

Flavors: fresh, peppery yet cooling, and sharp, with sweetness and subtle lemon

The cool, refreshing flavor of mint is known in practically every region of the world. Naturally, there are many varieties and hybrids, with flavors ranging from basil and apple mints to chocolate mint and the spicy Moroccan mint. But spearmint (*Mentha spicata*) is the number one choice for cooking. Peppermint (*Mentha peperita*) is cultivated for its oil and used in chewing gum, toothpaste, desserts, and teas, but it's generally too intense for typical culinary purposes.

Plant your own mint, and you'll get the added bonus of a built-in natural air freshener. Mint is the quintessential home fragrance—and one of the oldest in history!

HEALTH BENEFITS

Mint is a classic remedy for all sorts of stomach trouble. Menthol, one of its primary compounds, helps relax muscles along the digestive tract and can relieve gas, cramps, bloating, nausea, and diarrhea. Often consumed as a tea, mint is also useful in treating common respiratory ailments like sinus infections, coughs, congestion, and asthma.

In the Garden

Mint, a perennial, spreads quickly and aggressively by way of runners underground. You'll either need plenty of room for it, or you must devise boundaries to keep it contained. (For example, plant it in a pot first and then dig your pot into the garden soil; the rim should be aboveground so the mint can grow up while the roots are confined.) Alternatively, simply plant mint in a container and store it in a sunny spot near the kitchen. Sow seedlings in the spring, spacing them in your garden so they're about 2 feet apart.

Size: 1 to 3 feet tall
Container: At least 12 inches in diameter
Light: Full sun to partial shade

Soil: Moist, rich, well drained

Plant: Young plants or cuttings

Water: Regularly, to keep the soil consistently moist

Harvest: Gently pinch the stems and they'll easily snap off. For the best, most potent flavor, harvest right before the plant flowers.

Care: Trim off flower buds and harvest regularly to keep your mint plants thriving. Place mulch around outdoor plants to retain moisture.

PAIRINGS

Fruits and Vegetables: apples, avocado, cantaloupe, carrots, cranberries, cucumber, eggplant, honeydew, kiwi, lemon, lime, mangoes, onions, oranges, peas, pineapple, potatoes, raspberries, strawberries, tomatoes, watermelon

Proteins: almonds, beans, chicken, chickpeas, feta cheese, fish and seafood, lamb, lentils, pork, veal

Seasonings: basil, cardamom, chili peppers, cilantro, cinnamon, cloves, coriander seeds, cumin, dill, fenugreek, fish sauce, garlic, ginger, lemon juice and zest, lime juice and zest, marjoram, oregano, paprika, parsley, pepper, scallions, thyme, vanilla

Keep It Fresh

Mint leaves will freeze well, so pop them in the freezer for future use (see page 19). Mint is also often dried and used as a seasoning in some Mediterranean dishes, although it lacks the trademark sweetness of fresh mint.

In the Kitchen

Dishes: Salads, fruit salads, marinades, sauces, salsas, chutneys, curries, soups, chocolate dishes

Prep: Chop, crush, or use whole fresh leaves according to your recipe. Mint is a potent herb, so use sparingly at first and add more to reach your desired taste.

Serve: Mint brings its cool, fresh flavor to all kinds of dishes, including rich meats like lamb, chicken, and pork, vegetable-and-herb salads, grains like quinoa and couscous, cold soups like gazpacho, and hot Indian curries and dals. Use it in sauces for fish, wrap it up in fresh spring rolls, or stir it into plain yogurt to make a vibrant dipping sauce or salad dressing. It pairs well with a surprising range of flavors, from summertime herbs such as basil, cilantro, and dill, to spicy favorites cumin, ginger, and cardamom, to sweet desserts with fruit and/or chocolate.

OREGANO

Origanum vulgare
(subspecies *hirtum*)

Flavors: pungent, peppery, sharp

If you've ever enjoyed pizza (and who hasn't?), you know the peppery, robust flavor of oregano. An essential seasoning in Mediterranean cooking, oregano comes in many varieties and shares shelf space with several taste-alike and sound-alike herbs that aren't technically in the same family.

Marjoram (*Origanum majorana*), for example, is often categorized as oregano; although a member of the same genus, it is a different herb with a subtler, sweeter flavor (see page 64). The spicier Mexican oregano (*Lippia graveolens*) is not oregano at all, but rather a cousin of lemon verbena used in Latin American and Tex-Mex cuisines. If you want that typical oregano flavor beloved on pizzas and in tomato sauces, look exclusively for fresh Mediterranean oreganos at your local farmers market or specialty market, or pick up the dried herb in the spice aisle.

HEALTH BENEFITS

Oregano offers significant antibacterial powers: It's been known to help fight infection in the respiratory system and urinary tract, and also to relieve symptoms of the common cold and flu. Oregano contains thymol, the primary flavor component of thyme, which provides antibacterial, antiseptic, and antioxidant activity. It's commonly used in cough medicines, where it helps break up phlegm, as well as in mouthwashes and toothpastes to fight infection and tooth decay.

In the Garden

Oregano, a perennial, makes a great container plant; if you live in a seasonal climate, consider using a pot so you can bring it indoors in cold weather.

Size: 1 to 3 feet tall and 2 feet wide
Container: at least 6 inches deep
Light: Full sun
Soil: Moist, rich, well drained

Plant: Seedlings or cuttings
Water: Only when soil feels dry to the touch
Care: Harvest regularly to promote new growth.
Harvest: Simply snip off whole sprigs or pluck individual leaves. For dried oregano, wait just until the buds form, before flowering, and you'll get the best flavor.

SUBSTITUTIONS
- Marjoram
- Mint
- Basil
- Rosemary

PAIRINGS
Vegetables: bell peppers, carrot, celery, mushrooms, olives, onions, potatoes, tomatoes, zucchini
Proteins: beans, beef, cheddar cheese, chicken, eggs, feta cheese, fish and seafood, lamb, mozzarella cheese, Parmesan cheese, pork, sausage, veal
Seasonings: basil, bay leaf, cayenne, chili powder, cumin, garlic, lemon juice, mustard, paprika, parsley, red pepper flakes, thyme

Keep It Fresh
For longer storage, freeze oregano leaves in ice-cube trays (see page 19). You can also dry sprigs in bunches (see page 20); dried oregano will stay fresh for up to one year.

In the Kitchen
Dishes: Pizza, pastas, stews, tomato dishes and sauces, marinades, soups
Prep: Whole sprigs can be used for flavor when roasting, grilling, or baking: Simply place them on top of whatever you're cooking in the pan or on the grill. Leaves can be used whole or chopped and added to any dish. Dried oregano has an even stronger flavor than fresh and can be a handy substitute, as it's widely available in supermarkets. Remember to use only one-third the amount of fresh needed.
Serve: Pair oregano with other bold flavors and serve cooked for the best result. You'll find it on roasts, grilled meats, and roasted or baked vegetables, and in pastas, rich soups and stews, marinades, and tomato-based sauces.

PARSLEY

Petroselinum crispum

Flavors: fresh, tangy, lightly peppery

Parsley is so much more than just a garnish. Its fresh, green flavor enhances the flavors of other ingredients in a dish. It's an important component of classic herb mixtures like bouquets garnis and fines herbes (see page 250), and its stalks can be used to flavor all manner of soups, stocks, and stews. Parsley leaves, on the other hand, are more delicate and won't stand up to long cook times; they should be chopped and added at the very end of cooking or just before serving.

There are two main varieties found in most grocery stores: curly parsley and flat-leaf (or Italian) parsley. The pretty, ruffled leaves of curly parsley are less flavorful and more often used as garnish, since they're very easy to chop. Flat-leaf parsley has stronger flavor, but the two parsleys are, for the most part, interchangeable.

HEALTH BENEFITS

Used medicinally in ancient times, parsley has been known to aid in digestion and serve as a diuretic. Those diuretic properties can help relieve symptoms of urinary tract infections and kidney stones, while its digestive powers can help with stomach upset, gas, and constipation. Parsley also offers vitamins A, C, and K, as well as iron, magnesium, calcium, and potassium.

In the Garden
Parsley, a biennial, will thrive outdoors in the garden or indoors in a sunny window.
Size: 1 to 2 feet tall
Container: 6 to 10 inches deep
Light: Full sun to partial shade
Soil: Moist, rich, well drained
Plant: Seeds, soaked in water for at least one day before sowing. Parsley seeds are famously slow to germinate, so it might take a few weeks.

Water: Regularly, to keep the soil consistently moist
Harvest: Late in the spring season, leaves will be ready to harvest. Simply snip stems at the base of the plant, starting with the outer foliage.
Care: Prune your parsley in early fall to encourage new growth. After two seasons, the plants will flower and go to seed, and it'll be time to pull up and plant new ones.

SUBSTITUTIONS
- Chervil
- Celery leaves
- Cilantro
- Dill
- Fennel leaves

PAIRINGS
Vegetables: carrot, celery, eggplant, lettuce, mushrooms, onions, peas, potatoes, tomatoes, zucchini
Proteins: beans, beef, cheeses, chicken, eggs, fish and seafood, game, lamb, lentils, pork, sausage, veal
Seasonings: basil, bay leaf, cayenne, coriander seeds, cumin, dill, fennel, garlic, lemon juice, mint, oregano, paprika, red pepper flakes, sage, thyme, Worcestershire sauce

Keep It Fresh
Freeze parsley leaves as described on page 19. Dried parsley won't keep its flavor and is mostly useless, so opt for freezing instead.

In the Kitchen
Dishes: Stews, sauces, salads, soups, rice, roasts
Prep: Use whole leaves or chop, and sprinkle over a dish.
Serve: Parsley is a versatile, clean-tasting herb that complements almost any vegetable or meat dish.

ROSEMARY

Rosmarinus officinalis

Flavors: pungent, woodsy, with pine and subtle lemon

Long believed to possess medicinal, magical, and spiritual powers, rosemary certainly has some powers that are not so mysterious: robust flavor and fragrance. These piney shrubs come in many varieties, offering a range of scents and flowers in vibrant blue, purple, pink, or white.

Rosemary is used sparingly in many Mediterranean dishes for its warm, comforting herb flavor. This strong herb retains its flavor during cooking, making it perfect for any slow-cooked or high-heat dish. Rosemary is also an essential component in the herb mixture herbes de Provence (see page 250).

HEALTH BENEFITS

Rosemary has been used throughout history to improve memory, aid digestion, and alleviate symptoms of anxiety. Its oil has been shown to stimulate hair follicles when rubbed onto the scalp, suggesting the herb may help counteract hair loss. Rosemary oil is a staple of aromatherapy, used to tame stress and boost concentration; it's also applied to the skin to ease muscle and joint pain and stimulate circulation.

In the Garden

Healthy rosemary, which are perennials, shrubs need lots of sunlight and excellent drainage. If you live in a cold climate, consider growing rosemary in containers rather than planting it in the ground, so you can move the plant inside in winter. Placed in a sunny window, rosemary will thrive indoors if turned occasionally so the entire plant is treated to as much sunlight as possible.

Size: 3 to 5 feet tall and 4 feet wide
Container: 5 gallons
Light: Full sun

Soil: Light, loose, well drained

Plant: Cuttings, young plants, or seeds; cuttings and young plants are preferred, as seeds can be difficult to germinate.

Water: Regularly and evenly, when the soil feels dry; somewhat drought tolerant

Harvest: Snip off stems at the base.

Care: Prune regularly and snip off flowers to encourage new, bushier growth. Pruning also improves air circulation. Add mulch to the soil to retain moisture and protect the roots from extreme cold and extreme heat.

SUBSTITUTIONS
- Thyme
- Savory
- Oregano
- Basil

PAIRINGS

Vegetables: carrot, celery, eggplant, green beans, mushrooms, onions, peas, potatoes, tomatoes

Proteins: beans, cheeses, chicken, eggs, lamb, pork, salmon, tuna

Seasonings: balsamic vinegar, basil, bay leaves, chervil, garlic, honey, lavender, lemon juice, marjoram, oregano, parsley, sage, savory, tarragon, thyme

Keep It Fresh

Dried rosemary tastes much like the fresh herb, so drying is a great option for longer storage. Dry according to the directions on page 20.

In the Kitchen

Dishes: Stews, soups, marinades, roasts, breads, casseroles

Prep: Use whole sprigs or chop leaves very finely, as they are tough and sharp like pine needles.

Serve: Place whole rosemary sprigs in a roasting pan or on a grill alongside meat or fish. Use whole sprigs or chopped leaves in marinades and stews (remove whole sprigs before serving), and chop very finely when adding to casseroles, roasted veggies, sauces, and soups.

SAGE

Salvia officinalis

Flavors: pungent, woodsy, slightly bitter and warm with pine, cedar, mint, and lemon

Sage boasts more than nine hundred varieties, many of which are stunningly beautiful in the garden, with soft, velvety foliage and brightly colored flowers. For visual appeal, colorful plants like purple sage, golden sage, and tricolor sage can't be beat; for the tastiest herb, however, common sage and pineapple sage offer top flavor.

When it comes to food, you might be most familiar with sage in its common American incarnation—in the traditional Thanksgiving stuffing. It's also a frequent addition to the herb bundle bouquet garni (see page 250). Sage is a robust herb that withstands long cook times, although cooking does mellow the intense flavor.

HEALTH BENEFITS

Sage is known to promote healthy digestion, which is why it's so commonly paired with rich, oily meats. It's often consumed in tea form, used aromatically, or applied topically to treat various conditions, including inflammation, excessive sweating, sore throat, anxiety, and stress. Chewing leaves or drinking sage tea can heal inflammation inside the mouth and throat, while applying sage lotions can heal skin irritation. Tea is believed to soothe stomach upset and relieve gas and bloating. Research has shown that sage may also help improve memory, calm nerves, and boost concentration; it's even being studied for its potential effectiveness in treating symptoms of Alzheimer's disease.

In the Garden

Sage, a perennial, is a great candidate for indoor planting, as long as it receives plenty of direct light. It will take a year to really establish itself, so harvest only a bit the first year. In several years, sage plants (usually small shrubs) will lose their stamina and need to be removed and replaced. Simply replant fresh cuttings to start a new generation.
Size: Up to 3 feet tall and 2 to 3 feet wide

Container: 12 to 14 inches in diameter, or larger
Light: Full sun to partial shade
Soil: Light, loose, well drained
Plant: Seeds or cuttings
Water: Regularly, but only when the top layer of soil feels dry
Harvest: Snip sprigs and leaves only scarcely in the first year. Wait until the second season for a full harvest, then snip whole sprigs or individual leaves when needed.
Care: Prune in the spring after the last hard frost to encourage new growth.

SUBSTITUTIONS
- Marjoram
- Rosemary
- Savory
- Thyme

Keep It Fresh
Dried sage is usable for up to six months (see directions on page 20), but know that the flavor is more potent and should be used even more sparingly. If you prefer the flavor of fresh sage to dried, you can store fresh leaves for up to three or four months in the freezer (see page 19).

PAIRINGS
Fruits and Vegetables: apples, carrots, eggplant, onions, peas, potatoes, squash, tomatoes
Proteins: beans, beef, cheeses, chicken, duck, eggs, fish, lamb, pork, sausage, turkey, veal
Seasonings: basil, bay leaf, caraway, garlic, ginger, honey, lemon juice, lovage, marjoram, mint, nutmeg, oregano, paprika, parsley, pepper, savory, thyme

In the Kitchen
Dishes: Roasts, stuffings, stews, marinades, rubs
Prep: Use whole sprigs or leaves to flavor stews, soups, and roasts, then remove before serving and use as garnish, if you like. Use chopped or dried sage in a rub for meats and fish; you can even rub whole leaves onto the meat to impart sage flavor. Chop or mince leaves for other cooked dishes. If using lightly cooked sage leaves, chop finely or mince so they're not overly chewy (see chopping tips on page 26).
Serve: Sage pairs famously with rich, oily, fatty meats like beef, pork, duck, veal, and sausage. Italian cooks use it to season saltimbocca, the veal-prosciutto classic, as well as pastas and breads. It's also a great herb for infused oils, butters, and many cheeses. Use sparingly at first so it doesn't overpower your dishes; add more if needed, add more to reach your desired taste.

SCALLIONS

Allium fistulosum

Flavors: mild onion, fresh, subtly spicy; more pungent than chives

Also called green onions, Welsh onions, or bunching onions, these long, tasty herbs are slimmer cousins of the common bulb onion. They don't grow a bulb, but they *do* have that trademark onion aroma and flavor—just a bit subtler than the vegetable.

Scallions are often confused with spring onions and chives. To differentiate between them, know that spring onions will usually sprout a small bulb at the base, as they're actually just young bulb onions. Chives, on the other hand, are narrower and more tender. Scallions have a stiff, straight, white base and crisp, bright-green top. Their firm, white bottoms can be cooked briefly in stews, stir-fries, and even on their own as a side dish, while their mild green tops can be chopped finely and served as garnish.

> **HEALTH BENEFITS**
> Just like their close relatives in the onion family, scallions offer plenty of vitamins and minerals, including vitamins A and C as well as calcium, iron, potassium, manganese, and magnesium. Scallions also provide a whopping dose of vitamin K, believed to help with healthy blood clotting and to strengthen bones.

In the Garden

Scallions, a perennial, can be grown healthily indoors as a container plant if positioned in a sunny window. Note that they'll develop a more potent onion flavor the longer they're left in the soil, so harvest when they reach your desired taste.

Size: 10 to 12 inches tall
Container: At least 6 inches deep
Light: Full sun
Soil: Moist, rich, well drained
Plant: Seeds or seedlings
Water: Frequently and evenly, so the soil and roots are constantly moist

Harvest: Once your scallions reach about 8 inches tall, they're ready for harvesting. Simply dig out the roots and carefully remove from the soil. Start with the largest scallions first, and the smaller ones will have more room to grow.

Care: Weed regularly and gently by hand to protect your roots. Place mulch over the site to retain moisture and discourage weeds. Divide the roots every year or two and replant for a healthy, continuous crop.

SUBSTITUTIONS
- Chives
- Leeks
- Shallots
- Spring onions
- Onions

PAIRINGS

Vegetables: cabbage, carrots, celery, mushrooms, onions, peas, potatoes, tomatoes

Protein: bacon, cheeses, chicken, eggs, fish and seafood, ham

Seasonings: cayenne, chervil, chili peppers, cilantro, galangal, garlic, ginger, lemongrass, lemon juice, mustard, parsley, perilla, red pepper flakes, soy sauce

Keep It Fresh

For future use of the crunchy, flavorful white stems, chop and freeze them in ice-cube trays or plastic bags (see instructions on page 19).

In the Kitchen

Dishes: Salads, soups, stews, stir-fries, sauces, dressings, and marinades

Prep: Peel the outer layer of skin off the base and any additional layers if they're brown or wilting. Slice off the root end, then rinse scallions in cool water and dab dry with a paper towel. Either use whole, in long segments, or chopped. If scallions will be cooked, chop coarsely in thicker chunks; use kitchen shears for easier chopping. If serving raw, chop finely. For an elegant garnish, chop on a diagonal up the length of the scallion, or pull strips lengthwise from the green tops. See chopping tips on page 26.

Serve: Add scallions only at the end of cooking to retain their fresh, oniony flavor, or use raw in salads, eggs, and potato dishes.

TARRAGON

*Artemisia dracunculus
(sativa)*

*Flavors: sweet, spicy anise, with
subtle basil, mint, and pepper*

Tarragon is a crucial herb in French cuisine, where its distinct anise flavor is often partnered with fish and chicken, used in classic béarnaise sauce and the fines herbes and bouquet garni herb blends (see page 250). Use tarragon with some restraint, however, as it can be overpowering and will diminish other flavors if you use too much. Add to your dishes at the end of cooking to make sure it imparts its best flavor.

When shopping for tarragon, read labels carefully to make sure you're getting the tasty French version. If you see "Russian tarragon," skip it entirely. Although related and physically similar to French tarragon, it's seriously lacking in flavor and tastes rather grassy and bitter. If the plant isn't clearly labeled, try a taste test: French tarragon should be sweet, licorice-flavored, and leave a slight tingle on the tongue. On the other hand, Spanish or Mexican tarragon (*Tagetes lucida*)—an entirely different plant belonging to the marigold species—will be an apt substitute for French, with its similar but stronger anise flavor.

HEALTH BENEFITS
When eaten, tarragon leaves trigger a subtle numbing effect in the mouth, making it a natural treatment for toothaches. In fact, the herb contains the chemical eugenol, which is used in dentistry for its antiseptic and mild anesthetic abilities. Tarragon can also help prevent and alleviate digestive trouble, including gas and bloating.

In the Garden
Tarragon, a perennial, needs a dormant winter, so it's not an ideal herb for hot, humid regions. (Mexican tarragon is a great replacement.) In these climates, plant tarragon in a container to improve circulation and drainage. Consider growing tarragon in raised beds for optimal drainage, especially in regions that experience rainy seasons.
Size: 2 to 3 feet tall

Container: At least 12 inches deep
Light: Full sun to partial shade
Soil: Dry, loose, well drained
Plant: Cuttings or root divisions, about 2 feet apart
Water: Regularly and evenly until the plants are matured, then only every few days
Harvest: Pick individual leaves or snip full sprigs.
Care: Trim regularly to prevent flowering and promote new growth. Prune plants if they grow taller than 2 feet so they don't tip over. In cold climates, place mulch around the plants in late fall to protect the roots during winter weather. After the second or third season, divide plants in late winter or early spring and replant. Or, simply plant new cuttings.

PAIRINGS

Vegetables: artichokes, asparagus, carrots, celery, green beans, lettuce, mushrooms, onions, potatoes, shallots, spinach, tomatoes
Proteins: beef, cheeses, chicken, duck, eggs, fish and seafood, rabbit, turkey
Seasonings: basil, bay leaves, capers, cayenne, chervil, chives, dill, garlic, lemon juice, mustard, oregano, paprika, parsley, rosemary, thyme

Keep It Fresh

Tarragon loses its flavor when dried, so opt for the freezer if you want long-term storage (see directions on page 19). Alternatively, store leaves in a bottle of white vinegar for a tasty fusion of flavors.

In the Kitchen

Dishes: Dressings, marinades, roasts, stews, soups, salads, stuffings
Prep: Use whole leaves or chop before adding to any dish (see tips on page 26).
Serve: Place whole sprigs beneath chicken, game meats, or fish while cooking to permeate an entire dish with flavor. You can also infuse tarragon into vinegars, mustards, and herb butters: Chop and add to mustard or butter, and place whole leaves inside a vinegar bottle. Try pairing tarragon with the foods and seasonings on the pairings list for a complete meal.

THYME

Thymus vulgaris

Flavors: pungent, woodsy, spicy, with mint and clove

Thyme grows in hundreds of varieties, with common thyme (*Thymus vulgaris*) and lemon thyme (*Thymus citriodorus*) the most widely used in the kitchen. This Mediterranean herb often grows as a small shrub with stiff, woody stems and small, oval, green leaves. But its diverse species also includes plants that are taller, shorter, and more colorful. Try delicious flavors like orange, oregano, and caraway.

A staple in Italian, Mediterranean, French, Creole, and Cajun cooking, thyme is crucial to French herb blends such as fines herbes, herbes de Provence, and many bouquet garnis, as well as to the Middle Eastern blend za'atar (see recipes on page 250–251). With its robust flavor, thyme stands up beautifully to high temperatures and long cook times. Use in moderation—too much thyme can overwhelm other flavors in a dish.

HEALTH BENEFITS

Thyme has a long history of medicinal and superstitious uses. It was even included in herbal remedies believed to fight and prevent the Black Plague. Today, there's evidence that thyme in tea form can help respiratory illnesses like cough, bronchitis, and even asthma. Shown to possess antibacterial, antifungal, and antiseptic properties, the herb can also be made into a tincture to treat skin irritations, acne, minor wounds, and even nail fungus.

In the Garden

Thyme, a perennial, grows beautifully in containers, especially in clay pots, making it easy to bring indoors in extreme weather. Just make sure your container is the right size and offers adequate drainage holes. In humid climates or in heavy soils, improve drainage by using limestone gravel mulch.

Size: 6 to 15 inches tall and up to 15 inches wide
Container: at least 1 gallon
Light: Full sun

Soil: Sandy, extremely well drained soil
Plant: Cuttings or young plants
Water: Water thoroughly just after planting, and then only when the soil feels dry.
Harvest: Harvest whole stems often and regularly to keep the plant thriving through the growing season. For making dry thyme, harvest just before flowering for the best flavor. Divide root pieces and replant to keep your thyme thriving through a few seasons.
Care: Trim regularly to promote new growth. In cold climates, place mulch around the plants when the ground freezes to protect the roots.

SUBSTITUTIONS
- Marjoram
- Oregano
- Savory
- Basil
- Bay leaf

PAIRINGS
Vegetables: bell peppers, carrots, corn, cucumbers, eggplant, green beans, leeks, mushrooms, onions, peas, potatoes, spinach, tomatoes
Proteins: beans, beef, cheeses, chicken, eggs, fish and seafood, lamb, rabbit, sausage, turkey, veal
Seasonings: basil, bay leaves, garlic, honey, lemon, marjoram, mustard, oregano, parsley, rosemary, sage, savory

Keep It Fresh
For longer freshness, dry or freeze thyme according to the directions on page 19–20.

In the Kitchen
Dishes: Stews, casseroles, pâtés, soups, sauces, marinades, stuffings
Prep: Use whole sprigs for flavoring stews and roasts. Use whole leaves or chop and add to any savory dish.
Serve: Thyme is a fantastic match for tomato sauces, chili, potatoes, beans, and egg dishes. Add it to rubs for beef, pork, and lamb roasts, or infuse into butters, vinegars, mustards, or mayonnaise.

WATERCRESS

Nasturtium officinale

Flavors: pungent, peppery, slightly bitter

Hugely popular in English kitchens, watercress is one of the oldest veggies known to man. It's also one of the healthiest. Botanically, it's related to mustard, wasabi, and horseradish, which explains the spicy zip on your tongue when you eat it. Watercress adds a zesty crunch to salads, sandwiches, and cheese spreads. It's delicious in all manner of soups, from minestrone to wonton to French watercress soup, or *potage au cresson*. And it can be quick-cooked in stir-fries and egg dishes.

HEALTH BENEFITS

Watercress has been used over the centuries as a breath freshener, stimulant, and remedy for scurvy, blood disorders, and countless other conditions. As a tea, it's used to treat cough, flu, and bronchitis, and to improve digestion. Watercress is a cruciferous vegetable—a group of plants, along with broccoli, horseradish, and cabbage, currently being studied for its effect on cancer growth and prevention.

In the Garden

Watercress, a perennial, grows naturally and easily in shallow, slow-flowing water. If you can replicate these conditions, it will also grow in containers or in a shady, wet spot in the garden. You'll need a container large enough to hold soil-filled pots with drainage holes, so the water from the pots can drain into the container to form a pond-like environment. Or, try a makeshift "bog" in the garden (see instructions on opposite page). Watercress won't transplant easily, so make sure your pots and your bog are suitable for mature plants.

DIY GARDEN TIP

Build a Bog: To form a bog in the garden, dig a hole 2 feet in diameter and 1 foot deep, and line it with pond liner. Fill with soil, water deeply to create a bog environment, and plant the seeds or stems.

Size: Up to 2 feet tall
Container: At least 1 gallon
Light: Full sun or partial shade
Soil: Well drained potting mix with peat moss and perlite
Plant: Seeds or mature stems soaked in water under direct sunlight for several days first
Water: Refresh your pond water every 2 days and spray the plants and surface every other day.
Harvest: When the stems hit 5 or 6 inches tall, snip off with kitchen or garden scissors, leaving about one to two inches of stem on the plant. Harvest regularly.

SUBSTITUTIONS
- Arugula
- Endive
- Dandelion greens
- Mustard greens
- Salad burnet

Care: Trim regularly to promote new growth. Once established, watercress will withstand winters if placed under shelter.

PAIRINGS

Fruits and Vegetables: cabbage, corn, cucumbers, lemon, lettuce, mushrooms, onions, oranges, peaches, potatoes, tomatoes
Proteins: chicken, fish, and seafood
Seasonings: basil, fennel, ginger, lemon juice, parsley, sorrel

Keep It Fresh

Keep watercress dry if you plan to store it for later use. The tender, leafy green won't freeze or dry well, so use within two to three days.

In the Kitchen

Dishes: Salads, soups, sandwiches
Prep: Trim off thick stems, then chop or use whole in any dish.
Serve: Watercress pairs naturally with other salad greens, offering a spicy counterpoint to mild Romaine, spinach, Boston, and iceberg lettuces.

EXOTIC HERBS

These herbs will take a little more work to find, but they should be available at specialty markets, nurseries, or via the many herb catalogs online (see page 253 for an extensive list).

ANGELICA

Angelica archangelica

Flavors: warm, bittersweet, and earthy, with anise and celery

This cool-weather herb belongs to the parsley family but has a look, aroma, and flavor all its own. It can grow taller than 6 feet, bearing shiny green leaves, ribbed purplish stems, and globes of little light-green flowers that spread open over the plant like an umbrella.

In addition to its beauty, angelica's roots, stems, leaves, and flowers are all edible. Stems are often candied and used as decoration on desserts, while the roots can be cooked like a vegetable. Seeds are used to flavor wines, liquors, pastries, and ice cream.

HEALTH BENEFITS

Taken in tea form, angelica is a known natural remedy for digestive troubles, including ulcers, gas, and heartburn. Also used as an antispasmodic and stimulant, the herb eases stomach cramping, relaxes the nerves and muscles, and helps stimulate blood flow.

In the Garden

Angelica, a biennial, is not ideal for containers, as it grows quite tall and can become unstable in a pot. It won't transplant easily after the seedling stage, so choose wisely when selecting a spot for it.

Size: Up to 8 feet tall
Light: Partial shade to full sun
Soil: Moist, rich, well drained
Plant: Seeds or root divisions. Fresh seeds are preferred over old dried seeds, which need to be stratified in order to germinate (see page 14).
Water: Regularly, at the base of the plant

Harvest: Snip stems and leaves in the spring of its second year, and harvest seeds when they're mature. Flowers only bloom in the second year. To get the seeds, cut the flowers from the stems into a paper bag and let them dry. For the roots, dig up in fall of the second year.
Care: Weed regularly and snip flowers whenever you see them to prevent the plant from seeding. Prune back in summer to promote new growth. In hot, sunny climates, angelica will need some shade. Angelica will die after the flowers bloom and the plant seeds, usually in the second year; if trimmed regularly, it'll live longer.

SUBSTITUTIONS
- Lovage
- Tarragon
- Fennel
- Juniper berries

PAIRINGS
Fruits and Vegetables: apples, apricots, celery, dates, oranges, peaches, pomegranate, onions, pineapple, plums, pumpkin, rhubarb, squash, strawberries, tomatoes
Proteins: cheeses, chicken, eggs, fish and seafood, pork
Seasonings: allspice, anise, cardamom, cinnamon, cloves, coriander seeds, fennel, garlic, horseradish, juniper, lavender, lemon balm, lemon juice and zest, marjoram, mint, nutmeg, oregano, parsley, pepper, perilla, soy sauce

Keep It Fresh
For future use, freeze angelica leaves as described on page 19. If you want dried root, first scrub with a vegetable brush to thoroughly clean, then slice lengthwise into smaller segments to help them dry. Follow the oven-drying directions on page 21.

In the Kitchen
Dishes: Candy, desserts, marinades, sauces, salads, stuffings
Prep: Chop stems and leaves or use leaves whole in salads and other dishes. The dried, powdered root can be used to flavor cakes and pastries.
Serve: Angelica's delicate celery and anise flavors match well with fruit (rhubarb, in particular) and other sweets for preserves or pie fillings. It's also a nice complement for fish in a marinade. Stems and leaves can be added to salads, marinades, and sauces, or cooked and eaten on their own.

ANISE HYSSOP

Agastache foeniculum

Other common name: Agastache

Flavors: sweet, anise, subtle sweet mint

This fragrant herb is neither anise nor hyssop, though its lovely anise flavor and aroma might make you think otherwise. Its nickname, licorice mint, is more apt. A member of the mint family, anise hyssop bears leaves that look like mint and gorgeous spears of lavender or blue flowers. It's a favorite of hummingbirds and bees, and can grow quite tall, from 2 to 5 feet, making it a dramatic plant in the garden.

Leaves and flowers are both edible: Leaves add sweet anise flavor to teas, honeys, fruit salads, and marinades, while the flowers offer beautiful color as garnish for any dish. Also look for it under the names "lavender hyssop" or "blue giant hyssop."

HEALTH BENEFITS
Anise hyssop makes a delicious and healthful after-dinner tea, which can help stimulate digestion, calm stomach upset, and prevent or relieve gas. Thanks to its antibacterial properties, it's also effective in treating symptoms of cold and flu, including cough, sore throat, and congestion.

In the Garden
These stunning perennial plants thrive for 2 to 3 years, after which they can be divided and replanted in spring.
Size: Up to 5 feet tall
Container: At least 1 gallon
Light: Full sun or partial shade
Soil: Dry to moist, well drained. Mix compost or mulch into the soil to add nutrients and improve drainage.

Plant: Seeds, cuttings, or divisions. Seeds need to be stratified in the fridge before planting outside (see page 14).

Water: Moderately

Harvest: Pick or snip leaves and flowers when they're established. To harvest seeds, snip flower heads into paper bags, taking care not to drop any.

Care: Prune and snip dead flowers to encourage new growth. Self-seeds easily; collect seeds as you see them and plant where you like to control the growth of new plants.

SUBSTITUTIONS
- Anise + mint
- Fennel + mint
- Tarragon + mint

PAIRINGS

Fruits and Vegetables: apricots, beets, blueberries, carrots, grapefruit, green beans, lemon, lettuce, onions, oranges, peaches, pears, plums, raspberries, shallots, squash, sweet tomatoes, zucchini

Proteins: almonds, beef, chicken, eggs, pork, walnuts

Seasonings: anise, basil, bergamot, chervil, cinnamon, cloves, fennel, garlic, ginger, honey, lavender, lemon juice and zest, marjoram, parsley, salad burnet, tarragon

Keep It Fresh

Anise hyssop will stay fresh for up to five days in the fridge or longer in a vase or jar of water. Freeze for longer storage or dry if using for tea leaves (see directions on page 19–21). Alternatively, anise hyssop is a fantastic herb to preserve in honey, jam, or fruit syrup.

In the Kitchen

Dishes: Teas, cold beverages, baked desserts, marinades, sauces

Prep: Chop leaves and flowers, or use them whole.

Serve: Add to veggie salads, fruit salads, and marinades for fish, chicken, or pork. For baking, mince flowers and add to sugar or dough to make cakes, muffins, cookies, and other pastries.

BERGAMOT

Monarda didyma or
Monarda fistulosa

Other common name: bee balm

Flavors: warm, spicy citrus

Bergamot grows stunning, fragrant flowers that range in color from bright red to magenta to soft lilac. It's a favorite of hummingbirds, bees, and butterflies, an added bonus in summertime for many gardeners. Also called "bee balm" for its traditional use soothing bee stings, the herb goes by various other names, including scarlet bee balm, horsemint, and Oswego tea.

Leaves and flowers have been used for centuries to make delicious teas, dating back to northern Native Americans, who introduced their beloved citrus-spice tea to English colonists in the seventeenth and eighteenth centuries. Use bergamot in fruit jams, fresh fruit and veggie salads, refreshing summer beverages, and citrus-tinged dips, sauces, and salsas. Dried bergamot makes a wonderful potpourri.

HEALTH BENEFITS
Bergamot tea (also known as Oswego tea) has been used for centuries by various Native American tribes to relieve stomach trouble, nausea, gas, coughs, sore throat, and fever. Applied topically, this antiseptic herb can treat skin inflammations including bug bites and stings, rashes, and even pimples, and has been known to ease the pain of headaches and arthritis.

In the Garden
Bergamot, like most mints, is a perennial that tends to spread aggressively. To control spreading and keep roots from tangling, divide every few years in spring. You can also grow bergamot in a container to control its size.
Size: 1 to 4 feet tall and up to 3 feet wide
Container: Any size; transplant to larger containers as it grows
Light: Full sun to partial shade

Soil: Moist, rich, well drained. Add compost and mulch to help retain moisture.
Plant: Seeds or root cuttings
Water: Regularly, when soil feels dry
Harvest: Snip leaves all through the growing season and snip flowers when they bloom in summer. For seeds, wait until the flowers bloom and produce seeds, then cut the flowers from the stems into a paper bag and let them dry completely.
Care: Trim regularly and remove dead flowers to promote new growth. Prune heavily in the fall to protect from winter weather.

SUBSTITUTIONS
- Lemon balm
- Lemon verbena
- Makrut lime
- Mint
- Sorrel

PAIRINGS

Fruits and Vegetables:
apples, apricots, berries, broccoli, carrots, celery, grapefruit, kiwi, lemons, mangoes, melon, mushrooms, onions, oranges, papaya, pumpkin, shallots, tomatoes
Proteins: almonds, cheeses, chicken, cottage cheese, cream cheese, duck, eggs, fish and seafood, peanuts, pork, walnuts
Seasonings: chives, cinnamon, cloves, cumin, mustard, dill, fennel, garlic, ginger, honey, lemon balm, lemon juice and zest, lemongrass, lime juice and zest, mint, nutmeg, parsley, red pepper flakes, rosemary, soy sauce, thyme, turmeric, watercress

Keep It Fresh

Bergamot leaves and flowers should be used as soon as possible after harvesting. They dry wonderfully for use in teas and potpourris (see directions on page 20). To store fresh bergamot for future use, chop and freeze (see page 19).

In the Kitchen

Dishes: Teas, jams, dips, sauces, salads, beverages
Prep: Use both leaves and flowers whole or chopped in any dish. Dry them if making tea.
Serve: Sprinkle fresh bergamot sparingly over salads, add to rubs and marinades for meat and fish, or stir into yogurt, cream, or soft cheeses for luscious dips. It also adds an interesting spicy-sweet touch to homemade breads and cakes.

BORAGE

Borago officinalis

Flavors: fresh, cool, cucumber-like

With its delicate, star-shaped blue flowers and refreshing cucumber flavor, borage is a wonderful addition to any herb or flower garden. It makes a handy growing companion for other plants (especially tomatoes and strawberries), as it repels pests and attracts bees.

The fresh, young leaves and flowers are a welcome addition to salads, vegetable dishes, and pastas. Older, larger leaves have a prickly layer of hair that can be softened and made more palatable in stews and soups or when cooked like spinach. Flowers make a beautiful garnish for salads, cold summertime beverages, and baked sweets.

HEALTH BENEFITS
Known as the "star flower" and the "herb of gladness," borage has been used since ancient times for its mood-boosting effects, and has even been prescribed as an antidepressant and stress reliever. In fact, borage has been shown to positively affect the adrenal glands and calm the nerves. It's used to promote sweating in cases of fever, and treat coughs, infections, and inflammation throughout the body, including topically for skin conditions.

In the Garden
Borage, annual, grows healthily in containers. For a steady supply of leaves and flowers, sow seeds every month throughout the growing season.

Size: Up to 3 feet tall and 2 feet wide
Container: 12 inches deep and wide
Light: Full sun to partial shade
Soil: Rich, well drained, but will grow in almost any soil
Plant: Seeds

Water: Regularly

Harvest: Snip leaves any time throughout the growing season and pick flowers once they bloom.

Care: Trim regularly to promote branching and new growth. Borage self-seeds readily every season. To control growth, cut the flower heads once they turn brown and catch seeds in a paper bag.

SUBSTITUTIONS
- Cucumber
- Escarole
- Salad burnet
- Spinach

PAIRINGS

Vegetables: asparagus, carrots, celery, cucumber, leeks, lettuce, mushrooms, onions, potatoes, tomatoes

Proteins: cheeses, chicken, eggs, fish and seafood

Seasonings: arugula, chives, dill, garlic, lemon juice and zest, mint, parsley, red pepper flakes, salad burnet

Keep It Fresh

Use borage fresh and soon after harvesting. It won't freeze or dry well for future use in cooking, although it can be chopped and frozen in ice-cube trays for a pretty cocktail garnish. Use fresh leaves for tea instead of dried.

In the Kitchen

Dishes: Salads, soups, stews, preserves, beverages

Prep: Chop or shred young leaves before adding to any dish. Large, older leaves should be cooked like a vegetable to soften the texture and fuzzy coating.

Serve: Sprinkle fresh leaves and flowers over cooked veggies, potatoes, eggs, and pastas. It goes especially well with fatty fish, and is a cooling addition to chilled soups like gazpacho, cucumber, or asparagus. Flowers can be candied to make beautiful decorations for cakes, tarts, and other desserts.

CHAMOMILE

Chamaemelum

Flavors: pungent, sweet, floral, apple-like

Chamomile translates to "little apple" in Spanish and "earth apple" in Greek, presumably for the herb's apple-like fragrance in the garden. While there are many plants called chamomile, the two used most often as an herb are German chamomile (*Chamaemelum matricaria recutita*) and Roman chamomile (*Chamaemelum nobile*), both bearing flowers that look like daisies. Dubbed "the plant's physician," chamomile makes a great companion plant in the garden, as it repels pests and supports the health of neighboring herbs and veggies.

Best known for its soothing qualities in teas, chamomile can be added to all kinds of beverages for similar effect and floral flavor, including lemonades, smoothies, and liqueurs. It's also a popular herb in aromatherapy and a feature ingredient in many cosmetics, including soaps, hair products, lotions, and herbal baths.

HEALTH BENEFITS
Chamomile tea is a timeless remedy for digestive upset, nausea, sleeplessness, and the common cold. Its calming effects can alleviate symptoms of stress and anxiety, including nervous stomach, ulcers, and headaches or migraines. Chamomile also serves as an antispasmodic, taming both intestinal cramps and menstrual cramps as well as relieving gas and bloating.

In the Garden

Roman and German chamomiles grow in similar conditions and will both thrive in containers. The Roman variety is a perennial that grows close to the ground, with tiny daisy-like flowers and sweet, spindly foliage. German chamomile is an annual that sprouts upright to about 1 or 2 feet, growing larger daisy-like flowers.

Size: Roman, 3 to 6 inches tall and 9 to 12 inches wide; German, up to 2 feet fall and 18 inches wide

Container: 1 foot deep and wide

Light: Full sun or partial shade

Soil: Light, sandy, well drained

Plant: Seeds, plants, cuttings, or divisions. Seeds need light to germinate, so place them just under the surface of the soil.

Water: Regularly and evenly, especially in droughts, about one inch per week; do not overwater.

Harvest: Snip leaves through spring and summer. When in full bloom, snip individual flowers with a portion of stem attached. Or, if growing German chamomile, you can pull up the whole plant.

Care: Trim regularly and remove dead flowers to promote new growth. Place mulch around the plants to retain water and prevent the growth of weeds. German chamomile self-seeds readily, so either remove dead flower heads to control regrowth or let the plant grow back the following spring.

> **SUBSTITUTIONS**
> - Bergamot
> - Borage
> - Lavender
> - Lemon balm

Keep It Fresh

Leaves and flowers can be used fresh or dried for teas, though dried flowers are more potent. Dry chamomile according to the directions on page 20. Do not freeze fresh chamomile.

PAIRINGS

Fruits and Vegetables: apples, apricots, blueberries, grapefruits, lemons, oranges, peaches, pineapple, plums

Proteins: almonds, hazelnuts, pecans, walnuts

Seasonings: cinnamon, cloves, fennel, honey, lavender, lemon verbena, mint, nutmeg

In the Kitchen

Dishes: Teas, beverages, jellies, baked desserts

Prep: Use fresh leaves and flowers whole, chopped, or crumble dried.

Serve: In addition to tea, lemonade, smoothies, and other beverages, chamomile can be used creatively in baking: Infuse dried leaves into butter, milk, or honey, or grind them with sugar, and add to your batter. It also adds a floral essence to preserves, stewed fruit, pie fillings, panna cotta, dessert sauces like crème anglaise, and ice cream.

CULANTRO

Eryngium foetidum

Other common names: Mexican coriander, culangot, or long coriander
Flavors: pungent, sharp, earthy, cilantro-like but stronger

Despite being a wildly popular herb in the Caribbean, Latin America, and Southeast Asia, culantro is still under the radar in the United States, sold mostly in cities with large Latin American or Caribbean populations. It sounds and tastes somewhat like its famous cousin, cilantro, and the two herbs are often confused for those reasons. But they shouldn't be, as culantro *looks* like a completely different herb and *is* a completely different herb—with its long, serrated leaves, stronger flavor, and ability to withstand long cook times.

To add to the confusion, culantro also goes by several other names, such as long or spiny coriander, Mexican coriander, Mexican cilantro, *shado beni* in Trinidad, and *recao* in Central America.

HEALTH BENEFITS
Widely used in South America and the Caribbean as a medicinal herb, culantro is commonly prepared as a tea to treat indigestion, constipation, gas, fever, and the flu. Its stomach-calming effects help relieve diarrhea, nausea, and vomiting. Known to have anti-inflammatory and mild pain-relieving abilities, it's also been used historically as a treatment for epilepsy, as demonstrated in the nicknames "fitweed" and "spiritweed."

In the Garden
Culantro, a perennial, is a warm-weather plant that thrives in containers. It grows the most flavorful leaves when partially shaded from the sun. In peak summer temperatures and under hot full sun, the plant will flower quickly and stop producing leaves; so provide shade to keep those tasty leaves coming back.
Size: Up to 18 inches tall
Container: At least 4 inches deep and 8 inches in diameter, or 1 gallon

Light: Partial shade to full sun; partial shade is preferred for larger, more flavorful leaves and a longer growing season.

SUBSTITUTIONS
• Cilantro

Soil: Rich, well drained

Plant: Seeds, seedlings, or plants

Water: Regularly, when soil feels dry to the touch

Harvest: Snip outer individual leaves when you need them, or use a knife to cut off the entire plant at the base.

Care: Trim flower stalks when they sprout (about once a week) to keep the plant thriving and lengthen the harvest. Once culantro flowers, the leaves become too tough for cooking. Place mulch around the plants to retain moisture. Protect from frosts.

PAIRINGS

Fruits and Vegetables: avocado, carrots, corn, jicama, lettuce, mangoes, mushrooms, onions, peppers, plantains, shallots, tomatillos, tomatoes

Proteins: beans, beef, chicken, eggs, fish and seafood, pork

Seasonings: annatto, basil, chili peppers, cilantro, coriander seeds, cumin, curry powder, fish sauce, galangal, garlic, ginger, jalapeño, lemongrass, lemon juice and zest, lime juice and zest, makrut lime, marjoram, mint, oregano, parsley, pepper, red pepper flakes, turmeric

Keep It Fresh

Culantro dries well, unlike the more tender cilantro. It'll also hold up if chopped and frozen in ice-cube trays with a bit of olive oil (see directions on page 19–21).

In the Kitchen

Dishes: Curries, stews, soups, marinades, salsas

Prep: Chop and add to any dish. If you're using culantro in place of the milder cilantro, cut the amount in half to accommodate for the more intense flavor.

Serve: Culantro is essential to many Latin American and Caribbean dishes, including Puerto Rican *sofrito*. In Southeast Asia, it's increasingly used in curries, soups, chutney, and beef dishes, and it's a staple condiment in Vietnamese meals. Its robust flavor makes it a great swap for cilantro in meaty stews and curries.

CURRY LEAF

Murraya koenigii

Other common name: kadi patta

Flavors: pungent, warm, lemony, slightly bitter

Not to be confused with curry powder (see page 251) or the curry plant (*Helichrysum italicum*), which is not for cooking, curry leaf belongs to the same family as citrus. The tree bears small branches with shiny leaflets growing up both sides in pairs, in a pinnate, or feather-like, arrangement.

Curry leaves look a bit like bay leaves and are used similarly in cooking—to imbue aromatics in long-cooked dishes before being removed. However, curry leaves are also edible.

> **HEALTH BENEFITS**
> Curry leaves are prized in Ayurvedic medicine for a variety of conditions, including digestion trouble such as diarrhea, constipation, and loss of appetite, as well as skin inflammation, hair loss, and graying. Research has suggested that curry leaves may help lower cholesterol and regulate some cases of diabetes.

In the Garden

The curry leaf tree is native to tropical climates, so it should be grown indoors in a container if these conditions can't be met outside. Room temperature should be at least 65° F. Start a curry leaf tree in a small container with drainage holes, and increase the container size gradually over the years as it grows; a pot that fits is crucial to maintaining moisture and nutrients around the roots.

Size: 13 to 20 feet tall

Container: Depends on tree size. Start small and increase the size gradually every year or two; a mature tree, at around ten years old, might need a 30-gallon container.

Light: Full sun

Soil: Well drained potting mix

Plant: Young plants, leaves, or fresh seeds. Plants and leaves are preferred over seeds to avoid problems with erratic germination.

Water: Regularly, when soil feels dry two inches deep, about once a week; do not overwater. Unless in very hot climates, curry leaf plants often go dormant during winter (and lose their leaves); if this happens, only water when the soil dries out completely and do not fertilize.

Harvest: Start harvesting when a young plant reaches 1 foot tall and bears several leafy branches. Snip or pluck off whole stalks, or petioles, rather than individual leaves to keep your plant thriving and ensure optimal flavor.

Care: Trim regularly to remove dead leaves and promote new growth. Place mulch around the base of the plant to retain moisture in hot weather. Add fertilizer during the warm season. If keeping outdoors in summer, protect from frosts or winds and move indoors when the weather cools.

SUBSTITUTIONS

• Asafetida
• Basil
• Makrut lime leaves

*Note: There's no exact flavor match for curry leaves, so consider leaving it out of your recipe or altering the flavor with one of these substitutions.

PAIRINGS

Vegetables: cauliflower, coconut and coconut milk, green beans, onions, peas, potatoes, pumpkin, shallots, tomatoes

Proteins: beans, beef, cashews, chicken, fish and seafood, lamb, lentils, peanuts

Seasonings: cardamom, cayenne, chili peppers, cilantro, cinnamon, cloves, coriander seeds, cumin, fennel seeds, fenugreek, galangal, garam masala, garlic, ginger, lemongrass, lemon juice, lime juice, mint, mustard, paprika, pepper, tamarind, turmeric

Keep It Fresh

Store curry leaves (still on their stems) in a plastic bag in the refrigerator crisper for one to two weeks. For future use, place in a zip-tight plastic bag and store in the freezer. Leaves freeze well for up to four weeks and don't need to defrost before use in cooking. Curry leaves lose their flavor when dried.

In the Kitchen

Dishes: Curries, stews, soups, rice, lentils, dals

Prep: Use whole sprigs to flavor long-cooked dishes, or whole or chopped leaves in any dish.

Serve: Whole leaves are often fried quickly in oil or ghee along with Indian spices like asafetida, cumin, or mustard seed, and then added to curries or stews either at the start of cooking or at the very end. Leaves can also be chopped and cooked with potatoes or vegetables, or crushed with hot chili peppers, tamarind, and coconut to make chutney or relish.

ELDER

Sambucus nigra

Other common names: elderberry and elderflower

*Flavors: **flowers** sweet and floral; **berries** bitter and astringent when raw, mellower, sweeter, and tart after cooking*

Native to mild climates in Europe and North America, the elder shrub (or small tree) grows abundantly in the wild and bears flat clusters of fragrant, white flowers and juicy, black-purple berries. Both flowers and berries are edible, but the leaves, stems, and raw berries are poisonous: Berries must be cooked before eating.

In the Garden

Elder shrubs, which are perennials, grow healthily in containers but very likely won't reach full size; they should be pruned to control growth. These plants generally bear fruit after three to four years. When handling berries, wear gloves and an apron to protect your skin and clothes from juice stains.

Size: Up to 12 feet tall

Container: Any large size; transplant to larger containers as it grows

Light: Full sun to partial shade

Soil: Moist, fertile, well drained; but elder will tolerate varying qualities of soil. Mix compost into the soil to help retain water, add nutrients, and prevent weeds.

Plant: Young plants

Water: Regularly, about one inch per week

HEALTH BENEFITS

Called "the medicine chest of the country people," elderflowers and berries are a decongestant and diaphoretic—they stimulate sweating—making them useful against fever and in the detoxification process. With elderflower's natural astringency, it's popular in skincare products like lotions and toners. Elderberries have been used to fight colds and flu, and like other berries, they're high in antioxidants and help supercharge the immune system.

Harvest: After 3 or 4 years, when berry clusters are droopy and hanging downward, the plant is ready for harvest. Pick the flowers and ripe clusters of berries. Carefully remove the berries from the stems, as the stems are poisonous.

Care: At first, weed regularly by hand so you don't disturb the growing roots. Don't prune during the first two years; after that, prune only when the leaves and flowers die after the growing season in fall or winter.

PAIRINGS

Fruits and Vegetables, elderberries and flowers: apples, berries, cherries, figs, grapefruit, gooseberries, grapes, melon, oranges, peach, pears, plums, pomegranate, rhubarb; **just flowers:** cabbage, lettuce, onions, salad veggies, tomatoes
Proteins, elderberries and flowers: almonds, cheeses; **just flowers:** chicken, duck, eggs
Seasonings, elderberries and flowers: allspice, cinnamon, cloves, lavender, lemon juice and zest, lime juice and zest, mint, nutmeg, rose, sesame seeds, vanilla; **just flowers:** caraway, cilantro, garlic, mustard, vinegar

SUBSTITUTIONS
Flowers:
- Lavender
- Rose
- Squash blossoms
- Violets

Berries:
- Cranberries
- Lingonberries
- Gooseberries

Keep It Fresh

Store fresh-picked berries in a zip-tight plastic bag in the refrigerator until ready for use; use as soon as possible. Elderberries will freeze well in plastic bags for future use. Both berries and flowers can be dried (see directions on page 20).

In the Kitchen

Dishes: Cocktails, liqueurs, cordials, jams, syrups, chutneys, teas, sorbets, baked desserts

Prep: Fresh berries must be cooked before eating to kill toxic chemicals and improve flavor. Flowers can be served whole, chopped, or candied.

Serve: Elder is a perfect match for sweet-and-tart summer fruits like strawberries, blackberries, cherries, and rhubarb. In Germany, elderflowers are quick-fried on their stems to make *Hollerküchln*, or elderflower fritters, and they can be sprinkled over salads, pickled, or bottled with vinegar. Both flowers and berries can be baked into desserts and used in jams, chutneys, and pie fillings.

EPAZOTE

Dysphania ambrosioides

Flavors: pungent, earthy, lemony, bitter

A staple of ancient Aztec cooking, epazote is traditionally added to black beans, both for its flavor and its flatulence-relieving powers. It's also a common ingredient in salsas, mole verde, and quesadillas, and can be served raw or added at the end of cooking for optimal flavor.

Like that other popular Mexican herb cilantro, epazote is controversial: Some people hate the smell and the taste, while others find it addicting. In fact, the word *epazote* in Aztec means "skunk sweat." Taste-test with other members of your household to determine if epazote really lives up to its name. Use sparingly, as this herb is quite potent and is even poisonous in large quantities.

HEALTH BENEFITS

In addition to preventing and relieving gas, epazote is also an age-old remedy for intestinal worms (hence its other nickname, "wormseed"). Prepared as a tea or eaten with food, the herb is known to relieve stomach cramps and constipation as well as respiratory problems stemming from colds, the flu, and asthma. Epazote "water" can be applied topically to treat mild pain like arthritis: Soak leaves in water for a few days, then massage the infused solution into the skin.

In the Garden

In warmer climates, epazote grows back as a perennial. In wintry regions, plant epazote in a container to be moved indoors in cold weather.

Size: 3 to 4 feet tall
Container: At least 10 to 12 inches deep
Light: Full sun
Soil: Moist, sandy, well drained

Plant: Seeds or seedlings
Water: Occasionally, only when soil feels dry to the touch
Harvest: Pick off fresh leaves as needed.
Care: Trim regularly to prevent flowering and promote new growth. Epazote self-seeds freely and will spread if not monitored.

Keep It Fresh

Epazote dries well and the flavor is comparable to fresh, only weaker. It'll also hold up if chopped and frozen in ice-cube trays (see directions on pages 19–21).

SUBSTITUTIONS

There are no exact flavor matches for epazote, so cut it from the recipe if you want authenticity. You can try combining cilantro, oregano, and savory, or use any of the following.
- Ajwain
- Savory
- Parsley
- Cilantro
- Oregano

PAIRINGS

Fruits and Vegetables: avocado, chayote, corn, fennel, hominy, lime, peppers, mushrooms, onions, peas, potatoes, shallots, squash, tomatoes, tomatillos, zucchini
Proteins: beef, black beans, cheeses, chicken, chorizo, eggs, fish and seafood, pinto beans, pork, white beans
Seasonings: ajwain, bay leaf, cayenne, chili peppers, chipotle peppers, cilantro, cloves, cumin, garlic, habanero peppers, jalapeño, lime juice, marjoram, Mexican oregano, oregano, parsley, peppercorns, poblano peppers, rosemary, sage, serrano peppers, thyme

In the Kitchen

Dishes: Bean dishes, salsas, quesadillas, tamales, chilies, soups
Prep: Choose younger leaves to use in cooking, as older ones have even stronger flavor. Chop or use leaves whole in any cooked dish. Chop for salsas, but beware the flavor of raw epazote—it's potent.
Serve: If using dried epazote, cook for a bit longer than you would with, fresh, to soften the herb. To swap fresh for dried, use 1 teaspoon dried epazote for three or four fresh leaves. Note that cooking will mellow the intense flavor.

FENUGREEK

Trigonella foenum-graecum

Flavors: bitter, earthy, celery-like, with hints of maple

One of the signature ingredients in Indian cooking, fenugreek (or *methi*) is used as both herb and spice in many cuisines throughout India, the Middle East, and Northern Africa.

The clover-shaped leaves are fresh and zesty when young but grow bitter as they age, so older leaves can benefit from a little cooking to mellow the flavor. Dried leaves, called *kasuri methi*, are more potent in fragrance and flavor, so they should be used more sparingly. The seeds offer a distinct bittersweet flavor that's beloved in many spice blends and traditional dishes; they're even used to make imitation maple syrup.

HEALTH BENEFITS

Fenugreek has been used medicinally since ancient times. Fresh leaves offer iron, fiber, calcium, vitamin K, and lots of immune-boosting vitamin C, but dried leaves lose their C-content in significant quantity.

In the Garden

Fenugreek, an annual, grows successfully in containers if treated to plenty of sun. In cooler climates, bring potted fenugreek indoors during the winter months. They don't transplant easily, so choose a suitable container and stick with it.

Size: Up to 2 feet tall

Container: Any size

Light: Full sun

Soil: Moist, fertile, well drained. Mix compost into the soil for added nutrients.

Plant: Seeds, presoaked in warm water for 24 hours

Water: Moderately, only when soil feels dry to the touch

Harvest: For milder flavor, harvest leaves only in spring and fall; leaves harvested in hot summer weather are at peak bitterness. Simply pull plants out from the root. To harvest seeds, wait until fall, when the plant has died and the seedpods are mature; let them dry completely before picking.

SUBSTITUTIONS
- Celery leaves
- Watercress
- Spinach or kale

Keep It Fresh
Fenugreek leaves can be frozen or dried. Dried leaves offer more robust flavor than fresh, so store according to your flavor preference (see freezing and drying directions on pages 19-20).

PAIRINGS
Fruits and Vegetables: carrots, cauliflower, celery, coconut, lemon, eggplant, mango, mushrooms, okra, onions, peas, peppers, potatoes, shallots, spinach, tomatoes

Proteins: beef, beans, cashews, chicken, chickpeas, eggs, fish and seafood, lamb

Seasonings: allspice, anise, basil, bay leaf, cardamom, cayenne, chili peppers, cilantro, cinnamon, cloves, coriander seeds, cumin, curry leaf, curry powder, fennel, garam masala, garlic, ginger, jalapeño, lemongrass, lemon juice and zest, lime juice and zest, mint, mustard, nutmeg, paprika, parsley, pepper, poppy seeds, red pepper flakes, saffron, sesame seeds, tamarind, turmeric

In the Kitchen
Dishes: salads, stews, curries, breads, sauces, rice, chutneys

Prep: Chop fresh leaves and add to any savory dish.

Serve: Fresh leaves are delicious in veggie and meaty curries, rice, sautés, and stews, especially with potatoes and spinach. They're often baked into savory Indian breads, like naan, paratha, and chapati. Use the leaves toward the end of cooking. Use just a pinch of dried leaves for robust flavor in sauces and cooked dishes, along with onion, ginger, and garlic.

HOUTTUYNIA CORDATA

Houttuynia cordata

Other common names: fersh mint

Flavors: pungent, tangy, sour, fishy

Little known outside of Asia, these pretty, heart-shaped leaves are used abundantly in Vietnamese cooking. The Chameleon variety, with its dappled red-pink-yellow-green leaves, is an impressive ornamental and not generally used in the kitchen.

Called *rau diếp cá* in Vietnam, houttuynia is an acquired taste, to put it lightly—its common name, "fish mint," proves to be an apt description, though there's some cilantro in there too. However, note that the Japanese variety of houttuynia, *dokudami*, has a pleasant citrus aroma, while the Chinese plant bears the fishy scent.

HEALTH BENEFITS

In Japan, houttuynia is called *dokudami*, which translates to "poison-blocking plant." Used since ancient times to reverse the effects of poison, houttuynia has also proved effective against allergies, as it inhibits the body's production of histamines after an allergy is triggered. It's also antibacterial and anti-inflammatory, as well as a cough suppressant, mild pain reliever, digestive aid, and general immune booster. Applied topically for skin irritations and hemorrhoids, houttuynia's healthful qualities are also plentiful when prepared as a healing tea.

In the Garden

Houttuynia, a perennial, is an aggressive spreader, so unless you intend to grow it widely in an open area, it's best planted in a controlled space, like beside a wall or sidewalk or in a container. This herb is infamous for its pungent, fishy-cilantro aroma, so keep this in mind before starting your garden.

Size: 6 inches to 1 foot tall

Container: At least 8 inches in diameter, or 1 to 2 gallons

Light: Full sun to partial shade; the Chameleon variety needs full sun for the best color.
Soil: Moist to wet; pond or bog soil (see page 83)
Plant: Cuttings, root divisions, or young plants
Water: Regularly to keep soil consistently moist
Harvest: Leaves are ready for harvest from spring through fall; just snip them off the plant.
Care: In cold climates, place mulch around the plants to protect the roots during winter weather.

PAIRINGS

Fruits and Vegetables: carrots, celery, lemon, lettuce, lime, mushrooms, onions, potatoes, tomatoes
Proteins: beef, chicken, duck, eggs, fish and fish (especially whitefish) and seafood
Seasonings: basil, chili peppers, cilantro, coriander seeds, cumin, galangal, garlic, ginger, lemongrass, lemon juice, lime juice, mint, paprika, parsley, soy sauce

Keep It Fresh

To test freshness, bruise or crush leaves and check for that signature pungent aroma. Leaves can be dried for use in teas (see directions on page 20).

In the Kitchen

Dishes: salads, soups, stir-fries, sauces
Prep: Use leaves whole in salads; slice or chop in soups and cooked dishes. Add toward the end of cooking to retain that distinct flavor.
Serve: Houttuynia is commonly served raw in salads and spring rolls. The herb adds tangy flavor to stir-fries and fish sauce, and it also accompanies grilled or steamed meats and fish.

HYSSOP

Hyssopus officinalis

Flavors: minty, floral, bitter

Hyssop is a member of the mint family, like the similarly named anise hyssop (see page 88). But unlike its tall, sweet, distant cousin, this herb is a low-growing shrub with a bitter-mint, herb flavor. Long spears of blue, purple, pink, or white flowers attract welcome visitors—hummingbirds, butterflies, and bees—making this a charming addition to an outdoor garden.

Best known since ancient times as a medicinal and purifying herb, hyssop sneaks under the radar in the kitchen—but it shouldn't, as its unique flavor adds edge to everything from rich meats to fruity desserts. Its leaves, shoots, and flowers are all edible and also all pungent in flavor, so use only in pinches or teaspoons when cooking. Look for fresh hyssop at Middle Eastern markets or at online herb shops.

HEALTH BENEFITS

Hyssop has been used medicinally over the centuries in many ways, including for digestion problems, flatulence, and respiratory conditions like cough, bronchitis, and asthma. Taken as a tea, it's been shown to loosen mucus, help soothe a sore throat, and calm upset stomach. Hyssop is considered a purifying herb: its leaves can be added to herbal baths to stimulate sweating and clear out toxins.

In the Garden

Hyssop, which is a perennial, can be grown in containers and window boxes; just make sure the containers are a suitable size for the large roots.

Size: 2 to 3 feet tall
Container: 10 to 12 inches deep
Light: Full sun

Soil: Dry, poor, well drained

Plant: Seeds, cuttings, or divisions

Water: Regularly when young, until plants are established; drought tolerant, do not overwater.

Harvest: Harvest the leaves and flowers for use in the kitchen. For the seeds, wait until the pods dry out and turn brown. Take whole stems if you're drying sprigs.

Care: Trim foliage lightly throughout the season to keep the shrubs in shape. Prune back after the last frost in spring to promote new growth. The plant occasionally self-seeds. Replace after several years, especially in cold-winter climates. Divide mature plants and replant every three years in spring or fall.

PAIRINGS

Fruits and Vegetables: apple, apricots, beans, beets, cabbage, carrots, cauliflower, mushrooms, peaches, squash

Proteins: almonds, beef, cheeses, chicken, eggs, fish and seafood, game, lamb, lentils, turkey

Seasonings: anise, basil, bay leaf, chervil, chives, lemon juice, mint, parsley, sage, thyme

Keep It Fresh

Hyssop dries exceptionally well (see directions on page 20), but does not hold up frozen.

In the Kitchen

Dishes: Salads, soups, stews, sausages, beverages, fruit desserts, teas

Prep: Use fresh leaves and flowers in salads and soups. Dried leaves can be infused into liqueurs, beverages, fruit syrups and sauces, and creamy desserts (like pudding or ice cream), or prepared as a tea. Grind dried leaves to flavor stews, marinades, meat rubs, and even baking sugar.

Serve: Use dried hyssop in recipes that call for sage, rosemary, or mint, especially in seasoning for rich meats like pork, lamb, goose, and fatty fish. It's also delicious baked into savory breads and sweet desserts. Hyssop's bitter-mint flavor makes an interesting counterpoint for fruit jams, sorbets, and pie fillings; pair with tart summer fruits. Mix into soft creamy cheeses or herb butters.

LEMON BALM

Melissa officinalis

Flavors: lemon, mint

The delightfully fragrant lemon balm is enjoyed for its calming aroma, its refreshing lemony flavor, and its charms in the garden, where it attracts butterflies, bees, and birds. True to form, the herb's botanical name, *Melissa*, is Greek for "honeybee."

Lemon balm has been prized since ancient times for its mood-lifting abilities, and merely brushing against the leaves can offer a fresh, invigorating whiff of lemon. It's a popular herb in teas and summertime beverages like fruit punch and lemonade; it also flavors the herbal liqueurs Chartreuse and Bénédictine. Best used fresh, lemon balm loses flavor when cooked and should be added after cooking if possible.

HEALTH BENEFITS

Lemon balm is a classic feel-good herb, used for its calming qualities since antiquity. It's a popular sleep aid for people suffering from insomnia, specifically when prepared in a tea with other calming herbs like chamomile and valerian. Lemon balm tea can also ease symptoms of anxiety and stress, as well as stomach upset, gas, and cramps. Applied topically as an ointment, the herb's extract can quicken the healing of cold sores and help prevent them from spreading.

In the Garden

Lemon balm, a perennial, can reseed and spread aggressively in warm climates, so keep it contained in a pot or prune to keep it under control.

Size: 2 to 3 feet tall and up to 2 feet wide

Container: At least 8 inches deep

Light: Full sun to partial shade in the afternoon in very hot or dry climates

Soil: Moist, rich, well drained

Plant: Seeds, divisions, or young plants

Water: Regularly, to keep the soil consistently moist; somewhat drought tolerant, do not overwater.

Harvest: Harvest leaves often, as soon as they're ripe; they develop an unpleasant flavor if left to age.

Care: Prune heavily after flowering to prevent reseeding, control size, and promote healthy new growth. Prune after droughts and when the plant looks weak. Place mulch around the plant to nourish the soil and prevent reseeding. Divide roots in the fall or spring.

SUBSTITUTIONS
- Bergamot
- Catnip
- Lemongrass
- Lemon juice
- Lemon verbena
- Sorrel

PAIRINGS

Fruits and Vegetables: berries, celery, lettuce, melons, nectarines, onions, oranges, peaches, pears, pineapple, strawberries, tomatoes

Proteins: cheeses, chicken, eggs, fish and seafood, turkey

Seasonings: allspice, basil, bay leaf, borage, catnip, chamomile, chervil, cinnamon, cloves, dill, garlic, ginger, hyssop, lavender, lemon juice, lemon verbena, marjoram, mint, oregano, parsley, pepper, rosemary, sorrel, sweet cicely, sweet woodruff, tarragon, thyme, vanilla

Keep It Fresh

Lemon balm can be dried for potpourris (see directions on page 20), but it will lose flavor and is better used fresh for teas and food. It freezes well in ice-cube trays with a bit of oil or water (see directions on page 19).

In the Kitchen

Dishes: Teas, beverages, salads, soups, sauces, dressings and marinades, desserts

Prep: Use fresh whole leaves or tear them into smaller pieces before adding to any dish.

Serve: Since the mild flavor diminishes with heat, cold dishes will offer optimal lemon-mint flavor; add to cooked dishes just before serving. Lemon balm is ideal for fresh fruit salads, cold beverages, and hot teas, as well as sweet, fruity desserts like tarts, pies, custards, sorbets, and ice cream. Stir it into soft, spreadable cheeses like goat cheese and cream cheese, and add it to stuffings for chicken, turkey, or pork. Use it in marinades and sauces for fish dishes, and sprinkle it over eggs and potatoes.

LEMON VERBENA

Aloysia citrodora

Flavors: lemony and herbal

Grown naturally in the tropical climates of Latin America, lemon verbena is a summer-loving herb that brings elegant fragrance to the garden and refreshing lemon flavor to the dinner table. It's often found in scented lotions, soaps, and perfumes, as well as soothing hot teas.

Fresh-cut stems can be placed in a vase with water to serve as a natural air freshener. Lemon verbena is a tasty alternative to lemon peel or zest—it adds a "green" herbal flavor and lacks the tartness of the fruit.

HEALTH BENEFITS

Lemon verbena's soothing lemon-herbal scent makes it popular in aromatherapy, where it's used in oils and lotions to help calm nerves and relieve stress. Taken as a tea, the herb helps ease symptoms of stomach upset, including diarrhea, constipation, gas, and cramps.

In the Garden

In a temperate or wintry climate, where temps drop below 40°F, plant lemon verbena, a perennial, in a container so you can bring it indoors in cold weather; it will go dormant for the season and lose its leaves. Plants with shorter growing seasons won't flower or grow much taller than two to four feet in containers.

Size: 2 to 4 feet tall in a container up to 10 feet tall in the ground

Container: at least 1 foot in diameter

Light: Full sun to partial sun in tropical climates

Soil: Moist, loose, well drained

Plant: Seedlings or cuttings

Water: Regularly, to keep soil consistently moist. If wintering indoors while dormant, do not overwater.

Harvest: Snip stems regularly throughout the season.

Care: Trim throughout the growing season to keep the plant thriving and promote new growth. Prune heavily in fall. Fertilize regularly, but stop during the dormant winter season. In cold climates, return outdoors only after the last frost in spring, then prune.

PAIRINGS

Fruits and Vegetables: blueberries, celery, cherries, green beans, lemons, onions, oranges, raspberries, tomatoes

Proteins: almonds, cheeses, chicken, eggs, fish and seafood, pecans, pork, walnuts

Seasonings: basil, chamomile, cinnamon, cloves, garlic, ginger, honey, lavender, lemon juice and zest, lime juice and zest, mint, oregano, paprika, parsley, sage, thyme, vanilla

Keep It Fresh

Lemon verbena can be dried for tea or potpourri, or frozen in ice-cube trays for longer storage (see directions for freezing on page 19 and drying on page 20).

In the Kitchen

Dishes: Teas, cold beverages, desserts, jams, dressings and marinades, soups, sauces

Prep: Use leaves whole for flavor and remove before serving (they're tough to chew), or mince before adding to a dish.

Serve: Infuse lemon verbena leaves in vinegar, oil, jam, and milk (to make ice cream or custard). Chopped or minced leaves stirred into butter offers a fresh take on classic herb butter. Sprinkle them over cooked veggies, rice, and soups, or place whole leaves over fish and pork dishes while cooking. You can also store leaves in a container of sugar for a few days, then use to bake citrus-flavored breads and cakes. Alternatively, grind fresh or dried leaves and add to doughs, batters, and pie fillings.

LOVAGE

Levisticum officinale

Flavors: pungent, tangy, celery-like

Common in English kitchens, lovage is a large, elegant plant with a lot of flavor. The broad parsley-like leaves and thick stalks give it away as a member of the parsley, celery, and carrot family, and it can swap in for parsley and celery in any dish—just be sure to adjust amounts for the much stronger flavor.

The entire lovage plant can be used in the kitchen, from the leaves to the roots, so you'll get your time and money's worth with a specimen in your yard. Young leaves can be tossed fresh into salads, since they're milder, while stalks, seeds, roots, and older leaves are cooked to mellow out the flavor.

HEALTH BENEFITS

Lovage helps stimulate digestion and serves as a potent diuretic, helping to flush out the urinary tract, prevent or fight infection, and reduce inflammation. It also contains high quantities of the antioxidant quercetin, which can help fight inflammation and prevent the degeneration of cells due to aging.

In the Garden

Make sure you have plenty of room to grow lovage, a perennial, in your garden—it can reach anywhere between three and eight feet tall. To control its size, lovage can be grown in a large, deep container outside. The plants will go dormant over the winter, then grow back bigger and stronger the following spring. This is not an ideal plant for tropical climates, since it prefers cooler weather and an annual period of dormancy.

Size: 3 to 8 feet tall
Container: At least 10 inches deep
Light: Full sun to partial shade
Soil: Rich, fertile, well drained

Plant: Fresh seeds, seedlings, root divisions, or young plants

Water: Often during seedling stage, but less often once established

Harvest: Snip outermost stalks and leaves from the base. For the seeds, wait until they dry completely and turn brown, then use a bowl or paper bag to catch all of them.

Care: Trim stalks to promote new growth with optimal flavor (old foliage becomes too strong to eat). Cut the seed stalk to lengthen your leaf-and-stalk harvest, or let it grow if harvesting the seeds. If you experience harsh winters, place mulch around the plant to protect the roots.

SUBSTITUTIONS
- Celery leaves and seeds
- Angelica

PAIRINGS

Vegetables: asparagus, carrots, cucumbers, eggplant, leeks, lettuce, mushrooms, onions, peas, potatoes, shallots, tomatoes

Proteins: cheeses, chicken, duck, eggs, fish and seafood, lentils

Seasonings: bay leaf, capers, celery seeds, chervil, chives, fennel, garlic, lemon juice, mustard, oregano, parsley, pepper, sage, sorrel, tarragon, thyme

Keep It Fresh

Lovage can be dried, but know that the flavor becomes concentrated and even more potent, so use with caution. It will also hold up frozen (see directions on pages 19–21).

In the Kitchen

Dishes: leaves and stems soups, stews, braises, casseroles, pastas, salads, dressings and marinades; **seeds** breads, pickles, sauces

Prep: Use whole stalks (with leaves) to flavor long-cooked dishes like roasts and stews, or chop them up and add to casseroles, pastas, stews, or rice.

Serve: The clean veggie flavor of lovage goes remarkably well with potatoes, tomatoes, and eggs: Try potato soups, tomato-lovage frittatas and omelets, and lovage Bloody Marys (just nix the celery!). Place whole stalks in the pan with chicken or fish while cooking, or chop and add to pastas, lentil stews, stuffings, and casseroles. Toss young leaves into salads, dressings, and slaws. Seeds can be baked into breads or used in pickling spices, and even the roots can be cooked and eaten like a vegetable.

MARIGOLD

Calendula officinalis

Flavors: tangy, peppery, spicy, lightly bitter

The bright yellow-orange petals of marigold are put to work in the kitchen both for flavor and for coloring. A member of the daisy family, marigolds bring dazzle to the garden and have been used traditionally to dye cheese and butter, and to replicate the color of saffron. In regard to flavor, marigold has been dubbed "the poor man's saffron." But make no mistake: its flavor comes nowhere near that highly coveted spice.

Although not technically the same plant, other edible marigolds include the French marigold (*Tagetes patula*), one of the staple culinary herbs of the Georgian republic, and Mexican mint marigold (*Tagetes lucida*), whose anise flavor makes it a frequent substitute for tarragon in Mexican cooking.

HEALTH BENEFITS

Marigold can help fight inflammation, viruses, and bacteria. It's commonly used topically to moisturize the skin and treat minor cuts, burns, irritations, and other wounds. Marigold also offers antioxidant activity, which helps postpone or prevent age-related cell damage that can lead to degenerative conditions like heart disease and cancer.

In the Garden

Marigolds are annuals and like temperate climates and struggle in extreme heat. In hot climates, plan for peak seasons in early spring and fall. These flowers are some-what tolerant of drought and frost. They'll grow healthily in containers, too.

Size: 2 to 3 feet tall
Container: 6 inches deep
Light: Full sun to partial shade
Soil: Well drained; marigold will tolerate various qualities of soil.

Plant: Seeds or young plants
Water: Moderately; do not overwater.
Harvest: Snip stems regularly throughout the season.
Care: Trim dead flowers and harvest regularly to promote new, healthy growth. Marigold self-seeds freely and will return the following year if you let it.

SUBSTITUTIONS
• Nasturtiums
• Pansies

PAIRINGS

Fruits and Vegetables: cabbage, corn, cucumbers, lettuce, oranges, peaches, tangerines
Proteins: cheeses, chicken, eggs, fish and seafood
Seasonings: celery seeds, honey, lemon juice and zest, mustard, nutmeg, red pepper flakes, rose, vanilla

Keep It Fresh

Fresh marigold blooms should be used as soon as possible after harvesting, but they can be dried for longer storage (see directions on page 20). Dry petals individually to speed up the process.

In the Kitchen

Dishes: Salads, soups, sauces, pastas, rice, breads, desserts
Prep: Pluck petals from the stem and snip off the white ends, which taste bitter. Chop, puree, or use whole in any dish. Use dried marigold whole, crumbled, or ground into a powder.
Serve: Scatter petals over salads, soups, pastas, and rice. Their subtle, tangy flavor is delicious in herb butters, vinegars, spreadable cheeses, custards, and even baked into sweet breads and cakes. Quick-cook marigold in omelets, frittatas, and scrambled eggs, or stir into casseroles and stir-fries.

MYRTLE

Myrtus communis

*Flavors: **leaves** astringent, bitter, spicy, citrus; **berries** juniper, rosemary, allspice, black pepper*

Myrtle's sleek, green leaves and dark-purple berries are timeless seasonings on the Mediterranean islands of Corsica, Crete, and Sardinia. Although the leaves give off a luscious, sweet-spicy orange aroma, the taste is decidedly more bitter, so they're best used as flavoring and removed before serving. Mediterranean cooks most often use the leaves and sprigs to season meats and fish, whether roasted, grilled, broiled, or smoked. The branches even serve as firewood, imparting their spicy flavor to anything grilled over them.

Myrtle berries taste a bit like black pepper, with sweeter notes reminiscent of juniper berries. They're used much like both in cooking—added ground to hearty stews and meat dishes, or infused into liqueurs, syrups, and sweet sauces.

HEALTH BENEFITS

An ancient symbol of love and beauty, the myrtle plant has been used for health and healing for millennia. It was used to treat urinary conditions in ancient Egypt, and today myrtle is believed to have decongestant, antibacterial, and analgesic properties.

In the Garden

Myrtle, a perennial, grows successfully in containers and will conform to size; it can be grown as a shrub or a small tree. If you like, transplant to larger pots as the plant grows. If you live in a cold climate (temps lower than 20°F), bring it indoors in the winter.

Size: Dwarf shrub, 2 to 3 feet tall; tree, up to 16 feet tall and 10 feet wide
Container: Depends on tree size
Light: Full sun

Soil: Moist, well drained
Plant: Seeds or cuttings
Water: Regularly throughout the growing season; occasionally in dormancy, so the surface soil dries slightly between watering.
Harvest: Snip whole sprigs or individual leaves when needed.
Care: Prune in the spring. Protect from cold winds.

SUBSTITUTIONS

Leaves:
- Rosemary
- Allspice (leaves)
- Bay leaves

Berries:
- Juniper berries
- Black pepper
- Allspice (ground)

PAIRINGS

Vegetables: broccoli, carrots, celery, corn, mushrooms, okra, onions, peppers, potatoes, spinach, squash, tomatoes, zucchini
Proteins: beef, cheeses, chicken, duck, eggs, fish and seafood, game, lentils, pork, sausage, veal, venison
Seasonings: cayenne, celery seeds, fennel, garlic, lemon juice, mustard, paprika, parsley, savory, thyme, Worcestershire sauce

Keep It Fresh

Both leaves and berries are often dried (see directions on page 20).

In the Kitchen

Dishes: Roasts, broils, grills, stews
Prep: Use whole sprigs or leaves for flavoring, or chop leaves and add to stews and stuffings.
Serve: Place sprigs on the grill or in the roasting pan when cooking meat or fish. Sprigs can also be wrapped around cuts of meat to imbue flavor while cooking serving. Chop the leaves or grind the dried berries and add to stuffings, stews, and casseroles. Dried leaves can be added to pork rubs and marinades, while fresh berries will flavor sauces, syrups, and even cocktails.

NASTURTIUMS

Tropaeolum majus

Flavors: peppery, watercress-like

Also called Indian cress, nasturtium stays true to the "cress" name in flavor. It has a crisp, peppery bite much like watercress. But in appearance, nasturtium blows all other cresses out of the water. In summertime, vibrant bursts of orange, yellow, and red flowers grow just above the plant's emerald, lily pad–like leaves, making a stunning sight in any garden or yard. Nasturtium spreads, climbs, and grows quickly, while its leaves, flowers, and buds are all edible. They add zing to fresh green salads and serve as charming garnish.

As the summer sun gets hotter later in the season, nasturtiums' pepper flavor grows more potent right along with it, so adjust amounts in your cooking to accommodate for the added heat.

HEALTH BENEFITS
Nasturtium tea can help treat coughs, colds, the flu, and bronchitis. The leaves especially offer immune-boosting vitamin C and can help fight infections; they've most notably been used against infections in the urinary tract. When applied topically as a compress, nasturtium has been used to soothe minor skin irritations and muscle pain.

In the Garden
Nasturtiums, which are perennials, can either stay low and compact or climb over fences, trellises, and basket rims. Choose the variety that suits your garden's design. They grow healthily in containers and window boxes.

Size: Dwarf plants, 1 to 2 feet tall; climbers, up to 10 feet tall
Container: Depends on variety and size
Light: Full sun
Soil: Moist, somewhat poor, well drained; rich soils won't produce colorful blooms.

Plant: Seeds

Water: Regularly, when the soil feels dry to the touch

Harvest: Snip leaves and flowers throughout the season. Save seeds to plant the following spring; wait until they're completely dry and store in a paper bag.

Care: Weed regularly. Snip off dead flowers to promote new growth. If using a container, trim occasionally to control the growth.

PAIRINGS

Fruits and Vegetables: avocado, beets, carrot, celery, cranberries, cucumbers, grapes, lettuce, onions, oranges, peppers, potatoes, spinach, tomatoes

Proteins: almonds, cream cheese, chicken, eggs, fish and seafood, goat cheese, mascarpone, walnuts

Seasonings: arugula, balsamic vinegar, bay leaf, chili peppers, chives, cilantro, dill, fennel, garlic, honey, lemon juice, lime juice, marjoram, paprika, parsley, peppercorn, tarragon, watercress

SUBSTITUTIONS
- Marigold
- Pansies
- Violets
- Squash blossoms

Keep It Fresh

Leaves will keep in a plastic bag in the fridge for a few days, but blossoms should be used fresh, just after harvesting. Leaves and flowers do not dry or freeze well.

In the Kitchen

Dishes: salads, soups, sandwiches, dressings, garnish

Prep: Use leaves and flowers whole or chopped in any dish.

Serve: Fold chopped nasturtiums into soft, spreadable cheeses, butter, or mayonnaise, and spread onto sandwiches or crackers. Add young leaves and blooms to salads, soups, and sauces for fish and chicken (try nasturtium pesto!). Infuse into vinegar and make tangy nasturtium vinaigrette. Older leaves have a stronger flavor and will hold up to quick last-minute cooking in stir-fries, sautés, and pastas. The leaves and blossoms can be stuffed with cheese fillings for tasty finger food, and the buds can be pickled and swapped in for capers.

NEPITELLA

Calamintha nepeta

Other common name: lesser calamint

Flavors: pungent, minty, peppery, slightly bitter

A signature herb of Tuscany, Sicily, and Sardinia, nepitella grows in the wild in southern Italy, bearing a minty fragrance, shiny oregano-like leaves, and tall spears of lavender or white blooms. It's a favorite among hummingbirds, butterflies, and bees, and an easy charmer in the garden.

Also called basil thyme, mountain balm, and *mentuccia* in Italian, nepitella is often described as a cross between mint and oregano, flavoring regional dishes involving mushrooms, artichokes, roasts, grilled meats, and shellfish. It's a robust herb, so use sparingly at first until you know how much you like.

HEALTH BENEFITS
Nepitella can be prepared as a tea to aid in digestion, calm the nerves, and help clear congestion. It's also used to treat fever, insomnia, and symptoms of menstruation.

In the Garden

Nepitella is a small, perennial shrub in the mint family that, like its cousin, can spread fairly aggressively. Fortunately, it grows successfully in containers, which can help keep size under control.

Size: 1 to 3 feet tall and 2 feet wide (or more)

Container: At least 12 inches in diameter

Light: Full sun or partial shade

Soil: Moist, well drained

Plant: Seeds, cuttings, or divisions

Water: Occasionally, only when soil feels dry to the touch

Harvest: Snip leaves just before the plants flower for optimal flavor, or as needed.

Care: Nepitella self-seeds readily; pull up new seedlings when they appear to control spreading.

Keep It Fresh

Nepitella dries well for use over the winter (see directions on page 20).

PAIRINGS

Vegetables: artichokes, eggplant, mushrooms, peppers, potatoes, squash, tomatoes, zucchini

Proteins: beans, beef, cheeses, chicken, goat cheese, lamb, mozzarella, Parmesan, pecorino, shellfish

Seasonings: basil, chili peppers, cilantro, dill, garlic, lemon juice and zest, marjoram, oregano, parsley, pepper, thyme

In the Kitchen

Dishes: Sautés, roasts, soups, stews, teas
Prep: Use leaves whole or chopped.
Serve: Nepitella is traditionally sautéed with mushrooms, zucchini, and tomatoes in Tuscan cuisine. It's also a delicious companion for artichokes and goes particularly well in garlic and tomato sauces. Try it with porcini mushrooms, garlic, olive oil, and pecorino or Parmesan cheese. Stir it into soft, spreadable cheeses like goat cheese or cream cheese, and use it to season shellfish like scallops and shrimp.

PANDAN LEAF

Pandanus amaryllifolius

Other common name: screw pine

Flavors: sweet, warm, and nutty, with citrus and pine

Considered "the vanilla of the East," pandan leaves are ubiquitous in Southeast Asian cuisine. Their extract is commonly used in cakes, jellies, and other desserts, but their sweet, complex flavor is also enjoyed in savory dishes, either wrapped around meat for the grill or cooked in a pot of curry or rice.

The long, narrow leaves are prized for their bright-green hue in addition to their delectable flavors, and they're often used as food coloring. Extract from pandan flowers (*Pandanus tectorius*), called *kewra*, flavors rice, meats, and desserts in Northern India.

Sold fresh, frozen, or dried in some Thai and Vietnamese markets in the West, pandan is also sold as an extract or paste (opt for the extract over the paste, if possible).

> **HEALTH BENEFITS**
> Pandan leaf can be brewed as a tea to ease stomachache, aid digestion, and relieve sore throat and cough. Thanks to its antiseptic properties, it's also used to soothe irritated or stressed skin, including sunburns.

In the Garden

Pandan trees love tropical weather and will grow perennially in that climate. In wintry climates, where temps drop below 50°F for long periods of time, plant pandan in a container so you can bring it indoors in cold weather. Place in a sun-filled window or patio.

Size: 15 to 20 feet tall in ideal climate; 3 to 6 feet tall in container

Container: At least 12 inches deep at first, then transplant to larger containers as it grows

Light: Full sun

Soil: Moist, well drained

Plant: Cuttings or transplants

Water: Regularly, when top inch of soil feels dry, between 1 and 3 inches per week

Harvest: When the plant reaches about 2 feet tall, it's ready for harvest.

Care: If growing in a container, every two to three years, transplant in early spring to a larger container that accommodates the growing roots.

PAIRINGS

Fruits and Vegetables: apple, avocado, carrots, coconut, mangoes, mushrooms, oranges, peas, pineapple, potatoes, spinach, tomatoes

Proteins: almonds, beef, chicken, eggs, pecans, pine nuts

Seasonings: anise, basil, bay leaf, cayenne, chili peppers, cinnamon, cloves, coriander seeds, cumin, curry powder, fish sauce, galangal, garlic, ginger, honey, lemongrass, lemon juice and zest, lime juice and zest, lemon myrtle, mint, paprika, star anise, turmeric

Keep It Fresh

Pandan leaves are often sold frozen and will hold up well in the freezer. They can also be dried, but they won't be as flavorful (see directions on for drying on page 20 and freezing on page 19).

In the Kitchen

Dishes: Rice, curries, desserts

Prep: Pandan leaves are best used bruised or slightly wilted and dried for about two days after harvest, which releases the flavor. After crushing, bruising, or scratching a leaf with a fork, tie it in a knot and toss into a pot of rice, curry, or soup to cook. To make pandan extract, chop the leaves and combine with water in a food processor, then blend. Strain the liquid, which should be bright green, and use as you would vanilla extract.

Serve: Pandan is a beloved flavoring for rice, curries, and a traditional Southeast Asian sponge cake that's green thanks to the leaves. Wrapped around chicken, pork, or fish, the leaves are steamed, roasted, fried, or grilled to impart flavor.

PERILLA

Perilla frutescens

Other common name: shiso

Flavors: grassy, warm, spicy, and cilantro-like, with mint, basil, and cinnamon; **red perilla** *anise-like, less spicy*

One of the more prominent herbs in Japan, Vietnam, and Korea, perilla (also called *shiso*) comes in two varieties with distinct purposes in the kitchen. Red perilla, nicknamed "beefsteak plant" for its dark, red-meat appearance, is mostly used for pickling and coloring. Green perilla accompanies sushi and sashimi, and it flavors dishes in a similar fashion to basil, parsley, and cilantro. In fact, it's often dubbed "Chinese basil," since its leaves look similar (only bigger) and are sometimes substituted for those of its distant Mediterranean cousin. Perilla seeds are often ground and used in Japanese seven-spice powder, or shichimi (see page 250).

HEALTH BENEFITS
A Japanese folk remedy associates perilla with the prevention of food poisoning, perhaps explaining its longtime spot alongside raw fish. Perilla seed oil is extremely high in the ultra-healthy omega-3 fatty acids, which are believed to fight inflammation, reduce the risk of heart disease and cancer, and boost brain function. The leaves don't contain nearly as much, but the seeds are currently being researched for their medicinal uses.

In the Garden
Perilla, an annual, grows easily in gardens and in containers.
Size: 2 to 4 feet tall and 2 feet wide
Container: 1 to 2 gallons
Light: Full sun or partial shade
Soil: Moist, well drained
Plant: Seeds. Soak seeds in water for 24 hours before sowing; then sow seeds,

keep moist, and give plenty of sunlight to help them germinate.

Water: Regularly, to keep plants consistently moist

Harvest: Snip whole stems from the base of the plant.

Care: Regularly pinch off stems to promote new growth. Perilla self-seeds freely, so snip off flowers to control seeding, or let them drop for the following season.

PAIRINGS

Fruits and Vegetables: cabbage, carrots, celery, cucumber, daikon radish, leeks, lettuce, mangoes, mushrooms, potatoes, shallots, tomatoes, zucchini

Proteins: beef, cheeses, chicken, duck, eggs, fish and seafood

Seasonings: basil, chili peppers, chives, fish sauce, garlic, ginger, hoisin sauce, lemongrass, lemon juice, mint, miso paste, mitsuba, parsley, sansho, sesame seeds, soy sauce, wasabi, watercress

SUBSTITUTIONS
- Thai basil
- Rau Răm (Vietnamese mint)

Keep It Fresh

Fresh perilla can be frozen for up to three weeks (see page 19), then thawed and added to cooked dishes. Once thawed, they'll be too soggy to eat raw. Don't freeze if planning to use in salads. Perilla is often sold dried and added as seasoning to rice (see directions on pages 19–21).

In the Kitchen

Dishes: sushi, soups, stir-fries, salads, noodles, rice, sauces

Prep: Red perilla is almost exclusively used for pickling and coloring (especially plums). Green perilla leaves can be used whole or chopped.

Serve: Wrap whole green leaves around meat, fish, veggies, or rice. Chop or slice the leaves and add to salads, soups (like pho), noodles, rice, and spring rolls. Korean cooks pickle the leaves with garlic and hot chili peppers to make kimchi.

RAU RĂM

Polygonum odoratum

Other common name: Vietnamese mint

Flavors: cilantro-like but milder, spicy, peppery, with mint and citrus

Often compared and used interchangeably with cilantro, this Vietnamese herb has a spice all its own. Its nicknames include Vietnamese mint and Vietnamese coriander, but rau răm is related to neither mint nor coriander. It *is*, however, related to the sour-citrus herb sorrel (see page 138).

In Malaysia, the herb is known as "laksa leaf," for its significance in the traditional spicy noodle soup called laksa. Rau răm handles heat better than cilantro, so it can be added to dishes earlier in the cooking process to offer subtler flavor.

HEALTH BENEFITS
Rau răm is believed to aid in digestion, where it can prevent gas, soothe stomach cramps, and relieve diarrhea. It also offers antibacterial, anti-inflammatory, and astringent properties, which can be used topically to ease troubled skin.

In the Garden
Rau răm spreads, a perennial, easily and quickly in its ideal tropical climate. It grows successfully in containers and should be brought indoors in cold or very hot weather. Choose a pot large enough for its mature size—it'll stop growing fresh leaves in a too-small pot. Rau răm is a great substitute for short-lived cilantro in the garden.

Size: Up to 1 foot tall
Container: Transplant to larger containers as it grows throughout the season
Light: Partial shade
Soil: Constantly moist, rich, well drained
Plant: Cuttings or seeds. Cuttings placed in water for a few days will root and transplant easily.
Water: Regularly and thoroughly, to keep soil consistently moist

Harvest: Snip stems and leaves regularly.
Care: Trim regularly to promote new growth and control size.

SUBSTITUTION
• Cilantro + mint

Keep It Fresh
Rau răm can be frozen in ice-cube trays (see tips on page 19). Do not dry.

PAIRINGS
Fruits and Vegetables:
bean sprouts, cabbage, coconut, green beans, mangoes, onions, papaya, peppers, pineapple, shallots, spinach, tomatoes, water chestnuts
Proteins: beef, cashews, chicken, duck, eggs, fish and seafood, lamb, pork
Seasonings: basil, bay leaf, cardamom, chili peppers, chives, coriander seeds, cumin, curry powder, fish sauce, galangal, garlic, ginger, lemongrass, lemon juice, lime juice, makrut lime, mint, soy sauce, turmeric

In the Kitchen
Dishes: salads, soups, stir-fries, curries
Prep: Use leaves whole, shredded, or chopped.
Serve: Rau răm is used much like cilantro: added fresh to salads, soups, curries, and noodle dishes, as well as tacos, spring rolls, and stir-fries. In Vietnam, it accompanies meat dishes and is commonly served with duck eggs.

SALAD BURNET

Sanguisorba minor

Flavors: fresh, cool, cucumber-like, nutty

While this herb's common name reveals one of its primary uses in the kitchen, its botanical name, *Sanguisorba*, reveals one of its earliest medicinal uses: to support blood clotting (*sanguis* is Latin for "blood").

Salad burnet's thin stems grow from the ground in a pretty rosette pattern, bearing lacy, serrated leaves and eventually growing tiny, pink-purple tufts of flowers. A member of the rose family, this delicate-looking plant can be grown for its beauty and fragrance in the garden as well as its light, refreshing flavor. Use it as a garnish instead of parsley or in place of cucumber or borage in any dish.

HEALTH BENEFITS

Some *Sanguisorba* species were used in ancient Chinese medicine to control bleeding, but modern uses of the herb are exclusive to the kitchen. Salad burnet offers anti-inflammatory and astringent properties that encourage healthy digestion and can prevent or relieve symptoms of irritable bowel syndrome, ulcerative colitis, and diarrhea.

In the Garden

Salad burnet, a perennial, grows successfully in containers. It self-seeds readily, and the new plants are generally stronger in the second year.

Size: Up to 10 inches tall in the first year; 12 to 18 inches when flowering in the second year

Container: At least 4 inches deep

Light: Partial shade to full sun

Soil: Light, rich, well drained

Plant: Seeds or divided roots. Divided roots will yield a quicker crop, while seeds will need to grow for a year until the leaves are ready for harvest.

Water: Regularly, to keep soil consistently moist

Harvest: If growing from seed, wait until the second year to harvest, then snip leaves as needed and use shortly after. Snip outer leaves first to promote new growth.

Care: Weed regularly. Trim regularly to promote new growth. Snip flowers to control regrowth and keep plants thriving.

SUBSTITUTIONS
- Borage
- Parsley
- Watercress

PAIRINGS

Fruits and Vegetables: avocado, broccoli, carrots, celery, cucumber, lettuce, onions, potatoes, scallions, spinach, tomatoes

Proteins: almonds, beans, cashews, cheeses, chicken, eggs, fish and seafood, pecans, pork, turkey, walnuts

Seasonings: balsamic vinegar, basil, chervil, chives, cilantro, dill, garlic, lemon juice, lovage, mint, mustard, oregano, parsley, pepper, rau răm, rosemary, tarragon, thyme

Keep It Fresh

Use salad burnet fresh; it doesn't dry well. Leaves can be frozen for longer storage (see directions on page 19), but are best used in cooked dishes like soups.

In the Kitchen

Dishes: Salads, dressings, soups, sandwiches, sauces, cold beverages

Prep: Use leaves whole or chopped.

Serve: Stir chopped leaves into butter and soft, spreadable cheeses, or infuse whole leaves in vinegar and make herb vinaigrette. Salad burnet can be added to thick soups, eggs, casseroles, stuffings, marinades, and cream sauces for fish. Place whole leaves or sprigs in iced tea, lemonade, and other cold summer beverages. Older leaves can be tough and bitter, so these are best used in cooked dishes. Flowers are used only for garnish and not flavor.

SASSAFRAS

Sassafras albidum

Flavors: bitter, woody, citrus

The sassafras tree is a majestic sight: It grows up to 60 feet tall with leaves that turn dazzling colors in fall—from green-yellow to orange, pink, red, and purple. The leaves create a circular awning around the tree, offering shade and tasty nibbles for wildlife like deer, rabbits, caterpillars, and birds.

Tear a sassafras leaf in your hands, and you'll get a whiff of root beer. In fact, the original recipe for root beer used sassafras as a key flavoring. But not anymore: In the 1970s, the FDA prohibited use of the herb in foods thanks to a compound called safrole, believed to be a possible cause of cancer.

Sassafras leaves are safe to consume, and they're used to make filé powder, an essential thickening and flavoring agent in New Orleans–style gumbos.

HEALTH BENEFITS

Prized by Native Americans as a miracle medicinal herb, sassafras root extract was widely believed to heal everything from fever to measles to intestinal worms. These days, however, sassafras products must have the safrole removed before they're marketed for sale.

In the Garden

Sassafras trees can grow very tall, with a wide, leafy spread, so they'll need a spot that's far from other tall plants or structures. They have long taproots that aren't amenable to transplanting, so the initial planting site should be permanent. They'll grow healthily in containers that are several inches wider and deeper than the root ball.

Size: Up to 60 feet tall and 40 feet wide

Light: Full sun

Soil: Moist, rich, well drained

Plant: Seeds, root cuttings, or young plants. Seeds need to be stratified for at least 4 months in order to germinate (see page 14).

Water: Regularly when young, less frequently when established; mature sassafras is drought tolerant.

Harvest: Pick leaves or snip whole branches.

Care: Trim around the tree to prevent the growth of "suckers," which will turn into multiple trunks. Or let them grow in for a shrub rather than a tree.

PAIRINGS

Since filé is really only used to make gumbo, these pairings include typical gumbo ingredients.

Vegetables: artichokes, carrots, celery, collard greens, corn, mushrooms, mustard greens, okra, onions, peppers, tomatoes

Proteins: bacon, crab, crawfish, fish, ham, pork, sausage, shrimp, turkey

Seasonings: allspice, basil, bay leaf, Cajun seasoning, cayenne, chili peppers, cloves, cumin, garlic, jalapeño, lemon juice, mustard, old bay seasoning, oregano, paprika, parsley, pepper, sage, thyme, Worcestershire sauce

Keep It Fresh

Use dry leaves or sprigs to make filé powder (see the directions on page 20).

In the Kitchen

Dishes: Gumbo

Prep: To make filé powder, crush dried leaves in your hand, then crush into a powder using a mortar and pestle or food processor. Strain to remove large pieces and stems.

Serve: Sprinkle filé powder into gumbos just before serving, after the pot is removed from heat, and stir well.

SAVORY

Satureja

*Flavors: **summer savory** peppery and spicy, with thyme, mint, and oregano; **winter savory** spicier, piney, more pungent*

Savory is an aromatic, pungent herb that comes in two main varieties: summer savory (*Satureja hortensis*) and winter savory (*Satureja montana*). Summer savory is sweeter and mellower than its cold-weather cousin, and therefore appears more frequently at the dinner table. It's a common ingredient in classic herb blends fines herbes, herbes de Provence, and bouquet garni (see page 250). The potent winter savory proves valuable in the kitchen, too—as an evergreen perennial, it provides tasty flavor for hearty stews and meat dishes all year long.

HEALTH BENEFITS
Both savories are known to prevent and relieve flatulence, which is why they're so frequently paired with beans. They're also generally great for digestion and can help treat nausea, intestinal cramps, and diarrhea.

In the Garden
Summer savory grows as an upright annual, while winter savory is a woody perennial shrub. True to its name, winter savory can thrive well into the winter in temperate to cold climates (down to 10°F). Bring summer savory indoors when cool weather hits and place it in a sunny window.

Size: Summer savory, 12 to 18 inches tall; winter savory, up to 16 inches tall and wide
Container: 6 inches deep
Light: Full sun
Soil: Summer savory, moist, well drained; winter savory, sandy, well drained
Plant: Seeds; winter savory can also be started from cuttings.
Water: Regularly until plants are established; less often once mature

Harvest: Summer savory grows quickly and is ready for harvest at 6 inches tall; new winter savory plants will take more time to ripen. Snip whole stems or individual leaves as needed. Before the first frost in fall, harvest the entire summer savory plant to be dried.

Care: Harvest summer savory regularly to promote new growth and prevent flowering. After several years, old winter savory plants can be divided in spring or fall and replanted.

PAIRINGS

Vegetables: beets, broccoli, cabbage, carrots, celery, green beans, onions, peas, peppers, potatoes, spinach, tomatoes

Proteins: beans, beef, cheeses, chicken, eggs, game, fatty fish, fava beans, lamb, lentils, pork, sausage, turkey, veal

Seasonings: basil, bay leaf, cayenne, chives, coriander seeds, cumin, fennel seeds, garlic, lavender, marjoram, mint, mustard, oregano, paprika, parsley, rosemary, sage, tarragon, thyme

Keep It Fresh

Savory can be frozen or dried for longer storage (see directions on pages 19–21).

In the Kitchen

Dishes: Stews, soups, marinades, roasts

Serve: Summer savory pairs particularly well with eggs, poultry, and potatoes, while winter savory is more commonly used in stuffings and with heavy meats like sausage, lamb, game, and fatty fish. Both are excellent seasonings for beans: in German, savory is known as *Bohnenkraut*, "bean herb."

SCENTED GERANIUM

Pelargonium

Flavors vary widely: rose, lemon, apple, cinnamon, clove, mint, nutmeg, orange

Scented geraniums come in hundreds of varieties, many with delicious fragrances and beautiful blooms. Depending on the species, they might be grown for their scent, their flavor, or their attractive appearance. And sometimes all three!

Leaf shape and flower colors vary just as much as fragrance. The flowers themselves don't emit those lovely aromas—it's actually the leaves. The top choices for kitchen herbs include rose (*P. graveolens*), lemon (*P. crispum*), and peppermint (*P. tomentosum*), but you'll also find species offering strawberry, lime, nutmeg, apple, apricot, ginger, and coconut.

HEALTH BENEFITS

Scented geranium makes soothing, delicious teas similar in effect to classic chamomile. The herb can encourage healthy digestion, calm the nerves, and help relieve headaches (especially if stress-related). It's also antibacterial: a tonic made of infused leaves can be used on irritated or acne-plagued skin.

In the Garden

Scented geraniums, which are perennials, grow healthily in containers, making it easy to bring the plant inside in cool weather. They won't tolerate frosts (or temps below 45°F). Choose a pot with good air circulation and drainage, and place in a sunny window. Growing requirements differ between species, so check instructions on the plant you have at home.

Size: Up to 3 feet tall

Container: At least 6 to 8 inches in diameter, but larger depending on variety

Light: Full sun to partial shade

Soil: Moist, well drained; though some prefer dry, sandy soil.

Plant: Cuttings or seeds; cuttings are more reliable, as only natural varieties (not hybrids) can be grown from seed.

Water: Occasionally, around the base, only when the soil feels dry one inch deep. Don't let the roots sit in wet soil, but don't let them dry out completely either.

Harvest: Pinch or snip off leaves when needed.

PAIRINGS

Fruits and Vegetables:
apples, apricots, berries, lemons, peaches, plums
Seasonings: lemon balm, lemon basil, lemon verbena, mint

SUBSTITUTIONS
- Lemon verbena
- Mint
- Rose

Care: Trim occasionally to remove dead leaves and flowers, and promote new growth. Prune to control size and shape, especially in spring. Repot annually, or every two years, in the spring.

Keep It Fresh

Leaves make wonderful teas and potpourris when dried (see directions on page 20).

In the Kitchen

Dishes: Teas, jams, desserts, beverages, marinades

Prep: Use whole leaves for infusions and cooking. Flowers are edible and serve as pretty garnish.

Serve: Infuse scented geranium leaves into simple syrup, vinegar, or milk (for ice cream), or cook with fruits to make jams and jellies. Place a few leaves in the sugar container for a couple weeks to make a flavored sugar for baking. Or layer leaves on the bottom of a pan to flavor treats baked in the oven.

SORREL

Rumex acetosa

Flavors: refreshing, tart, tangy, citrus

Possibly derived from the old French word *sur*, or "sour," sorrel's unique tart-lemon flavor and spinach-like texture are beloved in French cooking; they bring dimension to rich, creamy foods. The distinct sour taste in raw sorrel comes from a chemical called "oxalic acid," which should not be consumed in large quantities; eat raw leaves in moderation or cook sorrel with other foods.

The two most widely used varieties are garden sorrel (*Rumex acetosa*) and French or buckler leaf sorrel (*Rumex scutatus*). The former has long, oval leaves and sharp flavor, while the French favorite bears smaller, shield-shaped leaves that are less sour and more smooth.

> **HEALTH BENEFITS**
> Sorrel has been used traditionally to treat respiratory problems including nasal congestion and bronchitis. Like most other herbs, it's also believed to encourage healthy digestion and serve as a mild diuretic.

In the Garden

Technically perennials, sorrel plants tend to grow bitter as they age and with prolonged exposure to hot sun, so you might want to plant new sorrel each year for optimal fresh flavor. Garden sorrel prefers cool, moist environments, while French sorrel likes its home warmer and dry. Both varieties grow successfully in containers.

Size: Garden sorrel, 2 to 3 feet tall; French sorrel, up to 12 inches tall

Container: At least 6 inches deep

Light: Partial shade

Soil: Moist, fertile, well drained. Add compost or mulch to prevent weeds and retain moisture.

Plant: Seeds, divided roots, or transplants

Water: Regularly, about one inch per week. Water more frequently and thoroughly in hot temperatures, as excess heat will increase bitterness and quicken flowering.

Harvest: When it reaches 6 inches tall, snip young outer leaves from the base of the plant; older leaves grow tough and bitter. Harvest large batches at a time (up to half the plant), and the leaves will grow back quickly.

Care: Weed regularly. Sorrel self-seeds freely, so snip off flower shoots to control propagation, or let the plant go wild. Divide clumps every 2 or 3 years in fall and replant in smaller batches, or simply sow fresh seeds every year for new young plants.

SUBSTITUTIONS
- Lemon juice + spinach
- Lemon verbena
- Arugula

PAIRINGS
Vegetables: beets, cabbage, cucumber, leeks, lettuce, potatoes, spinach, tomatoes
Proteins: beans, chicken, eggs, fish and seafood, lentils, pork, salmon
Seasonings: arugula, borage, chervil, chives, dill, lovage, parsley, tarragon, watercress

Keep It Fresh
Freeze sorrel for longer storage (see page 19).

In the Kitchen
Dishes: Salads, soups, sauces, marinades, omelets
Prep: Use leaves whole, chopped, or shredded.
Serve: Sorrel's tart, citrus flavor complements egg dishes, pork, and fatty fish like salmon. It's a main component in many European soups, like traditional Ukrainian green borscht and creamy French sorrel soup, often paired with potatoes and spinach. Sorrel sauces are a delicious accompaniment for fish. Small young leaves are mellower than larger ones, so use these raw in salads, and cook the large leaves to temper the strong taste. Sorrel shrivels when cooked, so use more to account for the reduced volume and add at the end of cooking.

SWEET CICELY

Myrrhis odorata

Flavors: sweet anise and celery

With its feathery leaves, clusters of delicate white flowers, and pleasant fragrance, sweet cicely is a welcome addition to the garden—for bees, butterflies, and humans alike. This herb's anise flavor is an obvious draw in the kitchen, where its sweetness can serve as a substitute for sugar, a major boon for diabetics and anyone monitoring their sugar intake. Roots, leaves, and seeds can all be eaten, with seeds offering a more potent anise taste. The leaves are tender and won't withstand heat for long, so add to dishes at the very end of cooking or just before serving.

HEALTH BENEFITS

Sweet cicely can stimulate healthy digestion, prevent or relieve gas, and serve as a mild diuretic. It's also believed to help clear up respiratory congestion and coughs by thinning mucus buildup in the airways.

In the Garden

This cool-weather, perennial herb is easy to grow, but starting from seeds is a little tricky, so consider purchasing young plants at a nursery. Sweet cicely develops a long taproot that makes container gardening difficult. Make sure any container you use is large and deep.

Size: 3 to 6 feet tall

Container: At least 12 inches deep, but the root may outgrow any pot.

Light: Partial shade to full shade

Soil: Moist, rich, well drained; tolerates poorer, dry soils, too

Plant: Young plants, fresh seeds, or divided roots. Plants are preferred, as seeds need to be stratified for at least two months in order to germinate (see page 14).

Water: Regularly, to keep soil consistently moist

Harvest: Snip leaves when needed throughout spring and summer, ideally just before using so they're fresh. Harvest young seedpods in summer, while they're green, flavorful, and still tender enough to eat raw. If using the root, dig it up in fall.

Care: Snip flowers regularly to promote new growth. If you let them bloom and seed, gather the fresh seeds for a new batch to plant the following season. Prune heavily after the plant flowers.

SUBSTITUTIONS

Leaves:
- Chervil
- Fennel
- Tarragon

Seeds:
- Anise seeds
- Fennel seeds

Keep It Fresh

Sweet cicely leaves should be used as soon after harvest as possible. They don't freeze or dry well. Seeds and roots can be dried and stored in containers for later use, while the flowers can be dried and used as potpourri (see directions on page 20).

PAIRINGS

Fruits and Vegetables:
apples, apricots, berries, carrots, gooseberries, lemons, nectarines, parsnips, peaches, pineapple, raspberries, rhubarb, shallots, strawberries, sweet potato, tomatoes

Proteins: almonds, cheeses, chicken, eggs, pecans, scallops, shrimp

Seasonings: allspice, basil, cardamom, chervil, cinnamon, cloves, cumin, garlic, ginger, honey, lemon juice, mint, nutmeg, parsley, vanilla

In the Kitchen

Dishes: Salads, desserts, breads, liqueurs, beverages, teas

Prep: Use leaves whole or chopped and seeds whole or ground. Stalks can be eaten raw or chopped and added to salads or soups, just like celery.

Serve: The flavor of sweet cicely is a wonderful counterpart for tart, acidic fruits like rhubarb and apricots; toss leaves or seeds into fruit salads, pie fillings, preserves, cakes, and breads. Add leaves to salads, soups, omelets, and creamy sauces for fish dishes. Seeds also make a tasty addition to custards and ice creams.

WASABI

Eutrema wasabi or *Wasabia japonica*

Flavors: strongly pungent, hot, sharp

Often called Japanese horseradish, wasabi bears a likeness to that herb in flavor and in form—both are roots with pungent, sinus-clearing, eye-watering heat. It's a treasured herb in Japan, where it grows along cold, flowing streams in the mountains. Wasabi is almost impossible to find fresh anywhere outside of Japan, since it's so difficult to grow and therefore quite expensive.

Supermarkets and sushi restaurants in the West carry wasabi as a paste or powder, but it's most likely an imitation made from horseradish, mustard, and food coloring. Check out Japanese markets or fine restaurants for real grated wasabi. Or search out fresh wasabi root (actually a rhizome) from growers in the Pacific Northwest and the Blue Ridge Mountains in the United States, or online.

HEALTH BENEFITS

Wasabi wields antibiotic powers over the digestive system, possibly explaining why the herb is traditionally served with raw fish. It's also an anti-inflammatory that can help clear up congested sinuses and other symptoms of allergies, as evidenced by that refreshing, head-rush feeling when eaten.

In the Garden

Wasabi's growing conditions are very specific and can be difficult to replicate, depending on your climate. This perennial herb needs consistent temperatures between 45°F and 70°F. If your local weather varies from that range, consider using a greenhouse for temp control.

Size: Up to 18 inches tall

Container: 10 inches deep

Light: Full shade to partial shade, preferably under trees, tall plants, or a canopy to block out direct sunlight

Soil: Rich, moist, well drained. Soil should be constantly moist but not waterlogged, so draining is crucial. Add plenty of compost to improve drainage.

Plant: Seeds, presoaked the night before planting, 1 to 2 inches apart; after they've grown a bit, separate seedlings to 12 inches apart to make room for growth. Transplanted rhizomes should be planted with their crowns above the soil line.

Water: Mist or spray with water regularly, and more frequently during drier months (several times a day).

Harvest: Dig up rhizomes after two years, when they're most flavorful and about 8 inches long. If you leave a couple in the ground, wasabi will self-seed.

Care: Weed diligently, every day if necessary. In hot, sunny climates, cover wasabi with a sheet or tarp.

PAIRINGS

Fruits and Vegetables: avocado, cabbage, carrot, chives, cucumber, daikon radish, edamame, lettuce, onions, potatoes, shallots

Proteins: beef, caviar, crab meat, cream cheese, chicken, raw fish, salmon, shrimp, tofu

Seasonings: chili peppers, cilantro, garlic, horseradish, lemon juice, lime juice, mustard, pickled ginger, sesame seeds, soy sauce

Keep It Fresh

Wrap fresh wasabi rhizome in a damp paper towel and store in the refrigerator for up to 2 weeks. Place leaves and stems (also edible!) in a zip-tight plastic bag in the refrigerator for up to 10 days.

In the Kitchen

Dishes: Sushi, sashimi

Prep: Peel off the layer of skin covering only the portion of rhizome you plan to use. Trim the root end only and grate finely from this point. As you grate, form a tight pile of wasabi shavings to retain flavor. Let sit for up to 2 minutes so the flavor develops, then enjoy within 20 minutes. If using wasabi powder, reconstitute with water and serve.

Serve: Wasabi is the classic accompaniment for raw fish, served with white rice and soy sauce. Pair it with foods that are also commonly used in sushi and popular Japanese dishes (see the pairings notes above).

WOODRUFF

Galium odoratum

*Other common name: sweet
woodruff*

Flavors: sweet vanilla, fresh hay

Sweet woodruff grows naturally in shady forests, spreading close to the ground in carpets of luscious foliage dotted with dainty white flowers. The bright-green leaves form pinwheels around its stems, and clusters of flowers sprout from the very tops, making this a gorgeous addition to otherwise dark spots in a garden.

Most often used for its sweet, hay-like fragrance, woodruff makes wonderful potpourris and perfumes. It's an important ingredient in the traditional German *Maiwein*, also called *Maibowle* or "May wine," enjoyed during May Day festivities. But woodruff's sweet-vanilla flavor can be added to any sweet beverages as well as marinades, dressings, and even fruit desserts.

Use only one or two stems per serving, as the herb contains a chemical called coumarin that's believed to be dangerous in large quantities.

> **HEALTH BENEFITS**
> Sweet woodruff makes a tasty, relaxing tea. It's often used to cure sleeplessness, relieve anxiety and symptoms of stress, and treat constipation as well as other digestive problems.

In the Garden
Sweet woodruff, a perennial, spreads aggressively in the garden via runners underground and self-seeding, so the plants will need some maintenance to create boundaries. It also grows well in containers, which will easily control its growth.
Size: Up to 8 inches tall
Container: Depends on preferred plant size
Light: Full shade to partial shade; leaves will burn in full sun, and plants will become dormant.

Soil: Moist, rich, well drained; tolerant of drier soils
Plant: Divisions, seedlings, or seeds. Divisions are preferred, as seeds are difficult to germinate and should be stratified for 3 to 4 months before planting (see page 14).
Water: Regularly, to keep soil consistently moist but not wet
Harvest: Pick leaves and flowers all through spring and summer for the best fragrance and flavor.

PAIRINGS
Fruits and Vegetables:
apples, berries, carrots, melons, oranges, peaches, pears, pineapples, raisins, sweet potatoes
Proteins: almonds, chicken, pecans, walnuts
Seasonings: caraway seeds, celery seeds, cinnamon, cloves, cumin, dill, garlic, ginger, honey, lemon juice, maple syrup, nutmeg, sage, thyme, vanilla

Care: Place mulch around the plants if they'll be exposed to sun. Woodruff self-seeds and sends out runners underground, so collect seeds as they develop and pull up stray runners to control spreading.

Keep It Fresh
Use fresh leaves within a couple days; the fragrance is best when they're slightly wilted, and even better when dried. They also freeze well (directions for drying on page 20 and freezing on page 19).

In the Kitchen
Dishes: Punches, teas, marinades, dressings, desserts, jams, sorbets, ice creams
Serve: Use whole stems fresh or dried to infuse woodruff's flavor, and then remove before serving. Remember to only use one or two stems per serving.

SPICE GUIDE

From your backyard to the far corners of the globe, spices are the universal truths for delicious dishes.

COOKING WITH SPICES

The importance of spices in human history cannot be overstated: They've provoked wars, inspired the exploration of continents, served as currency, and treated countless medical conditions. (Fun fact: Most spices have at some point been touted as aphrodisiacs.) Although their uses and price points have evolved over time, spices are still indispensible in every cuisine on the planet.

For the best flavor, spices should always be purchased whole, never ground. Grinding or crushing spices releases their flavorful oils, which immediately begin to lose their pungency. If you do buy pre-ground or powdered spices, be sure to renew your stock at least once per year. Test freshness by observing their color and fragrance: If that paprika or cayenne has turned from bright red to dull brown, it's probably time to toss it. If that once-sharp aroma is now a bland shadow of its former self, pop it in the trash.

In addition to dried seeds and berries, spices come in several other forms that require specific preparation. Rhizomes like ginger, galangal, and turmeric can be sliced, chopped, grated, or juiced (see tips on page 189). Fresh and dried chili peppers can also be prepared in a variety of ways. Chop fresh chili peppers or use them whole; crush dried chili peppers to form flakes, or grind them to a powder using a spice grinder, blender, or mortar and pestle.

Most spices, however, are dried seeds and berries. These can simply be ground before serving, or cooked quickly beforehand to enhance their flavors and soften them for grinding. See the specific prep instructions in each spice profile, and use the following techniques when applicable.

Preparing Spices

Spices can be readied for cooking in a few different ways. In Indian cuisine, a technique called *tadka*, or "tempering," involves frying whole or ground spices in hot oil or ghee before they're incorporated with other ingredients. Cooking the spices in fat enriches their flavors and is also believed to activate their nutritional compounds. Dry-roasting is another quick-cooking method that *alters* flavors rather than simply enhancing them—roasted spices taste, essentially, "roasted." The prep method is entirely up to the cook and the recipe. Here are quick tips for getting the most out of your spices.

Frying in Oil

Whether frying a single spice or several, take special care to avoid burning them, which will ruin the overall flavor. Smaller spices and ground spices will need less cooking time—sometimes just a few seconds will sufficiently fry them. Others may need a full minute. Prepare all ingredients for the final dish so they're ready to be combined with the just-fried spices. (If adding spices at the start of cooking, have your raw ingredients ready; if adding spices at the end of cooking, have your cooked dish ready to receive them.)

- Heat 1 to 2 tablespoons of vegetable oil, grapeseed oil, sunflower oil, or ghee in a heavy pan. Wait until it's lightly smoking before adding spices.
- Start with larger, whole spices, then gradually add smaller spices or ground spices, which require less cooking. Watch carefully to prevent burning.
- Fry until the spices darken and crackle in the hot oil, then remove from heat and prepare according to your recipe.
- Fried spices can be crushed or ground before adding to a dish or used whole.

Dry-Roasting (or Toasting)

Dry-roasting is exactly what it sounds like. All you need is a dry pan—no oil or fat required. This method is intended to dry out the spice, making it easier to grind. The spices will become earthier, deeper versions of themselves, and they can be combined into spice blends or used individually.

- Preheat a heavy pan over medium heat.
- When it's hot, add whole spices and stir frequently until fragrant, about 2 to 3 minutes for 1 tablespoon. The larger the batch, the longer they'll need to cook.
- Watch carefully. When they become darker and begin to smoke, transfer to a separate dish and let them cool.
- Use roasted spices whole or grind them in a spice grinder or a with mortar and pestle.

For a batch of spices that's too large for a frying pan, roast them on a baking sheet in the oven at 500°F, stirring occasionally as they cook.

Grinding, Grating, and Crushing

A blender or food processor may *seem* like a good idea when it comes to grinding spices, but in fact, you'll get a much more even texture using a spice grinder or a good-old mortar and pestle.

A spice grinder or coffee grinder will easily handle larger quantities. If using a coffee grinder for spices, just make sure to restrict its use exclusively to the spice rack. (You won't want coffee in your steak rub or mustard in your cappuccino!)

SPICE PASTES

Used in many cuisines around the world, spice pastes typically combine fresh moist ingredients with dried ground spices or herbs. Any spice blend can be prepared as a paste simply by adding crushed fresh ginger or garlic, and then enough oil to reach the desired consistency.

Laksa paste (Malaysia): red chili peppers, coriander seeds, paprika, cumin, turmeric, onion, lemongrass, galangal or ginger, cashews, garlic, shrimp paste, peanut oil

Harissa: dried hot chili peppers, coriander seeds, cumin, caraway, garlic, salt, olive oil

Chili garlic paste: ground red chili peppers or chili powder, garlic

Curry paste: dried hot chili peppers, fresh hot chili peppers, coriander seeds, cumin, turmeric, paprika, garam masala, lemongrass, peppercorns, galangal or ginger, makrut lime leaves, cilantro, garlic, shrimp paste, shallots

A mortar and pestle is ideal for smaller quantities. Pounding the spice with your own hands gives you total control over its texture: Crush into coarse bits or grind to a powder.

A rolling pin is a great alternative to a mortar and pestle. Spread the spices over a rimmed baking sheet to keep them contained, or place them in a zip-tight plastic bag. Then roll over them to crush.

A microplane grater will come in handy when grating nutmeg, cinnamon sticks, lemon and lime zests, and rhizomes like ginger and turmeric.

FLAVOR CHEAT SHEET

Looking for a particular flavor? Use this list to find a spice that fits the bill.

- **Licorice-y:** anise, fennel seeds, licorice, star anise
- **Bitter:** ajwain, capers, celery seeds, fenugreek seeds, mastic
- **Earthy or warm:** annatto seeds , cardamom, black cardamom, caraway, cumin, nutmeg, saffron, turmeric
- **Fruity, tart, or citrus:** amchoor, barberry, makrut lime, sumac, tamarind
- **Nutty:** mahlab, nigella, poppy seeds, sesame seeds
- **Pungent:** allspice, asafetida, chili peppers, cloves, galangal, ginger, grains of paradise, mustard, pepper, Sichuan pepper
- **Sweet:** cassia, cinnamon, coriander seeds, juniper berries, paprika, rose, vanilla

COMMON KITCHEN SPICES

These spices are easy to find at the grocery store or farmers market, or may already be in your kitchen.

ALLSPICE

Pimenta dioica

Flavors: warm, sweet, pungent, and peppery, with cinnamon, cloves, and nutmeg

Native to the tropical climates of the Caribbean and Central America, allspice berries are harvested exclusively in that part of the world, with Jamaica's crop considered the gold standard. They grow on trees and are dried and cured before being sold.

Though whole berries look like over-sized peppercorns and their botanical name is *Pimenta* (Spanish for "pepper"), allspice is *not* related to pepper. The common name "allspice" was chosen for its warm flavor combination of cinnamon, nutmeg, and clove. Allspice is a favorite ingredient in baked goods and many spice blends, from curry powders to pumpkin pie spice to jerk seasoning (see page 251).

HEALTH BENEFITS

Allspice is a known digestive aid, helping to alleviate gas, cramps, and other stomach troubles. It can also help lower blood pressure, relieve nerve pain, and prevent and fight viruses, infection, fungus, and inflammation. On top of all that, research has shown that compounds in allspice may help protect against several forms of cancer.

In the Garden

Allspice trees need tropical or subtropical climates and both male and female specimens in order to grow their tasty berries. But they can also be planted in other climates and used for their leaves rather than for the spice. (Leaves have a similar aroma and flavor, and they can be used in cooking like bay leaves.) The tree will grow in a large container so it can be brought indoors in cooler weather.

Size: 5 to 8 feet tall in containers; 40 to 60 feet tall in ideal conditions in the ground
Container: At least 20 inches deep and 2 feet in diameter; at least 5 gallons
Light: Full sun to partial shade

Soil: Moist, well drained

Plant: Seeds, extracted from fresh berries and soaked in water for 24 hours before sowing

Water: Regularly, when soil surface feels dry

Harvest: Berries are picked while unripe and still green, though they should be at their mature size. Leaves can be snipped, if using instead of the fruits.

Drying: After harvesting, the berries are laid out on a concrete surface and dried in the sun.

Care: Weed regularly. Trim regularly to remove dead or decaying foliage and branches.

SUBSTITUTION
- Cinnamon + cloves + nutmeg

PAIRINGS

Fruits and Vegetables: apples, carrots, currant, eggplant, onions, pumpkin, raisins, squash, sweet potatoes

Proteins: almonds, beef, chicken, eggs, fish and seafood, game, pecans, turkey, walnuts

Seasonings: cardamom, cayenne, chili peppers, cinnamon, cloves, coriander seeds, cumin, garlic, ginger, honey, lemon juice and zest, mustard, nutmeg, pepper, rosemary, thyme, vanilla

In the Kitchen

Dishes: Rubs, marinades, sauces, roasts, curries, rice, mulled beverages, pickling spices, desserts

Prep: Use allspice berries whole and remove before serving, or grind them into a powder.

Serve: For centuries, the leaves and wood from the allspice tree have been used in Jamaica to smoke meat barbecue-style. But the spice is incredibly versatile: Whole allspice berries are infused into stews, marinades, and mulled beverages (and removed before serving), while ground allspice is added to cakes, pies, fruit desserts, and other sweets. It's a common ingredient in ketchup, chutney, sauerkraut, and sausages, and it pairs well with just about any fruit.

ANISE

Pimpinella anisum

Flavors: sweet, warm, licorice

Anise flavor is found frequently in nature—in fennel, dill, tarragon, chervil, sweet cicely, and, of course, licorice root. While all the credit usually goes to the flavor and aroma of "licorice," in reality, what you're smelling and tasting is probably anise, even in licorice candy!

Anise plants grow delicate feathery leaves, white blooms, and sweet fruits or "seeds." Anise seeds have tons of commercial uses. Their extracted oil is crucial in anise-flavored liqueurs like anisette, ouzo, pastis, and Sambuca, as well as in toothpaste, chewing gum, lozenges, and cough medicine. In the culinary department, anise flavors everything from cakes to curries to candy.

HEALTH BENEFITS

Anise is an age-old digestive aid, helping to relieve gas, stomach cramps, nausea, loss of appetite, and constipation. In India and parts of Europe, anise seeds is chewed after meals to stimulate digestion and freshen breath; it's also prepared as a tea. Long valued as a treatment for colds and coughs, anise is a common ingredient in modern-day cough suppressants.

In the Garden

Anise, an annual, needs at least 4 months of hot summer weather in order to generate seeds. They'll grow healthily in containers with adequate drainage. However, the seedlings develop taproots and aren't amenable to transplanting, so choose a suitably sized pot and stick with it.

Size: Up to 2 feet tall

Container: At least 8 inches deep

Light: Full sun

Soil: Loose, somewhat rich, well drained; soil must be warm, around 70°F, for seeds to germinate

Plant: Seeds, soaked overnight in water before sowing
Water: Regularly until established, to keep soil consistently moist; after seedlings appear, water less frequently, only when soil feels dry.
Harvest: Seeds are ready for harvest when they're a ripe, grayish brown. Snip off flower heads into a paper bag and hang to dry; the seeds will fall to the bottom of the bag.
Care: Protect from winds.

PAIRINGS

Fruits and Vegetables: apricots, carrots, celery, cranberries, currants, figs, lemon, oranges, pears, pineapple, pomegranate, potatoes, shallots, turnips

Proteins: almonds, beans, beef, cheeses, chicken, eggs, fish and seafood, peanuts, pecans, pork, walnuts

Seasonings: allspice, basil, caraway seeds, cardamom, cayenne, chervil, chili peppers, cilantro, cinnamon, cloves, coriander seeds, cumin, epazote, dill seed, fennel seed, fenugreek, garlic, ginger, honey, jalapeño, lemon juice and zest, lime juice and zest, mint, nutmeg, pepper, saffron, sesame seeds, star anise, turmeric, vanilla

In the Kitchen

Dishes: Breads, desserts, stews, curries, salads, teas

Prep: Whole anise seeds can be roasted or quick-fried in oil to improve aroma and flavor before being ground to a powder (see pages 150–151).

Serve: Add ground anise seeds to everything from stews, curries, and lentils to candies, cakes, and rye breads. It adds warm flavor to sausages and stews with fish, pork, and vegetables. It's a natural partner for root vegetables, fruits, nuts, and creamy cheeses. Anise leaves, with their milder flavor, can also be used in salads and teas, and sprinkled over eggs.

CAPERS

Capparis spinosa

Flavors: pungent, sharp, tart, salty

Used generously in Italian, Spanish, and North African cooking, capers are actually young flower buds that have been pickled in vinegar or preserved in dry, coarse salt. They're never eaten raw, as their signature refreshing flavor only reveals itself through these preservation methods. If left on the plant to bloom, buds grow into pretty white-pink flowers that die within one day.

Capers are graded for quality: The tiniest capers, nonpareils from France, are considered the best-tasting and most valuable, while other varieties move down the list according to size. Caper bushes also bear edible berries, which are likewise preserved in vinegar and have similar flavor, but are larger, plumper (like olives), and less pungent.

HEALTH BENEFITS
Capers may offer significant benefits for health, especially for carnivores: Their antioxidant powers make them a great partner for rich meats, as they protect against the harmful effects of oxidation during the digestion of meat. This translates to lower risk of cancer and heart disease.

In the Garden
Native to regions surrounding the Mediterranean, perennial caper shrubs grow in warm, dry climates. Plant a bush in a mound or raised bed to ensure efficient drainage, or use a container to bring indoors in cold weather. Caper seedlings and bushes don't transplant well; if transplanting, try to keep the soil around the roots intact for minimal disturbance, then water and place a plastic bag over the top until the new plant settles in.

Size: Up to 5 feet tall and 4 feet wide

Container: Up to 1 gallon for seedlings; at least 15 gallons for maturing and full-grown shrubs

Light: Full sun

Soil: Poor, loose, extremely well drained

Plant: Cuttings, young plants, or seeds. Cuttings and plants are preferred, as seeds are difficult to germinate and need to be stratified in a moist cloth in the fridge for 2 to 3 months before sowing (see page 150).

Water: Occasionally until established, once per week or less; once established, rarely if ever; tolerates drought

Harvest: Pick unripe flower buds and caperberries throughout the season. If you let them be, buds will bloom into pretty light-pink flowers that die quickly.

Care: Place mulch around the plants to protect from cool weather. After two years, prune established plants completely in late fall or early winter; they go dormant during the winter months and will sprout new shoots in spring.

SUBSTITUTIONS
- Green olives
- Pickled nasturtium seeds
- Chopped pickles

Keep It Fresh

To pickle fresh capers, first wash them thoroughly and place them in a small jar. Add water and seal the lid, then soak for 3 days, refreshing the water once each day. Drain, then place back in the jar. In a pot, combine 1 part wine vinegar, 1 part water, and a little salt (1 tablespoon salt per 1 cup brine); heat until boiling. Let the brine cool, then pour over the jarred capers. Seal tightly and store for 3 days or until they reach your desired flavor. Pickled capers should be stored in the refrigerator in their brine.

PAIRINGS

Fruits and Vegetables: artichokes, celery, cucumbers, eggplant, lettuce, mushrooms, olives, onions, potatoes, shallots, tomatoes

Proteins: anchovies, beef, cheeses, chicken, fish and seafood, lamb

Seasonings: basil, dill, garlic, lemon juice and zest, mustard, oregano, parsley, red pepper flakes, thyme

In the Kitchen

Dishes: Sauces, dressings, salads

Prep: Rinse capers before serving to tone down the saltiness.

Serve: Capers pack a fresh, tangy punch when paired with rich meats, fatty fish, smoked fish, salad veggies, creamy sauces, and tomato sauces like puttanescas. They're an important component in tartar sauce, Niçoise salad, tapenade (anchovy and olive paste), caponata (eggplant salad), and piccata dishes.

CARAWAY

Carum carvi

Flavors: pungent, warm, earthy, spicy, bittersweet, with subtle citrus and anise

The caraway plant has the distinctive look of its relatives in the parsley and carrot family, with delicate, fern-like leaves and clusters of tiny flowers sprouting from the top. The roots and leaves are edible, but it's the sharp, pungent seeds that do the heavy lifting in the kitchen. Caraway "seeds" are actually fruits, comprised of two seed halves that are brown, ribbed, and crescent shaped, like cumin.

Believed to be one of the world's oldest spices, caraway is integral in German, Austrian, Scandinavian, and Jewish cooking. They're also used frequently in Indian and North African seasonings, including garam masala, the Tunisian chili paste *harissa*, and the North African blend *tabil* (see recipes on 150 and 251).

HEALTH BENEFITS
Caraway seeds have been used through the ages to relieve gastrointestinal issues, including gas, cramps, heartburn, and constipation. In fact, seeds are often served after meals to stimulate digestion and freshen breath, and they're even an additive in some mouthwashes. Thanks to its antispasmodic properties, caraway is also used to treat menstrual cramps.

In the Garden

Caraway plants like temperate climates and grow as biennials; they produce ripe seeds in their second season. With their long taproot, they are not amenable to transplanting, so choose a suitable spot in the garden or a deep container with good drainage.

Size: Up to 2 feet tall

Container: At least 8 inches deep

Light: Full sun to partial shade (in hot climates)

Soil: Light, loose, fertile, well drained

Plant: Seeds, soaked in water for 3 to 6 days and dried before sowing

Water: Regularly when young, to keep the seedlings consistently moist; less frequently when established, when the soil feels dry. Water at the base of the plant and not over the leaves.

Harvest: Snip full stems if harvesting the leaves. Once the seeds are ripe in the second year (they should be dark brown), snip the flower heads into a paper bag, taking care not to lose any seeds. Dry them for up to 10 days, then separate the seeds. You can also dig up the roots to cook as a vegetable.

Care: Place mulch around the plants to provide nutrients and protect from the cold. Weed regularly, especially when young. Protect from winds. Prune heavily in fall to protect from winter weather, and the plant will grow back in spring.

PAIRINGS

Fruits and Vegetables: apples, Brussels sprouts, cabbage, carrots, celery, cucumbers, green beans, onions, potatoes, tomatoes, turnips

Proteins: bacon, beef, cheeses, duck, eggs, pork, sausage

Seasonings: allspice, cardamom, cinnamon, cilantro, cumin, dill, fennel seeds, garlic, honey, juniper berries, lemon juice and zest, mustard, paprika, parsley, pepper, thyme, turmeric

In the Kitchen

Dishes: Breads, stews, sauerkraut, pickles, curries, rice, pastas, liqueurs

Prep: Split harvested fruits in half to obtain the crescent-shaped seeds, which can be used whole or ground. Toast whole seeds to bring out their flavor before adding to a dish (see page 150).

Serve: The anise flavor of caraway balances out the richness of fatty meats, such as pork, sausage, and duck, and also pairs wonderfully with apples, cabbage, and cheeses. Whole seeds are baked into crackers, cakes, and breads, especially rye and pumpernickel, and infused into liqueurs like *akvavit* and *kümmel*. They're a central seasoning in coleslaw and sauerkraut, as well as heavy meat stews like goulash. Seeds grow bitter when cooked for a long time, so add at the end of cooking for optimal flavor.

CARDAMOM

Elettaria cardamomum

Flavors: pungent, warm, floral, bittersweet, with lemon, menthol, and camphor

Native to India, cardamom is now so prized around the world that it's an essential spice in countries ranging from Ethiopia to Russia and Scandinavia. It's also one of the most expensive spices, along with vanilla and saffron.

Grown from a shrub, green cardamom seedpods contain up to 18 small, sticky seeds, which are either ground before cooking or used whole for flavor. Green cardamom is also used in curry powder, chai, Ethiopian berbere, North African ras el hanout, and Yemeni zhug (see recipes on page pages 250–51).

Like all spices, cardamom should always be purchased as whole pods and ground just before using.

> ### HEALTH BENEFITS
> An ancient medicinal spice, cardamom has long been used as a digestive aid, treating gas, stomach cramps, constipation, and heartburn. It's also a boon for the immune system, offering antibacterial, antifungal, and antioxidant powers, the latter of which help protect against damage to DNA and, consequently, conditions like cancer and heart disease.

In the Garden

Cardamom, a perennial, needs rainy, humid, tropical climates to survive outdoors, but can be grown successfully indoors in a container if its conditions are met. Plants grown in containers indoors will very likely never flower or produce seeds, but they can be used for their long, flavorful leaves instead. Adequate temps range from 72° to 80°F.

Size: Up to 10 feet tall

Container: At least 10 to 15 inches deep

Light: Filtered sun or partial to full shade

Soil: Moist, rich, well drained

Plant: Seeds, cuttings, or rhizome divisions. Cuttings and rhizomes are preferred, as seeds are difficult to germinate.

Water: Regularly, to keep the soil consistently moist. Mist with water from a spray bottle to simulate the humidity in the tropics.

Harvest: Snip leaves when needed. After 3 or 4 years, snip off unripe, green seedpods—if left on the plant too long, they'll ripen and break open, spilling out the seeds. Pods are sun-dried (or "cured") for several days, or dried in heated sheds.

Care: Since plants rarely seed in nontropical conditions, to propagate, dig up the rhizome, divide, and replant.

SUBSTITUTIONS
- Cinnamon + nutmeg
- Nutmeg + cloves
- Ginger

Note: There's no close flavor match for cardamom, so these substitutes will not replicate the real thing.

PAIRINGS

Fruits and Vegetables: apples, oranges, pears, sweet potatoes, tomatoes

Proteins: almonds, cashews, eggs, lentils, pistachios, walnuts

Seasonings: allspice, anise, Indian bay leaf, caraway, chili peppers, cinnamon, cloves, coriander seeds, cumin, fennel seeds, ginger, lemon juice, nutmeg, paprika, pepper, rose water, saffron, star anise, turmeric, vanilla

In the Kitchen

Dishes: Stews, curries, rice, breads, cakes, desserts, ice creams, coffee, teas

Prep: Use whole seedpods for flavor and remove before serving, or grind the seeds. Seedpods should be bruised to release the aromatic oils; just split open the shell with a pestle or the back of a spoon, then cook and discard. Or, grind seeds to a powder: Use a mortar and pestle rather than a spice grinder, which doesn't handle the oily seeds as well. Simply break the seedpod, discard the shell, and grind the seeds. Ground cardamom is potent, so use sparingly.

Serve: Green cardamom flavors both sweet and savory dishes, everything from pastries, puddings, and cooked fruit to braised meats (*kormas*) and curries.

BLACK CARDAMOM

Amomum subulatum

Other common name: Nepal cardamom

Flavors: pungent, warm, camphorous, piney, earthy, smoky

Black cardamom, also called Nepal or brown cardamom, is a slightly larger, "hairy," dark-brown seedpod with a smokier flavor than the more commonly used green cardamom. The distinct aroma and taste come from the different drying method: Black cardamom seedpods are dried over an open fire rather than in the sun. This deep flavor is exclusively suited to rich, savory dishes, as opposed to green cardamom's affinity for sweets.

Less expensive than its highly coveted green cousin, it's also found in various spice blends, including garam masala, curry powder, and tandoori spices (see pages 250–251).

HEALTH BENEFITS
An ancient medicinal spice, cardamom has long been used as a digestive aid, treating gas, stomach cramps, constipation, and heartburn. It's also a boon for the immune system, offering antibacterial, antifungal, and antioxidant powers, the latter of which help protect against damage to DNA and, consequently, conditions like cancer and heart disease.

In the Garden
Black Cardamom, a perennial, needs rainy, humid, tropical climates to survive outdoors, but can be grown successfully indoors in a container if proper conditions are met. Plants grown in containers indoors will very likely never flower or produce seeds, but they can be used for their long, flavorful leaves instead. Adequate temps range from 72° to 80°F.

Size: Up to 10 feet tall

Container: At least 10 to 15 inches deep

Light: Filtered sun or partial to full shade

Soil: Moist, rich, well drained

Plant: Seeds, cuttings, or rhizome divisions. Cuttings and rhizomes are preferred, as seeds are difficult to germinate.

Water: Regularly, to keep the soil consistently moist. Mist with water from a spray bottle to simulate the humidity in the tropics.

Harvest: Snip leaves when needed. After three or four years, snip off unripe, green seedpods—if left on the plant too long, they'll ripen and break open, spilling out the seeds. Pods are sun-dried (or "cured") for several days, or dried in heated sheds.

SUBSTITUTIONS

- Cinnamon + nutmeg
- Nutmeg + cloves
- Ginger

Note: There's no close flavor match for cardamom, so these substitutes will not replicate the real thing.

Care: Since plants rarely seed in non-tropical conditions, to propagate, dig up the rhizome, divide, and replant.

PAIRINGS

Vegetables: carrots, onions, potatoes

Proteins: chicken, lamb

Seasonings: ajwain, allspice, chili peppers, cinnamon, cloves, coriander seeds, cumin, ginger, mustard, paprika, pepper, star anise, turmeric

In the Kitchen

Dishes: Stews, curries, rice, sauces, marinades, rubs, roasts

Prep: Use whole seedpods and remove before serving, or break open the pods and grind their seeds using a mortar and pestle.

Serve: Black cardamom plays more of a smoky, background role, used with other bold flavors in long-cooked dishes like hearty stews, biryanis, or anything cooked in the tandoori.

CELERY SEEDS

Apium graveolens

Flavors: pungent, warm, bitter, grassy, earthy, celery-like

Although it smells like celery, tastes like celery, and is called "celery," celery seed don't come from that thick-stalked, produce-aisle staple at your local supermarket. The potent, brown seeds are actually from a related species called smallage, or wild celery, an ancient plant whose stalks are slender, exceedingly bitter, and inedible.

Common celery is actually derived from wild celery, but they bear little resemblance to one another. Wild celery *seeds*, however, taste remarkably like a concentrated version of the juicy vegetable. Its bitter leaves can be used like parsley, but skip those skinny bitter stalks!

HEALTH BENEFITS
The bold flavor of celery seed makes them a healthy substitute for salt in any dish, a great perk for those who are watching their salt intake. The seeds are good for digestion and helpful against inflammation, able to alleviate symptoms of arthritis and gout. Celery seeds can also help ease cramps, lower blood pressure, relieve anxiety, and improve sleep.

In the Garden
Wild celery is a biennial that produces seeds in its second year. It likes temperate climates and will grow healthily in a container, so it can be brought inside during extreme heat or cold.

Size: 12 to 18 inches tall
Container: At least 12 inches in diameter
Light: Full sun to partial shade
Soil: Moist, rich, well drained
Plant: Seeds
Water: Regularly, to keep the soil consistently moist

Harvest: Once the flower heads have turned brown in the second year, snip them off into a paper bag to catch all the seeds. Hang the bags upside down to dry, or spread the flowers onto a flat surface in a warm, shady, airy location. When dry, remove the seeds.

SUBSTITUTIONS
- Celery salt
- Dill seeds

Care: Place mulch around the plant to prevent weeds and retain moisture; mulch heavily to help the plant withstand cold winters. Weed regularly and with care so you don't accidentally pull up the wild celery roots. If you like, let the plant self-seed for a new crop the following year.

PAIRINGS
Fruits and Vegetables: cabbage, carrots, celery, cucumbers, lettuce, onions, peppers, potatoes, tomatoes
Proteins: beans, beef, cheeses, chicken, eggs, fish and seafood, pork
Seasonings: basil, cayenne, cumin, dill, garlic, ginger, lemon juice, mustard, oregano, paprika, parsley, sage, soy sauce, thyme, turmeric, Worcestershire sauce

In the Kitchen
Dishes: Salads, dressings, marinades, rubs, coleslaw, soups, casseroles, breads, juices

Prep: Use seeds whole or grind them in a spice grinder. Combine ground celery seeds with salt to make celery salt.

Serve: Celery seeds are used in pickling spices, rubs, and spice blends for meat, fish, and chicken, sometimes ground into celery salt like in Old Bay Seasoning. Seeds are also tossed into a variety of salads, from mixed greens to coleslaw to potato salad, tuna salad, and chicken salad. They're a perfect complement to tomatoes, and are often added to tomato and vegetable juices.

CHILI PEPPERS

Capsicum

Flavors: range from mild and sweet to fiery hot

Though they're called "peppers," chili peppers are not at all related to the true black pepper (*Piper nigrum*), which is native to India. They're actually fruits, cousins of the mild and juicy common bell pepper.

With nearly two hundred types of chili peppers hailing from all corners of the globe—including Thailand, Mexico, Africa, and California—their flavors, shapes, and colors range wildly, from large and mild to tiny and fiery. Convention says that the smaller the pepper, the hotter the spice; but there are plenty of big peppers packing lots of heat, too. Drying chili peppers changes their chemistry and their flavor, upping the heat and introducing hints of smokiness or sweetness reminiscent of dried fruit.

Chili peppers can be prepared for cooking in many ways, whether as straightforward and fresh, dried whole, ground, chili flakes, powdered blends, oils, sauces, and pastes.

HEALTH BENEFITS

All peppers are packed with vitamin C and vitamin A, but it's chili peppers that boast the positive health effects of capsaicin, the substance that puts the "hot chili" in "hot chili pepper." Capsaicin helps boost the metabolism, stimulating fat-burning and improving appetite, and has been shown to lower cholesterol and triglycerides. It can also clear up sinus and nasal congestion, making it an easy and natural treatment for the common cold.

In the Garden

Chili peppers grow best in hot climates and won't tolerate contact with frosts. The ideal growing temperature is between 70° and 85°F. They'll grow successfully in containers indoors if positioned in a sun-filled windowsill. When you notice roots growing out of the drainage holes, it's time to re-pot into a larger container. When transplanting, try to keep the soil around the roots intact for minimal disturbance.

Germination and flowering times vary by type of pepper, so check the plant's growing instructions for its specific requirements and schedule.

Size: Varies by species

Container: At least 4 inches in diameter; larger depending on plant size

Light: Full sun

Soil: Moist, well drained. Add plenty of compost to the soil and place mulch around the plants to retain moisture.

Plant: Seeds, soaked overnight in warm water. (Either slice open a pepper and use its seeds, or buy seeds in any variety you like.)

Water: Regularly, to keep the soil consistently moist

Harvest: Snip off peppers with some stem attached.

Care: If your plants grow tall and skinny, consider staking them so they have upright support and protection from winds.

CHILI PEPPER PROTECTION

Chili peppers contain a chemical called capsaicin, which gives them their fiery heat. In super-hot varieties, it's so fiery that it can burn your skin. If you're using hot chili peppers, always wear gloves for protection, avoid touching your face and eyes, and wash your hands after handling. Wash the counter and any utensils thoroughly. Treat any chili pepper burns on the skin by submerging in ice-cold water. Note: The next time a too-hot chili pepper sets fire to your mouth, don't reach for that glass of water! Skip the soda and beer, too, as all three of these cold beverages will only fan the flames. Instead, reach for yogurt, milk, oil, peanut butter, sugar, rice, or bread.

Drying Chili Peppers

Chili peppers are often dried for future use, because dried chili peppers offer delicious flavors and can be even hotter than fresh ones. If drying indoors, make sure the room is well ventilated: Open the windows and bring in a fan, as the pepper vapors can irritate your eyes and nostrils. If air-drying, keep the peppers whole and either lay them flat or hang them from a string. If using the oven, follow these tips:

Oven-Drying

Protect your skin: Wear gloves to avoid contact with skin. Wash your hands if you touch the peppers, and avoid touching your face and eyes.

Prepare the peppers: Slice off the stems, slice the peppers in half lengthwise, and remove seeds and veins to reduce the spiciness. Spread over a baking sheet.

Bake at 110° to 140°F: Leave the oven door open. Drying time varies according to size, so check on them often and turn every 60 minutes. Chili peppers are dried when their skin is wrinkled and brittle.

Don't let them cook: Feel the peppers to make sure they're not softening or browning where their skins touch the pan. If they are, lower the oven temperature, keep the oven door open even wider, and turn them more frequently.

Store dried chili peppers whole in a sealed jar, or prepare as directed below.

Storage: Reconstituting Dried Chili peppers

You can rehydrate your stored dried chili peppers and use them to make sauces and pastes.

In a frying pan over low heat, toast the dried chili peppers for a couple minutes, turning them and making sure they don't burn. Skip the toasting step for less heat in your chili sauce.

Submerge the chili peppers in a bowl or pot of hot water (not quite boiling), and let sit for up to 20 minutes, until they soften.

Remove the skins, then crush or puree and add to sauces or pastes.

In the Kitchen

Dishes: curries, stir-fries, sauces, salsas, chutneys, guacamole, pastes, oils

Prep: Remember to wear disposable gloves if you'll be handling hot chili peppers. Remove seeds and membranes to tone down spiciness.

Slice, chop, or use small fresh chili peppers whole (if you dare). Whole peppers can be roasted in a pan, on a grill, in the oven, or over a flame on the stove. Dried chili peppers can be crushed finely to make dried pepper flakes, or ground in a spice grinder for a chili powder. Infuse whole dried chili peppers in a jar of oil for hot chili oil.

Serve: Chili peppers are used around the world to spice up bland foods like

PAIRINGS

Fruits and Vegetables:
carrots, celery, corn, cucumber, mushrooms, onions, peas, potatoes, tomatoes

Proteins: beans, beef, cheeses, chicken, eggs, fish and seafood

Seasonings: basil, bay leaf, cilantro, coriander seeds, fish sauce, garlic, ginger, lemon juice, lime juice, oregano, paprika, parsley, rau răm, soy sauce, thyme

potatoes, rice, and beans. Add fresh chopped chili peppers to stir-fries, curries, salsas, and sauces. Use dried chili peppers in any long-cooking stew or curry. Fats and oils help tone down the heat. Use sparingly at first and add more chili as you go, according to taste.

TYPES OF CHILI PEPPERS

Here are some of the most popular chili peppers from around the world, along with estimated heat levels.

Anaheim: mild
Large, often stuffed in Mexican cooking, like chiles rellenos

Bird's Eye: extremely hot
Small, often used in Southeast Asian stir-fries

Habanero: hottest
Dried, sweet, citrusy, used in Mexican salsas and long-cooked dishes

Jalapeño: hot
Medium-sized, used in Mexican salsas; the dried, smoked version is called chipotle, used in adobo sauce

Malagueta: extremely hot
Small, used in stews and poultry dishes in Portuguese, Brazilian, and Mozambican cooking

Poblano: mild
Large, often stuffed in Mexican cooking; the dried version is called ancho pepper, often ground

Scotch bonnet: hottest
Small, smoky, used in Caribbean jerk seasonings and sauces

Serrano: hot
Small, fruity, popular in Mexican salsas

Tabasco: extremely hot
Small, sharp, used in the ever-popular sauce

Thai: extremely hot
Small, red, used in curries and stir-fries

    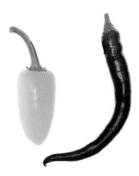

CASSIA

Cinnamomum cassia

Flavors: pungent, sweet, spicy, slightly bitter

The spice that most people know as "cinnamon" is actually cassia, culled from a different species of tree and offering stronger flavor and a lower price tag. To distinguish cinnamon quills from cassia quills, take note of the way they're rolled: If rolled in one direction from end to end, it's cinnamon; if rolled inward toward the center from opposite ends, like a scroll, you've got cassia. Cassia is also darker and redder.

Cassia is an integral ingredient in Chinese cuisine, where it's mostly used in savory, slow-cooked dishes containing heavy meats, lentils, and rice. The braising technique known as "red-cooking" calls for cassia either in whole form or in traditional five-spice powder (see page 250). Saigon cassia is considered the finest quality.

HEALTH BENEFITS

Cassia cinnamon has been studied for its ability to help stabilize blood sugar, making it a potential natural aid for people with type 2 diabetes. It's also used to treat a variety of gastrointestinal issues, including cramps, gas, nausea, diarrhea, and decreased appetite, as well as symptoms of the common cold.

In the Garden

Cassia trees are very similar to cinnamon trees, needing year-round warmth to grow. You can keep cassia in a container indoors, and the tree will grow according to your container size. However, most people who want to grow this type of spice at home plant a true cinnamon tree.

In the Kitchen

Dishes: Braises, rice, curries, compotes

Prep: Use cassia quills to flavor long-cooked dishes and remove before serving, or grind into a powder and add to dish, any savory or sweet.

Serve: Unlike delicate cinnamon, cassia is pungent and better suited to savory dishes, including rich meats, curries, and lentils. Use it in braises, curries, and rice, as well as in sauces for meat, duck, and chicken. Cassia also pairs well with lentils and hearty winter vegetables like pumpkin and squash. The aromatic leaves from a related cinnamon tree, tejpat leaves or Indian bay leaves (*Cinnamomum tamala*), are used widely in Indian cooking (see page 40).

SUBSTITUTIONS
- Cinnamon
- Nutmeg
- Allspice
- Indian bay leaves (crushed)

PAIRINGS

Fruits and Vegetables: apples, celery, cucumber, onions, plums, prunes, pumpkin, shallots, squash, sweet potatoes, tomatoes

Proteins: almonds, beans, beef, chicken, duck, game, lentils, pork

Seasonings: allspice, anise, caraway, cardamom, cayenne, chili peppers, cloves, celery seeds, coriander seeds, cumin, fennel, garlic, ginger, honey, Indian bay (tejpat) leaf, mustard, nutmeg, paprika, pepper, sesame seeds, Sichuan pepper, star anise, tamarind, turmeric

CINNAMON

Cinnamomum verum

Flavors: sweet, warm, slightly woody, with clove and citrus

One of the most recognizable flavors in the world, cinnamon is an ancient, valuable spice from Sri Lanka made from the bark from an evergreen tree. However, the "cinnamon" found in supermarkets is very likely not this particular spice, also called Ceylon or true cinnamon. Common cinnamon is actually cassia (see page 172), from a different species of tree and bearing more pungent flavor.

Sri Lankan cinnamon is subtler, with a hint of clove. In spice shops and well-stocked supermarkets, you might find cinnamon in a few different forms: whole quills, smaller "quillings" (quills broken in transit), or ground cinnamon. The best-quality ground cinnamon will be lighter in color.

HEALTH BENEFITS

Cinnamon is antibacterial and antifungal, and its extracts have been used to treat candida and other infections. A long-prized medicinal herb, it can improve digestion and relieve gas, diarrhea, and vomiting, while its aroma and flavor are thought to enhance brain function.

In the Garden

Cinnamon trees are native to tropical climates but will grow successfully elsewhere if protected from cold winter weather (temperatures below 40°F).

Size: 30 to 50 feet tall
Container: As large as you like
Light: Full sun to partial shade
Soil: Dry, sandy, well drained
Plant: Seeds, cuttings, transplants, or divided roots
Water: Occasionally and lightly, only when the soil feels dry two inches deep
Harvest: After two years, cut the tree to about 6 inches tall, leaving up to six shoots on the plant so they continue to grow; new growth will be bushier. Harvest from the cut branches that are ½ to 1 inch in diameter. Cut the branches into 4-inch segments that are easy to work with then follow these steps:

1. Peel off the brown outer bark to reveal the pale inner bark.
2. Use a sharp knife to score a line along the length of the branch. Don't cut too deep; you just want to loosen the top layer.
3. Wedge the knife or a spatula beneath the outer layer of bark, then gradually pry it up and peel.
4. Dry your fresh cinnamon bark in a warm, airy location away from sunlight. It will curl up naturally as it dries. For a dense quill, layer several thin segments of bark on top of one another so they curl up together.

SUBSTITUTIONS
- Cassia
- Allspice
- Nutmeg

Care: Add humus to the soil for added nutrients. Wait another two years after the first cutting—until the new shoots are 5 to 6 feet long and ½ to 1 inch in diameter—then harvest again. Cut and harvest every two years.

Keep It Fresh

Store cinnamon quills in a sealed jar or other container for several years. Ground cinnamon won't last as long—and flavor will diminish with time.

PAIRINGS

Fruits and Vegetables: apples, apricots, bananas, eggplant, onions, oranges, peaches, pears, pumpkin, raisins, sweet potatoes

Proteins: almonds, chicken, lamb, pecans, walnuts

Seasonings: allspice, cardamom, chocolate, cloves, coriander seeds, cumin, ginger, honey, lemon juice, nutmeg, tamarind, turmeric, vanilla

In the Kitchen

Dishes: Desserts, compotes, curries, rice, mulled wine, coffee, teas

Prep: Use whole quills to infuse cinnamon flavor into long-cooked dishes like stews, compotes, and curries. Grind quills in a coffee grinder and add ground cinnamon to baked goods, puddings, and spice blends.

Serve: A major player in sweet dishes, cinnamon pairs wonderfully with chocolate and a variety of fruits. In Middle Eastern, Indian, and Moroccan cooking, it's added to stews, curries, and tagines containing lamb and chicken. Ground cinnamon is also a common ingredient in curry powders, masalas, and sweet spice blends like pumpkin pie spice. The leaves from the cinnamon tree can also be used as an aromatic spice, placed in baking tins to infuse a pastry with cinnamon flavor.

CLOVE

Syzygium aromaticum or
Eugenia carophyllata

*Flavors: pungent, warm, sharp,
spicy, sweet*

Cloves are the dried, unripe buds of an evergreen tree native to the Banda Islands (or the Spice Islands) of modern-day Indonesia. A whole dried clove is dark, reddish-brown, with a thick stem cradling a round bud at one end, somewhat reminiscent of a tiny torch.

One of the most coveted spices throughout history, clove is integral to cuisines from around the world, used in spice blends including garam masala, Chinese five-spice powder, berbere, and quatre epices (see pages 250–251). Its flavor is one of the boldest in the spice rack, thanks to the high quantity of eugenol, a chemical found in other warm spices like nutmeg, cinnamon, and allspice. Use cloves sparingly in cooking, as you'll get lots of flavor from just a few buds.

> **HEALTH BENEFITS**
> The substance that gives cloves their trademark flavor is eugenol, an antiseptic, anti-inflammatory, and local anesthetic frequently used to treat toothaches. In fact, eugenol is often present in painkillers used at the dentist. Cloves also offer bacteria-, fungus-, and yeast-fighting properties, and can help treat nausea, diarrhea, bloating, and gas.

In the Garden

Clove trees thrive in wet, tropical climates with high humidity; low temperatures must be above 60°F. In nontropical or temperate regions, a greenhouse or in-home terrarium is a necessity. Full-grown trees can reach 33 feet tall, and they may take 8 years (or longer) to grow buds. The plus side: a healthy tree will continue producing cloves for 50 years or more!
Size: 25 to 33 feet tall

Container: 6 to 8 inches for seedlings; transplant to larger containers as necessary, but these large trees are more likely to grow full-size in the ground

Light: Partial shade

Soil: Moist, rich, well drained. Add compost to the soil for improved drainage.

Plant: Fresh seeds or cuttings; soak seeds in water overnight to remove the outer layer.

Water: Regularly, to keep the soil consistently moist but not wet or soggy; ½ to 2 inches per week

Harvest: Pick clove buds when they're full size, ½ to ¾ inch long, and just starting to change color from green to reddish-pink. They should be spread out to dry completely under hot tropical sunlight for several days, protected from rainfall.

SUBSTITUTIONS
• Allspice
• Cinnamon
• Nutmeg

PAIRINGS

Fruits and Vegetables: apples, beets, cabbage, carrots, onions, oranges, pumpkin, squash, sweet potatoes

Proteins: almonds, beef, cheeses, eggs, ham, lamb, pecans, pork, walnuts

Seasonings: allspice, bay leaf, cardamom, cinnamon, chili peppers, coriander seeds, cumin, curry leaves, fennel, garlic, ginger, honey, lemon juice, mustard, nutmeg, tamarind, vanilla

Care: If starting from seed, only transplant at the seedling stage and no later, as the growing roots are delicate and don't tolerate disturbance well.

In the Kitchen

Dishes: Curries, sauces, marinades, relishes, breads, baked sweets, fruit pies, dried fruit dishes, mulled wine

Prep: Use cloves whole to infuse flavor into a sauce or broth, and remove before serving. Or grind them in a spice grinder; however, they can be difficult to grind, so consider grabbing a jar of ground cloves in addition to whole ones.

Serve: Cloves are a natural companion for other foods and spices containing eugenol, like cinnamon, allspice, vanilla, and red wine. Used often in both sweet and savory dishes, they're essential to fruit pies (especially apple), traditional glazed ham, stewed fruit, mulled wine, and Christmas desserts. Cloves bring warmth to many spice blends used to season rich meats like pork, as well as to Asian and Indian curries.

CORIANDER SEEDS

Coriandrum sativum

Flavors: mild, warm, and sweet, with orange and lemon peel

Coriander seeds come from the plant that bears the pungent leafy-green herb known as cilantro (see page 48). However, while cilantro offers sharp, eye-opening flavor, coriander seeds are subtle, sweet, and versatile, bringing mild citrus flavor to both sweets and savory dishes alike. Their flavor is so agreeable that they can be used in great quantity without overdoing it. Coriander is considered an "amalgamating" spice, meaning it can bring disparate flavors together to harmonize in a dish; for this reason, it's a common ingredient in many spice blends and pastes, including garam masalas, curry powders, curry pastes, and pickling spices, as well as berbere and zhug (see pages 250–251) and harissa (see page 150).

HEALTH BENEFITS

Coriander is touted for its anti-inflammatory qualities, helpful for ailments like arthritis, rheumatism, and skin conditions such as eczema and psoriasis. It's also been shown in studies to improve cholesterol levels *and* lower blood sugar. On top of that, research has found that an antibiotic compound found in coriander may fight off food-borne bacteria like salmonella.

In the Garden

Coriander, which are annuals, plants do best in mild climates between 60° and 80°F. They'll produce foliage (cilantro) and seeds through the winter if your region doesn't experience frosts. The plants grow healthily in containers, but they're fussy if uprooted, so choose a suitable, permanent container. The seeds develop their sweet citrus flavor upon drying; while still ripe, they'll taste like cilantro.

Size: 2 feet tall
Container: 18 inches wide and 10 to 12 inches deep
Light: Full sun

Soil: Moist, well drained

Plant: Seeds. To help germination, gently squeeze each seed until its halves split, then soak in water for 2 to 3 days and let dry completely before planting.

Water: Regularly, to keep soil consistently moist, about 1 inch per week

SUBSTITUTIONS

- Cumin
- Cardamom
- Caraway

Harvest: Let the flowers develop and dry. When the seeds turn from green to tan or light brown, snip off the stems and place in a paper bag, making sure to collect all the seeds. Hang them to dry for several days, then remove the seeds and let dry for longer, if necessary.

Care: Weed regularly or place mulch around plants to prevent weeds. Either let the plant self-seed, or sow fresh seeds every few weeks for a steady supply. Pull up plants after they seed to make room for new ones.

PAIRINGS

Fruits and Vegetables: apples, carrots, celery, mushrooms, onions, oranges, pears, plums, potatoes, pumpkin, shallots

Proteins: almonds, beans, beef, chicken, duck, fish, game, ham, lamb, lentils, pork, sausage

Seasonings: allspice, anise, bay leaf, caraway, cardamom, chili peppers, cilantro, cinnamon, cloves, cumin, fennel seeds, fenugreek seeds, garlic, ginger, lemon juice and zest, lime juice, mustard, paprika, parsley, pepper, nutmeg, sesame, thyme, turmeric

In the Kitchen

Dishes: Curries, tagines, stews, stocks, marinades, sausages, chutneys, spice pastes, breads, compotes, stewed fruit

Prep: Dry-roasting (see page 150) whole coriander seeds will bring out their intense flavors. Seeds can be used whole, chopped, or ground in any dish. Whole and chopped coriander seeds are suitable for dishes with longer cook times, as the heat will gradually soften the seeds; or, simply remove them before serving. Grind seeds using a mortar and pestle or a spice grinder.

Serve: The ever-adaptable coriander can flavor anything from pumpkin pie to red-hot curries, from meat-stuffed casseroles to fruit compotes. It pairs deliciously with fall-season fruits like apples and pears, as well as pungent seasonings like garlic, chili peppers, and ginger. Dry-roast seeds when using in any dish with intense flavors or rich ingredients, like meaty curries and fatty fish.

CUMIN

Cuminum cyminum

Flavors: pungent, warm, earthy, slightly bitter

Cumin ranks only behind black pepper as the second-most popular spice on the planet. It's essential to a diverse range of high-spice cuisines, from Spain to Lebanon to Mexico to India, and found in many curry powders, masalas, and chili powders, as well as spice blends and pastes like Ethiopian berbere, Moroccan harissa paste (see page 150), Middle Eastern baharat, and Egyptian dukka.

While the seeds look like caraway—long and oval with lengthwise ridges—their flavor is decidedly more pungent, with a slightly bitter edge. Add cumin at the start of cooking for a deep flavor that penetrates an entire dish, or toss in seeds at the end for fresher seasoning.

> **HEALTH BENEFITS**
> Cumin has been used throughout history as a digestive aid, thanks to its powers in taming indigestion, gas, cramps, diarrhea, and nausea (it's even prescribed for morning sickness). It's also high in iron, which is great for energy and the immune system, and particularly important for people with anemia.

In the Garden

Cumin plants, which are annuals, like hot and moist climates, similar to their native home in Egypt's Nile valley. In temperate climates, start seeds indoors and transplant seedlings outside once temperatures are consistently above 60°F. Cumin plants don't fare well when transplanted, so use biodegradable pots to minimize the disturbance. They'll grow successfully in containers indoors positioned in a sun-filled window.

Size: 6 to 20 inches tall, depending on climate conditions
Container: 6 inches in diameter and 4 inches deep
Light: Full sun

Soil: Light, fertile, well drained. Mix compost into the soil for added nutrients and better drainage.

Plant: Seeds. Soak in water overnight to help them germinate. After sowing, mist with water from a spray bottle to keep moist.

Water: Regularly and thoroughly, when soil feels somewhat dry but not completely dry; soil should be moist but not wet.

Harvest: After about 4 months or longer, seedpods will grow ripe and turn brown, while stems will dry and become brittle. Snip stems into a paper bag, then hang to dry.

Care: Weed regularly. Protect from frosts and winds.

SUBSTITUTIONS

- Chili powder (contains cumin)
- Coriander seeds
- Caraway seeds

PAIRINGS

Fruits and Vegetables: cabbage, carrots, celery, corn, cucumbers, eggplant, onions, peppers, potatoes, squash, tomatoes

Proteins: beans, beef, cheeses, chicken, fish, game, lamb, lentils, pork, turkey, venison

Seasonings: ajwain, allspice, anise, bay leaf, cardamom, chili peppers, cilantro, cinnamon, cloves, coriander seeds, curry leaves, fennel seeds, fenugreek seeds, garlic, ginger, lemon juice, lime juice, mustard, nutmeg, oregano, paprika, pepper, tamarind, thyme, turmeric

In the Kitchen

Dishes: Curries, rice, chilies, stews, soups, sausages, breads, pickling spices, chutneys

Prep: Enhance the flavor of whole seeds by dry-roasting or frying before use (see pages 149–150). Use seeds whole or grind using a mortar and pestle or spice grinder.

Serve: Ubiquitous in curries and many Indian dishes, cumin creates well-rounded overall flavor when used with other pungent spices. Pair it with potatoes, squash, or carrots, whether roasted or in stews and soups. Cumin is especially delicious with lamb, couscous, beans, and chickpeas, and is a common ingredient in Mexican and Tex-Mex chili. Fresh cumin leaves can add a little spice to salads.

DILL SEEDS

Anethum graveolens

Flavors: pungent, warm, and tangy, with anise and caraway

Dill plants work double-duty in the culinary department. Not only are their leaves delicious (see page 50), but their seeds—actually fruits—are, too. Each offers a distinct flavor, with the leaves reminiscent of light anise and parsley, and the seeds bearing sharp, caraway-like tones. Seeds are oval, ribbed, and practically weightless; they appear only after the plant has flowered and stopped producing leaves. In North America, perhaps the most familiar use of dill seeds is in dill pickles, but they're also often added to breads, just like caraway seeds.

HEALTH BENEFITS

Dill's use as a medicinal herb dates back to ancient times. It's still believed to improve digestion; many people chew on dill seeds to stimulate appetite, calm stomach upset, and relieve gas and heartburn. As an antibacterial, dill seeds also help clean the digestive tract and the mouth, while their flavor freshens breath.

In the Garden

Dill plants, which are annuals, don't transplant well due to their long taproot, so choose a location that will be adequate for a full-grown plant.

Size: Up to 3 feet tall

Container: At least 12 inches deep

Light: Full sun

Soil: Light, rich, well drained

Plant: Seeds or transplants. These plants form sturdy, thick roots, so transplant only young potted plants with roots and soil together.

Water: Frequently at first, but less often when established; when the soil feels dry

Harvest: Let the plant flower and the seeds develop. When the seeds are ripe and turn light brown, snip off the stems or the seed heads and place in a paper bag. Hang to dry.

Care: Protect from winds or support with stakes in the ground. To grow more dill, let some seeds drop so the plant can reseed, or sow new seeds every few weeks to ensure a steady supply of leaves and seeds in the kitchen.

SUBSTITUTIONS
- Caraway seeds
- Fennel seeds
- Dill leaves

PAIRINGS

Fruits and Vegetables: cabbage, carrots, celery, corn, cucumbers, eggplant, onions, peppers, potatoes, squash, tomatoes

Proteins: beans, beef, cheeses, chicken, fish, game, lamb, lentils, pork, turkey, venison

Seasonings: ajwain, allspice, anise, bay leaf, cardamom, chili peppers, cilantro, cinnamon, cloves, coriander seeds, curry leaves, fennel seeds, fenugreek seeds, garlic, ginger, lemon juice, lime juice, nutmeg, mustard, oregano, paprika, pepper, tamarind, thyme, turmeric

In the Kitchen

Dishes: Pickling spices, stews, soups, breads, baked sweets

Prep: Use dill seeds whole or ground. They can be toasted, fried, or added to long-cooked dishes to impart deep, mellow flavor. The longer they cook, the softer the flavor; add at the end of cooking for greater pungency.

Serve: Dill seeds are essential in pickling spices; they're used generously in "dill pickles," a signature food of New York City. They're also used in brines for pickling beets and carrots. The seeds pair deliciously with root vegetables like potatoes, beets, carrots, and onions, as well as fatty fish like salmon. Add them to rich, creamy soups, traditional borscht, and rubs and marinades for any kind of meat.

FENNEL SEEDS

Foeniculum vulgare

Flavors: pungent, fresh, warm, strong anise

The fennel plant offers a variety of culinary uses as both herb and spice, thanks to its fresh, tasty leaves (see page 52) and anise-flavored seeds. Stronger in flavor than the leaves, fennel seeds are a versatile spice in Eastern cuisines, where they often flavor meat, poultry, and beans. They're used in Chinese five-spice powder, and some versions of garam masala (see recipes on pages 250–251).

The seeds are oval and ridged, resembling both cumin and caraway, only greener. In fact, the greenest seeds have the best, unadulterated fennel flavor, so check color when selecting seeds for cooking. The flavor of fennel seeds is often mistaken for that of anise seeds, but the latter is more pungent.

HEALTH BENEFITS
Chewing on fennel seeds can help alleviate gas, bloating, and acid reflux, promote digestion, and even freshen breath after meals (this is a common post-dining practice in India).

In the Garden
Fennel, a perennial, thrives in temperate climates and will grow successfully in containers. It doesn't transplant easily, so find a suitable spot and stick with it.
Size: Herb fennel, 4 to 6 feet tall; Florence fennel, 2 feet tall
Container: At least 1 foot deep
Light: Full sun to partial shade
Soil: Rich, moist, well drained
Plant: Seeds, soaked in water for 5 days before planting; or divided roots
Water: Regularly until the plant is established, when cutting it for harvest or replanting, and during drought. Drought tolerant; don't overwater or your roots may rot.

Harvest: Let the fennel grow until the flowers turn from yellow to brown and the seeds are green-yellow; cut the flowers from the stems into a paper bag and let them dry completely in the shade.

Care: Keep fennel far from any dill plants in the garden, as they can interfere with one another and produce unpleasant flavors. Fennel self-seeds readily; let them drop for a new crop.

PAIRINGS

Fruits and Vegetables: beets, cabbage, carrots, celery, cucumbers, mushrooms, onions, peppers, potatoes, shallots, spinach, tomatoes

Proteins: beans, chicken, fish and seafood, pork, sausage

Seasonings: anise, basil, bay leaf, cardamom, cayenne, cinnamon, cloves, coriander seeds, cumin, fennel leaves and bulb, garlic, ginger, lemon juice, mustard, oregano, paprika, parsley, red pepper flakes, rosemary, thyme, turmeric

In the Kitchen

Dishes: Salads, dressings and marinades, rubs, soups, sauces, breads, pastas, casseroles, pickling spices, beverages

Prep: Use seeds whole, crushed, pounded, or ground in any recipe. Roast whole seeds before adding to a dish to develop a sweet-spicy flavor (see page 150).

Serve: Fennel seeds give Italian sausages their distinctive flavor, and are a common ingredient in dry rubs for meats and fish. Seeds are also used as a pickling spice and flavoring for teas, syrups, anise-flavored liquors (like absinthe), and even toothpastes. They're often baked into breads, incorporated into stuffings and sauerkraut, and partnered with garlic, tomatoes, cucumbers, and beans.

GINGER

Zingiber officinale

Flavors: **fresh** *pungent, tangy, sweet, and ranging from warm to fiery;* **dried** *warm, lightly spicy, and sweet, with lemon*

Ginger is a beautiful, tropical plant that has a thick, knobbed rhizome growing underground. It's the rhizome that produces one of the world's most popular spices, with a pungent flesh that changes in flavor as it ages and offers countless uses in the kitchen.

Fresh rhizomes should be plump and solid with smooth, taut skin. Ginger can be prepared and sold in a variety of tasty ways: pickled, preserved in syrup, crystallized or candied, dried, and juiced. Sushi lovers know pickled ginger as the pink, thinly sliced condiment served alongside wasabi in Japanese restaurants; this preparation is known in Japan as *gari*. Dried ground ginger is commonly used in pie spices and baked sweets (like gingerbread!), as well as in many savory spice blends from around the world, including curry powders, barbecue seasonings, Ethiopian berbere, Moroccan ras el hanout, and French quatre épices (see page 250).

HEALTH BENEFITS

Ginger is a traditional go-to remedy for nausea and vomiting, particularly when caused by motion sickness, morning sickness, surgical procedures, and medications. But it has many other health benefits, too: Its anti-inflammatory and analgesic properties help relieve symptoms of arthritis, muscle pain, and cramps. Consumed as a tea, ginger warms the body from the inside and can help reduce fevers.

In the Garden

In temperate climates, plant ginger, which is a perennial, in a container to bring indoors in cooler weather. Rhizomes harvested while they're young are sweeter, juicier, and softer, while those allowed to age grow coarse, fibrous, and more pungent; harvest times will vary according to your tastes. The longer you let your ginger grow and hold off harvesting, the larger the harvest will be.

Size: 2 to 3 feet tall

Container: At least 15 inches in diameter

Light: Partial, filtered sun to full shade

Soil: Moist, rich, loose, well drained. Mix compost into the soil for added nutrients and to retain moisture. If growing outdoors in a garden, add plenty of mulch, which retains water, adds nutrients, and prevents weeds.

Plant: Rhizomes obtained in early spring. Plant whole rhizomes or break into 3-inch sections to grow more plants; each section should have at least one bud. Soak in water overnight before planting. Sow with bud-end up, just under the surface of the soil.

> ## SUBSTITUTIONS
>
> Dried:
> - Allspice
> - Cinnamon
> - Nutmeg
>
> Fresh:
> - Crystallized ginger (with sugar washed off)
> - Galangal (more potent)
>
> Note: There's no exact flavor match for ginger, so consider leaving it out of your recipe or altering the flavor of your dish with one of these substitutions.

Water: Regularly, to keep the soil consistently moist but not wet or soggy. Ginger loves humidity, so in dry climates, mist with water using a spray bottle. Plants go dormant in winter, so there's no need to water then; they'll perk back up in spring.

Harvest: After 4 months of growth, you can harvest small portions of the rhizome by simply digging them out and breaking them off; note that younger rhizomes are less pungent in flavor. After 8 to 12 months, once the leaves die away, the whole rhizomes will be ready to harvest. If you're not harvesting everything for the year, break off the parts you need and replant the rest.

Care: Protect from winds and frosts.

Keep It Fresh

Wrap fresh ginger rhizome in paper towels and store in a plastic bag in the refrigerator's crisper, where it should keep for up to 10 days. For longer freshness, slice, chop, or mince ginger, and store in the freezer.

Dried ginger will be usable for about one year, and it has many uses in the kitchen. Fresh rhizomes can be peeled and dried in the sun. For quicker drying, slice the rhizome into thin coins (less then ¼ inch thick). Spread onto a baking sheet and bake on your oven's lowest temperature setting, 130° to 150°F. Keep the oven door open to ensure the lowest amount of heat. Dried ginger slices can be grated to a powder for use in the kitchen (see tips for Roots and Rhizomes on page 189).

In the Kitchen

Dishes: fresh stir-fries, curries, soups, salads, sauces, marinades, relishes, chutneys, beverages; **dried ground** marinades, rubs, stews, cakes, pies, cookies, fruit desserts, beverages

Prep: Chunks or thick slices of fresh ginger can be used for flavoring long-cooked dishes and marinades then removed before serving. This will infuse mellow ginger flavor. For more intensity, thinly slice, chop, shred, or grate the ginger and add at the end of cooking. Fresh ginger can also be juiced for sauces and marinades.

Serve: Fresh ginger is essential in Cantonese cooking, as part of the traditional aromatic blend of ginger, garlic, and scallions used in countless dishes. Among its many tasty uses, ginger also serves to balance out the strong odors of fish and meat, especially in Asian cuisines. Dried ground ginger flavors so many baked sweets in Western cooking, it's nearly impossible to name them all; it's essential in pumpkin pie spice, apple pie spice, many cakes and cookies, and—of course—anything labeled "ginger," like gingerbread and gingersnaps. Dried ginger also stars in savory spice blends used in Asian and Middle Eastern dishes.

PAIRINGS

Fruits and Vegetables: apples, beets, broccoli, cabbage, carrots, celery, chives, leafy greens, onions, peppers, pumpkin, scallions, squash, sweet potatoes

Proteins: beef, chicken, duck, eggs, fish and seafood, ham, nuts, pork

Seasonings: allspice, cardamom, cassia, chili peppers, cinnamon, cloves, coriander seeds, cumin, curry leaf, fennel seeds, galangal, garlic, honey, lemongrass, lemon juice and zest, lemon myrtle, lime juice and zest, mustard, nutmeg, paprika, sesame seeds, star anise, soy sauce, turmeric, vanilla

ROOTS AND RHIZOMES

Some herbs and spices come from a plant's rhizome, or the plump, hard root, including horseradish, galangal, and turmeric. As usual, the best flavor derives from the whole fresh ingredient rather than store-bought ground or chopped versions. So if you want the freshest seasoning available, look for whole rhizomes or roots and then prepare as called for in your recipes.

- **To peel:** Use a spoon, *not* a knife or vegetable peeler. Both are unwieldy for peeling around the knobs and into the narrow crevices of a rhizome. On top of that, they'll remove too much of the delicious flesh that would be much better used in your cooking. A regular spoon is safer and easier to maneuver, and it will only remove the outer layer of skin. Peel only the segments that you need to keep the remaining root fresh.
- **To slice:** Use a sharp kitchen knife to slice thin rounds from the end of the root or a "finger."
- **To shred or julienne:** Place several slices flat on top of one another, and carefully cut through the stack to form matchstick-size slivers.
- **To chop or mince:** Align the slivers or form them into a mound, and chop crosswise down the length of the bundle to form small cubes.
- **To grate:** Hold a knob in one hand and rub it against a microplane grater, being careful when you get to the end of the knob so you don't cut yourself. Place a bowl or plate on the counter to catch any juice as you work.
- **To juice:** Collect the juice extracted from grating in a bowl, then wrap the grated ginger in cheesecloth and wring it out into the bowl. You can also use a garlic press or a juicer, if you have one.

MUSTARDS

Brassica alba (yellow or white), *Brassica juncea* (brown), *Brassica nigra* (black)

Flavors: **hot mustards** *pungent, sharp, biting, and hot;* **mild mustards** *tangy and smooth*

Mustards make up an entire class of condiment. Whole seeds offer little in the way of fragrance, but they unleash their trademark heat when crushed. Yellow mustard seeds are on the mild end of the heat spectrum, often found in pickling spices and marinades. Brown and black seeds, on the other hand, bring fiery heat to Indian dishes and Bengali spice pastes and cooking oils. Mustard seeds are used in many curry powders, pickling spices, and mustard powders.

However, it's when these seeds are combined with liquids—water, grape juice, wine, or vinegar—that they form the range of mustard condiments beloved in cuisines from India and Europe and beyond. These liquids temper the heat of mustard seeds to varying qualities, from the smooth and subtle Dijon to the eye-popping hot mustard offered at Chinese restaurants. The greater the acidity, the milder the flavor; therefore, water yields the hottest mustard while vinegar mellows it out.

> **HEALTH BENEFITS**
> Like its relatives in the *Brassica*, or cruciferous, plant family, mustard scores an A+ in the health department. It encourages healthy digestion and improves respiratory conditions by clearing out nasal passages and breaking up phlegm. Mustard also boosts blood circulation and serves as an effective anti-inflammatory, especially when applied in a compress over sore muscles and arthritic joints.

In the Garden

Mustard plants are annuals, grow well in containers, and produce tasty mustard greens, another culinary bonus to growing your own. A cool-weather crop, mustard will go to seed quickly in hot temperatures (over 75°F), resulting in subpar seed quality. To avoid this in hot climates, sow seeds in fall for a cool winter harvest.

Size: Up to 4 feet tall

Container: At least 12 inches deep

Light: Full sun

Soil: Moist, rich, well drained. Mix compost into the soil for added nutrients and to retain moisture.

Plant: Seeds or seedlings

Water: Regularly, to keep the soil consistently moist; about 2 inches per week

Harvest: When seedpods turn from green to brown, snip off the stems or seedpods into a paper bag. Let dry for 2 weeks, and the pods will eventually open and release the seeds. You can also spread them out over a mesh screen or muslin fabric to dry completely.

PAIRINGS

Fruits and Vegetables: cabbage, carrots, cauliflower, celery, coconut, cucumber, leafy greens, mushrooms, onions, peas, peppers, potatoes, spinach, tomatoes

Proteins: beans, beef, cheeses, chicken, fish and seafood, game, lentils, ham, pork

Seasonings: allspice, bay leaf, asafetida, cardamom, cayenne, celery seeds, chili peppers, cilantro, cinnamon, cloves, coriander seeds, cumin, curry leaf, curry powder, dill, fennel seeds, fenugreek seeds, garlic, ginger, honey, lemon juice, nigella, paprika, pepper, red pepper flakes, star anise, tarragon, turmeric

SUBSTITUTION
• Horseradish

In the Kitchen

Dishes: Curries, stir-fries, soups, pickling spices, rubs, marinades, sauces, dips

Prep: Use whole seeds in curries, soups, and stir-fries. Fry seeds in hot oil before adding to any dish (see page 149); the seeds will pop while they're cooking, releasing their flavorful oils, and will stop when they're ready. Dry-roast whole seeds for pickling (see page 150). For prepared mustards, grind seeds and add liquids—vinegar, wine, or water—to adjust the flavor.

Serve: Experiment with prepared mustards by adding other herbs and seasonings into the mix, like honey, chili peppers, tarragon, and garlic. Add mustard to marinades, rubs, and glazes for any variety of meat or fish. Combine with robust cheeses, or stir into salad dressings or mayonnaise for sauces and dips.

NUTMEG

Myristica fragrans

Flavors: pungent, warm, bittersweet, woody, with clove

Nutmeg is the fruit of a tropical tree native to the Banda Islands (or Spice Islands) of Indonesia. Like a plum or peach, the fruit contains a hard seed at its center, and it's this seed that gives us the scrumptious, powerful spice we call nutmeg. The nutmeg shell is covered with a red webbed coating, an aril or placenta—this is mace, another spice entirely with distinct uses in cooking. Mace is subtler and sweeter than nutmeg, with hints of citrus and cinnamon.

Whole nutmeg seeds are sold at specialty markets and health-food stores, and they're worth seeking out for the superior flavor of freshly ground nutmeg. Pre-ground nutmeg holds up well, too, so it's a fine alternative. Spice shops sell mace in ground form and, sometimes, in larger segments called "blades," which are preferred.

HEALTH BENEFITS

Nutmeg has been used traditionally to treat digestive troubles like gas, nausea, vomiting, and diarrhea, and to soothe toothaches and sores in the mouth. Its mild calming effect can be helpful for anxiety and insomnia, while its essential oil contains compounds believed to wield antioxidant and anti-inflammatory powers.

In the Garden

Nutmeg loves tropical climates with plenty of rainfall and humidity. The trees are dioecious, or single-sexed, meaning they need both male and female specimens in order to bear fruit; unfortunately, the tree's gender isn't revealed until it's 5 years old, so the best way to begin a nutmeg crop is to plant several trees and hope there is a male in the mix. The tree begins producing fruit after 5 to 8 years, but it'll continue offering up delicious spices for another 50. If growing indoors, position the plant where it will receive lots of sunlight.

Size: Up to 60 feet tall

Container: At least 2 feet in diameter and 20 inches deep

Light: Partial sun or light shade in the first few years, then full sun

Soil: Moist, rich, extremely well drained

Plant: Fresh seeds, soaked in water for 24 hours before sowing. Start seeds in a container and transplant outdoors when 10 inches tall, taking care not to disturb the taproot. Space at least thirty feet away from other plants.

Water: Regularly, to keep the soil consistently moist but not wet. Mist with water from a spray bottle to simulate the humidity in the tropics.

Harvest: When ripe, the seed's outer husks will split open. The husks, flesh, and mace should be removed and the seeds dried in the sun for up to 2 months. When shaken, a completely dried nutmeg seed will rattle inside the shell. Remove the shell to reveal the seed.

Care: Mulch the soil for added nutrients, especially for seedlings and young plants. Weed regularly. If planting permanently in a container, transplant to a container that's at least 2 inches wider than the previous one, and repeat as the tree grows.

PAIRINGS
Fruits and Vegetables: apples, cabbage, carrots, cauliflower, onions, potatoes, pumpkin, raisins, spinach, sweet potatoes

Proteins: cheeses, chicken, eggs, fish and seafood, lamb, mutton, pecans, veal, walnuts

Seasonings: allspice, cardamom, cinnamon, cloves, coriander seeds, cumin, garlic, ginger, honey, lemon juice, mace, pepper, rose, thyme, vanilla

Keep It Fresh
Whole nutmeg seeds will keep for years if sealed in an airtight container.

In the Kitchen
Dishes: Baked desserts, cakes, cookies, pies, puddings, stews, sauces

Prep: Grind whole nutmeg using a microplane grater.

Serve: A signature holiday-season spice in the United States, nutmeg is used widely in cakes, cookies, puddings, milkshakes, eggnog, and mulled wine; it's integral to sweet spice blends for pumpkin pie and apple pie. It also pairs nicely with cooked root vegetables like beets, carrots, and potatoes, as well as squash and spinach. Outside the United States, nutmeg is often added to meaty stews, pasta sauces, and veggie purees; it's used in the savory blends quatre epices and ras el hanout (see page 250).

PAPRIKA

Capsicum annum

Flavors: range from sweet and smoky to pungent and hot

An assortment of red chili peppers are cured and ground to create paprika, a bright-red spice that comes in a range of flavors depending on the blend and preparation. It's an essential spice in Hungarian and Spanish cuisines. Hungary produces several varieties, ranging from mild and sweet to pungent, hot, and bitter. Spanish paprika, or *pimentön*, comes from two regions in Spain: La Vera and Murcia. Pimentön de la Vera is the favorite, bearing a smoky flavor completely distinct from the Hungarian spice; the chili peppers are smoked over an oak-burning fire rather than air-dried.

Paprika's heat is determined by the type of pepper used and whether or not the spicy stems, veins, and seeds are included in the grinding process. Remove all three from the equation to reduce the heat-carrying substance capsaicin, resulting in the mildest paprika.

> ## HEALTH BENEFITS
> Thanks to capsaicin, the heat-carrying chemical present in all hot chili peppers, hot paprika can help clear up congestion, cool down body temperature, reduce blood pressure, relieve indigestion, and stimulate healthy digestion and fat burning. Paprikas with the most capsaicin are also the hottest, but milder paprika provides its share of healthy perks, too. All varieties are loaded with carotenoids, which improve vision and offer powerful antioxidant properties.

In the Garden

To make your own paprika, choose peppers based on your flavor preferences. Like your spices hot? Go for Alma peppers, which sneak a little heat into their overall sweet flavor. Dulce Rojo, Kalosca, and Boldog peppers are predominantly sweet.

Chili peppers grow best in hot climates and won't tolerate contact with frosts. Ideal growing temperature is between 70° and 85°F. They'll grow successfully in containers indoors if positioned in a sun-filled window. When you notice roots growing out of the drainage holes, it's time to re-pot into a larger container. When transplanting, try to keep the soil around the roots intact for minimal disturbance. Germination and flowering times vary by type of pepper, so check the plant's growing instructions to know its specific requirements and schedule.

Size: Varies by species

Container: At least 4 inches in diameter; larger depending on plant size

Light: Full sun

Soil: Moist, fertile, well drained. Mix compost into the soil and place mulch around the plants for added nutrients and to retain water.

Plant: Seeds or seedlings

Water: Regularly, to keep the soil consistently moist

Harvest: When the peppers are a solid color, they're ready for harvest. Snip off peppers with some stem attached.

Care: Protect growing plants from frosts and winds.

Making Paprika from Dried Peppers

Dry your fresh paprika peppers as directed on page 169. Once completely dried, select some peppers for the paprika and store the others in the freezer for later use. (Ground spices lose their flavor over time, so only grind a

PAPRIKA VARIETIES

When shopping for paprika, keep this rule in mind: The redder the powder, the milder the spice. Bright-red paprika will be mild and sweet, while pale-red and brown varieties pack more heat. Paprikas produced in the United States are generally all mild, while Hungarian varieties can be hotter than Spanish.

HUNGARIAN

Különleges ("special delicate"): mild, very sweet, and bright red

Édesnemes ("noble sweet"): the most common paprika; sweet, slightly hot, and bright red

Delicatessen ("delicate"): slightly hotter and pale red

Félédes ("semisweet"): medium hot, less sweet

Rósza ("rose"): hot and light red

Erös ("stong"): hottest, bitter, dark red to brown

SPANISH

Dulce ("sweet"): smoky, tangy, and dark red

Agridulce ("bittersweet"): sharp, pungent, and bitter

Picante ("hot"): sharp and hot

SUBSTITUTIONS
- Chili powder
- Cajun spice
- Cayenne (very hot)
- Chipotle powder

batch that you're sure to use within a couple months.) Remove stems, veins, and seeds to reduce the heat level, or use the whole peppers for super-hot paprika. Break the brittle peppers into smaller pieces that fit in your spice grinder, blender, or mortar and pestle. Grind to a powder.

In the Kitchen

Dishes: goulash, stews, soups, chili, marinades, sauces, rice, noodles, casseroles

Prep: Paprika can be sprinkled over dishes before serving, but the true, complex flavors are released during cooking. Fry the spice with onions and olive oil to make a base for stews or goulash.

Serve: Paprika flavors potato and vegetable dishes, as well as virtually any meat, whether smoked, grilled, or roasted. It's an important spice in many sausages, especially Spanish chorizo, and is integral to the Moroccan fish marinade called *chermoula*. Paprika is employed in Indian cooking for its bright-red hue, particularly in tandoori dishes.

PAIRINGS

Vegetables: carrots, celery, mushrooms, onions, peppers, potatoes

Proteins: beans, beef, cheeses, chicken, duck, eggs, lamb, pork, sausage

Seasonings: allspice, basil, caraway, cardamom, celery seeds, cumin, garlic, ginger, lemon juice, oregano, parsley, pepper, rosemary, saffron, thyme, turmeric, Worcestershire sauce

PEPPER

Piper nigrum

*Flavors: **black** pungent, hot, sharp; **white** pungent, fiery, and sharp, with slight sweetness; **green** fresh, pungent, and hot; **red** fresh and sweet*

One of the most coveted spices since ancient times, pepper is still the world's number one seasoning. Grown on a tropical flowering vine, peppercorns are actually the plant's fruit, or berries, and they're harvested at different times to produce black, white, green, and red varieties.

Peppercorns turn bright green when full-grown and bright red when ripe. Unripe green berries are harvested and dried outdoors, where they adopt the familiar black, wrinkled appearance and pungent flavor of black peppercorns. The variety sold as green peppercorns is either freeze-dried or preserved in brine to retain their green color and distinct hot flavor. They can also be dried after heating in boiling water for 20 minutes.

For white peppercorns, the berries are picked later, as they're ripening from yellow to red; after harvesting, the outer coating is removed to reveal the white kernel inside, which has less aroma but sharper flavor. Ripe red peppercorns offer the sweetest flavor, most like a fruit but with a little hot-pepper kick; they're preserved in brine.

> **HEALTH BENEFITS**
> Black pepper helps stimulate healthy digestion, urination, and sweating, all functions that aid in detoxification. Its biting heat can clear out congestion and improve symptoms of the common cold, making it the perfect seasoning for good ol' chicken soup.

In the Garden

Pepper vines are perennials that love the hot, rainy climates of India and Southeast Asia. It's not impossible to grow pepper in subtropical regions, like the southern United States, but a greenhouse environment would be better than attempting to grow it outdoors year-round. However, it'll grow successfully as a container plant if brought indoors in cool weather and given its required conditions. Pepper needs high humidity (at least 50 percent at all times) and temps between 75° and 85°F; it won't survive under 65°F. Vines are obviously natural climbers, so they'll need a structure to support their growth habit indoors; consider growing it as a hanging plant or installing a stake or trellis.

Size: Up to 15 feet long

Container: 3 to 7 gallons

Light: Full or filtered sun

Soil: Moist, rich, well drained. Mix compost into the soil for improved drainage, or plant in raised beds.

Plant: Seeds, soaked overnight in water before sowing.

Water: Regularly and thoroughly, to keep the soil consistently moist. Mist regularly with water from a spray bottle to simulate the humidity in the tropics. After the plant flowers, water constantly to encourage the berries to sprout.

Harvest: Peppercorns may take up to 3 or 4 years to develop. When they do, harvest according to your desired ripeness, either when green and full-sized, or later.

PAIRINGS

Pepper pairs well with all proteins.

Seasonings: allspice, basil, caraway, cardamom, chili peppers, cinnamon, cloves, coriander seeds, cumin, curry leaf, fennel seeds, fenugreek, garlic, ginger, lemon juice, lime juice, marjoram, oregano, paprika, parsley, rosemary, sage, savory, thyme, turmeric

Keep It Fresh

Dry fresh peppercorns in the sun for several days or on low heat in an oven or dehydrator for a few hours.

In the Kitchen

Dishes: Pepper can be used to season any savory dish.

Prep: Pepper can be used to season any savory dish. Use whole peppercorns for flavor and remove before serving, or grind in a pepper mill and add to any dish.

Serve: Sprinkle freshly ground black pepper into any dish. It's integral to many spice blends, including curry powders, jerk and barbecue spices, pickling spices, garam masala, quatre épices, ras el hanout, and berbere (see pages 250–251). It pairs well with all herbs and spices.

PEPPER VARIETIES

Cubeb or Java pepper (*Piper cubeba*): *pungent, piney, and peppery, with allspice or nutmeg.* Native to Indonesia, cubeb is used mostly in that cuisine and in Moroccan dishes, where it's paired with lamb and other meats and included in the spice blend *ras el hanout* (see page 250).

Hoja santa (*Piper auritum*): *peppery with anise, mint, and nutmeg.* This is the aromatic leaf of a pepper plant native to Central America. Its nickname, "root beer plant," aptly describes its flavor. Hoja santa is used abundantly in Mexican cooking, in mole verde, tamales, soups, and beverages.

Long pepper (*Piper longum*): *peppery, sharp, and hot yet sweet and earthy.* Also called Indian or Indonesian long pepper, this variety grows in small spikes that are used to flavor stews, pickles, and meat dishes.

Lá Lót (*Piper sarmentosum*): Another aromatic leaf related to pepper, lá lót is used raw in Southeast Asian cooking as a salad herb and as a wrapper for meats and various fillings.

POPPY SEEDS

Papaver somniferum

Flavors: nutty and sweet

They might have a nefarious reputation in some circles, thanks to the poppy plant's use in producing opiates, but poppy seeds themselves are a delicious and beloved seasoning for all sorts of baked goods. The tiny dark specks adorn bagels, rolls, and muffins in bakeries throughout the United States and Europe. With their subtle nutty flavor, they're also widely used in savory dishes in India and parts of the Middle East.

Although poppy seeds look black, they're actually a dark blue; Indian cooking uses white seeds, while Middle Eastern and Turkish cooks use brown. White poppy seeds are an important component in Japanese seven-spice powder, or shichimi togarashi (see page 250), used to flavor soups and udon.

HEALTH BENEFITS

Poppy seeds contain high quantities of dietary fiber, which encourages healthy digestion and can help lower cholesterol and blood sugar. They also offer a significant dose of good-for-your-bones calcium. However, poppy seeds should not be eaten in large quantities, as they *do* contain trace amounts of psychoactive chemicals known as opiates.

In the Garden

Because of their association with opiate production, growing poppy plants is illegal in the United States, so check your local supermarket or spice shop for fresh seeds to use in the kitchen. White and brown varieties will more likely be sold in specialty stores and spice shops.

Keep It Fresh

Poppy seeds contain high quantities of oil, so they'll go bad quickly. To keep them fresh for longer, store in the freezer for up to a year.

In the Kitchen

Dishes: Breads, cakes, baked sweets, curries, stews, sauces, dressings
Prep: Dry-roast seeds (see page 150) for 2 to 3 minutes to enhance their nutty flavor before adding to a dish, especially if they won't be cooked. If they'll be ground, a quick dry-roast will also make them easier to grind, as they're too small for a typical spice grinder when raw. Grind roasted seeds using a mortar and pestle or spice grinder. If making a poppy seed paste, soak the fresh seeds in boiling water for about an hour so they expand and soften; grind the seeds in their liquid to create the paste.

Serve: Poppy seeds pair remarkably well with carbohydrates and cheeses. Sprinkle dry-roasted seeds over cheesy potato dishes, pastas, and casseroles. Bake them into crackers, cookies, cakes, and muffins, especially in combination with lemon, like the popular lemon–poppy seed cake. Ground seeds are cooked with honey and sugar to form a thick paste filling for traditional Jewish hamantaschen. They're tossed into Indian spice blends as a thickener curries, kormas, stews, and sauces, and also used in Bengali cooking to flavor stews and vegetables.

PAIRINGS

Fruits and Vegetables: cauliflower, eggplant, green beans, lemons, lettuce, onions, oranges, potatoes, strawberries, zucchini
Proteins: almonds, cashews, cheeses, chicken, eggs, ham, pork, walnuts
Seasonings: allspice, cardamom, cassia, cinnamon, cloves, coriander seeds, garlic, ginger, honey, lemon juice and zest, mustard, nutmeg, sesame seeds, sumac, vanilla

SESAME SEEDS

Sesamum orientale

Flavors: nutty and earthy

One of the oldest cultivated crops on the planet, sesame plants not only produce richly flavored seeds, but they're also harvested for their tasty, nutty oil, the most popular cooking oil in Asian cuisines. The sleek, glossy seeds come in several varieties, including black, brown, red, and creamy white, the most common sesame seed in the West. Black sesame seeds have a nuttier flavor and are most often used in Asia.

Sesame oil is a key ingredient in Asian stir-fries and dressings. White sesame seeds are ground to make tahini paste, an essential ingredient in classic Middle Eastern hummus and the sweet confection, halvah. They're also used in various spice blends, including Middle Eastern za'atar, Egyptian dukkah, and Japanese seven-spice powder, or shichimi togarashi (see pages 250–251).

> **HEALTH BENEFITS**
> Sesame contains a lot of oil, which explains its slick, shiny coating; but that oil happens to be the healthy kind, high in the cholesterol-lowering monounsaturated and polyunsaturated fatty acids. Sesame seeds are also packed with nutrients, such as copper, manganese, magnesium, calcium, iron, and zinc.

In the Garden

Sesame is a heat-loving, annual tropical plant that needs warm soil, at least 70°F, for healthy growth. They'll grow in containers, but will not be as tall as those grown in the ground. Sesame plants need 90 to 120 days of consistently hot weather to develop ripe seeds, so in cooler climates they may not be fruitful. Fresh-off-the-plant sesame seeds have edible hulls that are often removed mechanically before being packaged and sold; they are slightly bitter and sometimes darker in color than hulled seeds, but still delicious.

Size: 3 to 6 feet tall

Container: 6 inches
Light: Full sun
Soil: Medium to light, rich, well drained
Plant: Seeds
Water: Regularly while the seedlings and young plants are developing; less frequent and lighter watering once established; somewhat drought tolerant
Harvest: When seedpods turn brown, but before they pop open, they are ready for harvest. Collect the pods and spread them onto a flat surface in a dry, shady location; when completely dry, the pods will split and free the seeds. Let the seeds dry completely before storing.
Care: Weed regularly. Protect from frosts.

SUBSTITUTIONS
- Poppy seeds
- Chopped nuts (almonds, peanuts, or cashews)

PAIRINGS
Fruits and Vegetables: broccoli, cabbage, carrots, eggplant, lettuce, mushrooms, onions, peas, peppers, scallions, tomatoes, zucchini
Proteins: almonds, beans, chicken, fish and seafood
Seasonings: allspice, cardamom, cassia, cinnamon, chili peppers, cloves, coriander seeds, garlic, ginger, honey, lemongrass, lime juice, nutmeg, oregano, paprika, pepper, soy sauce, sumac, thyme, vanilla

In the Kitchen
Dishes: Breads, stir-fries, dressings, marinades, baked sweets, ice cream
Prep: To bring out their flavor, dry-roast (or toast) sesame seeds briefly, until they pop, become fragrant, and look lightly tanned. They burn easily, so cook with caution. Baking also enhances their flavor. Grind using a spice grinder, blender, or mortar and pestle.
Serve: Sprinkle toasted sesames into soups, salads, cooked veggie dishes, and cheesy dips and sauces. Add raw seeds to breads and pastry doughs before baking. Black sesame seeds make a crunchy coating for fish and chicken, and a tasty addition to noodle and rice dishes. Seeds and oil are perfect partners for traditional Asian seasonings, especially ginger, lemongrass, garlic, and chili peppers.

VANILLA

Vanilla planifolia

Flavors: sweet, fruity, and smooth, with subtle caramel

Perhaps fittingly, the rich, elegant flavor of vanilla derives from a beautiful orchid. Though it's one of the most recognizable spices in the world, vanilla is also one of the most expensive, thanks to its complicated and rigorous growing, drying, and curing processes.

Vanilla seedpods, or "beans," are long, thin, and green when fresh. They're also odorless and flavorless, only developing their vanilla essence while curing, which stimulates the production of vanillin. Cured vanilla beans appear dried, wrinkly, and dark brown, and they carry the distinct sweet aroma of vanilla. Sliced open lengthwise, they'll reveal their tiny, flavorful seeds.

Vanilla extract is made by soaking beans in alcohol. Store-bought extract varies widely, but the best by far is "pure vanilla extract," with 35 percent alcohol. Skip the imitations, which contain artificial flavorings that taste bitter and obviously chemical.

HEALTH BENEFITS
Famous for its calming fragrance, vanilla is used widely in aromatherapy and in scented products like soaps, lotions, and candles. Vanilla also works as a stimulant, helping to boost mental clarity and mood. It's been used traditionally to calm stomach upset, relieve stress, and improve sleep.

In the Garden
Vanilla beans, which are perennials, grow on a climbing tropical orchid native to Mexico and parts of Central America. These plants are a major long-term investment, as they need humid, tropical conditions all year round in order to produce beans, which can take 3 to 4 years. Optimal conditions include high humidity of at least 60 percent and consistent temps around 80° to 85°F, and no lower than 70°F. Vanilla

orchids also need vertical structures to support their climbing habit, so grow alongside a fence or trellis, or install a stake or trellis in a container indoors.

Note: Homegrown orchids need to be pollinated by hand. But there's a catch! Flowers bloom and die within one day—yep, just *one day*—and they must be pollinated at this time. Flowering will begin after 2 to 3 years (or longer). Consult a local garden shop for help pollinating orchids.

Size: 25 to 50 feet tall

Container: 1 gallon

Light: Filtered sun to partial shade

Soil: Moist, rich, well drained

Plant: Cuttings or plants; cuttings should be at least 1 foot long.

Water: Regularly, to keep the soil consistently moist. Mist regularly with water from a spray bottle to simulate the humidity in the tropics.

Harvest: After flowering and pollination, the seedpods take 5 to 9 months to develop and ripen.

Care: Mix mulch into the soil a few times every year for added nutrients. After a few years, the plant will flower and must be hand-pollinated to ensure the growth of seedpods.

Curing Vanilla Beans

Fresh seedpods are heated during the day then covered indoors overnight to "sweat"; this process can continue for a month and will stimulate the chemical reaction that gives vanilla its flavor. After that, they're stored for 3 to 6 months, during which time they shrivel up, turn dark brown, and finish developing their flavor.

Store vanilla beans in an airtight container away from sunlight for 2 years.

In the Kitchen

Dishes: Ice cream, pudding, baked sweets, syrups, compotes, poached fruit

Prep: Use whole beans to infuse vanilla flavor and remove before serving; slit open the pod for extra flavor. Beans used for infusions are reusable; just give them a rinse and let dry. If you have a high-performance blender, like a Vitamix, you can grind the entire bean, pod and all, and add to any dish. First, chop off the ends; then chop crosswise down the length of the bean and add to the blender along with any other ingredients.

To open the bean and remove the tiny seeds, first chop off the ends then carefully slice down the length of the bean using a sharp knife. Only slice through the top layer—not all the way through—to reveal the inner seeds. Scrape out the sticky seeds using a spoon or the dull side of the knife.

For vanilla extract, infuse 5 whole beans in 8 ounces of vodka for up to 2 months. Slice open the beans before adding to the alcohol, and use more or fewer according to your taste. Try another type of alcohol for slightly different flavor—rum, bourbon, or brandy will do. Shake the mixture occasionally while infusing.

Serve: Vanilla flavor complements virtually any sweet dish, whether it contains fruit, chocolate, caramel, creamy pudding, or nuts. Add to coffee, tea, cocoa, and even sodas for fresh vanilla-tinged beverages. Place the whole beans in a container of sugar to make a delicious vanilla sugar, which can be used in any sweet treat. Or infuse into boiling milk to make milk-based dishes. Use vanilla extract sparingly (1 teaspoon, max), as it's very potent.

PAIRINGS

Fruits and Vegetables: apples, berries, bananas, cherries, lemon, melon, oranges, peaches, pears, pineapples, plums, raspberries, rhubarb

Proteins: almonds, hazelnuts, pecans, walnuts

Seasonings: allspice, anise, cardamom, cinnamon, cloves, elderberries, ginger, honey, lavender, lemon balm, lemon verbena, licorice, marigold, mint, nutmeg, pandan leaf, poppy seeds, rose, sesame seeds, sweet cicely, woodruff

EXOTIC
SPICES

These spices will take a little more work to find, but they should be available at spice shops, specialty markets, or via the many spice merchants online (see page 253 for an extensive list).

AJWAIN

Trachyspermum ammi

Other common name: carom seeds

Flavors: pungent, hot, bitter, with strong thyme

As a member of the parsley family, ajwain plants grow in similar form, with clusters of seed-bearing flowers growing from lanky green stems. The seeds, or fruits, look somewhat like their relatives cumin, dill, and caraway: ribbed, oval, and gray-brown, only smaller.

Although mostly used in Indian cooking, this spice offers flavors that will be familiar to Western palates. The seeds contain high quantities of thymol, the essential oil also present in the herb thyme, giving them a distinctly thyme-like flavor. But while thyme has a lighter, sweeter flavor, ajwain is stronger, sharper, and bitter.

Also called ajowan, carom, or bishop's weed, ajwain is integral in chaat masala and the Ethiopian spice blend berbere (see pages 250–251).

HEALTH BENEFITS

Ajwain contains high quantities of the volatile oil thymol, giving it many uses in both Ayurvedic and Western medicine. It stimulates digestion, eases stomach upset, and helps prevent and relieve gas, which explains ajwain's traditional pairing with beans in the Indian kitchen. Used in medications for coughs and bronchitis, thymol helps break up and clear out phlegm. It's a common ingredient in mouthwashes and toothpastes for its powerful antiseptic and antifungal properties; it helps prevent infection and tooth decay while also freshening breath.

In the Garden

Ajwain is a cool-weather, annual plant that grows easily in temperate climates and in containers. Ideal conditions are between 60° and 75°F, but the plant will also thrive in lower (but not freezing) temps.

Size: Up to 3 feet tall
Container: 6 to 10 inches deep
Light: Full sun to partial shade
Soil: Light to heavy, but rich and well drained
Plant: Seeds or cuttings
Water: Regularly, when the soil feels dry, about once a week

Harvest: Once the flowers and seeds turn brown, they are ready for harvest. Snip off flowers into a paper bag and hang to dry. When completely dry, remove the seeds from their husks.

Care: Weed regularly. The plants can withstand cooler temperatures, but protect from hard winter frosts.

PAIRINGS

Vegetables: cabbage, carrots, cauliflower, eggplant, green beans, onions, peas, potatoes, pumpkin, spinach, squash
Proteins: beans, cheeses, fish, lentils
Seasonings: amchoor, asafetida, cardamom, chili peppers, cinnamon, cloves, cumin, curry leaf, fennel seeds, garlic, ginger, pepper, turmeric

In the Kitchen

Dishes: Curries, stews, sauces, breads, pickling spices, chutneys

Prep: In Indian cooking, ajwain seeds are often "tempered" before adding to a dish. This method involves frying the spice in hot oil or ghee, and then incorporating with other ingredients either at the start of cooking or at the very end. Frying in fat tones down ajwain's pungency and brings out its complex flavors. The seeds are also often dry-roasted, though very rarely (if ever) served raw. Seeds can be ground to a powder using a mortar and pestle or spice grinder, but they're just as flavorful whole.

Serve: Use sparingly so the strong ajwain flavor doesn't overpower your dish. Long cook times will mellow out its intensity, while adding at the end of cooking results in sharper flavor. Ajwain is commonly paired with root vegetables and beans, added to veggie and fish curries, and baked into savory breads. It's also a regular seasoning for fried Indian staples like samosas (stuffed pastries) and pakoras (fritters).

AMCHOOR

Mangifera indica

Other common name: mango powder

Flavors: tart, sweet, fruity

Amchoor is unripe green mango fruit that has been dried and ground to a powder. Unlike the sweet and succulent mango, this spice is tart and acidic, closer to lemon or lime juice and tamarind than its fully ripened fresh fruit. In fact, amchoor makes a great dry substitute for lemon or lime juice when your recipe needs less liquid. It can be found sliced or in powder form. Dried slices are light brown and hard.

In the Garden

Native to India, the tropical evergreen mango tree can grow up to 100 feet tall and produce fruit for more than 100 years in ideal conditions. Dwarf varieties are reasonably easy to grow in small gardens or containers, and they also bear delicious fruit. In more temperate climates, plant a dwarf tree in a container to bring indoors in cooler weather; the plant won't tolerate temps lower than 40°F.

Size: Dwarf trees, 4 to 8 feet tall; full-size trees, up to 65 feet tall

Container: At least 20 inches in diameter and depth

Light: Full sun

Soil: Light to medium, rich, well drained

Plant: Young grafted trees from a nursery; seeds of store-bought mangoes will not germinate.

> **HEALTH BENEFITS**
> Amchoor boasts all the benefits of the ultra-nutritious mango: Packed with iron as well as vitamins C, A, and E, mango also offers high quantities of dietary fiber, which is crucial for a healthy digestive tract. It's a great source of beta-carotene, an antioxidant found in orange-colored fruits and vegetables that can help boost the immune system and reduce the risk of heart disease and cancer.

Water: Regularly, when the soil feels dry; more frequently in lighter soils and drought conditions, less frequently for mature trees

Harvest: Depending on its age and health, a mango tree may take 3 to 7 years to flower and bear fruit. About 3 months after flowering, the mangoes should be ready for harvest. Pick while they're still green.

Care: Protect from winds and frosts. Install stakes to support the growing tree and its branches. Prune to control size. If growing in the ground, make sure the soil is deep, as mango trees grow a long taproot.

PAIRINGS

Vegetables: cauliflower, eggplant, guava, okra, onions, peppers, potatoes, squash, tomatoes, zucchini

Proteins: beans, chicken, fish, lentils, nuts, pork

Seasonings: ajwain, asafetida, cayenne, chili peppers, cinnamon, cloves, coriander seeds, cumin, fennel seeds, garlic, ginger, lemon juice, lemongrass, mint, mustard, paprika, pepper, star anise, turmeric

Drying Mango to Make Amchoor

Peel the unripe mangoes, then cut into thin slices or chip-size strips. Let sit in the sun for several days, turning occasionally, until completely dry. To oven-dry, spread the mango slices onto a baking sheet and heat in the oven on the lowest temperature setting until completely dry; prop open the oven door to prevent cooking and turn them occasionally. Repeat every day until the mango is light brown and crisp. Then grind to a powder in a spice grinder.

Dried mango slices will stay fresh for up to 4 months, while the powder will last for up to a year in an airtight container.

In the Kitchen

Dishes: Curries, soups, meat rubs, marinades, chutneys

Serve: Use whole slices for flavor and remove before serving, or add ground amchoor to a dish at the end of cooking. It's a popular ingredient in vegetarian curries and soups. The tartness and acidity of amchoor balances the sweetness of fruit compotes and syrups. It adds zest to marinades and rubs for pork, chicken, and fish, while its acids help tenderize the meat. Amchoor makes a great substitute for lemon or lime juice in any recipe. Use sparingly, as it's much sharper: 3 tablespoons lemon juice roughly equals 1 teaspoon amchoor.

ANNATTO SEEDS

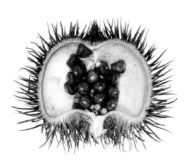

Bixa orellana

Other common name: achiote seeds

Flavors: earthy, subtle, peppery

With their vibrant red hue, annatto, or achiote, seeds have been used since pre-colonial days to make dye for foods, textiles, and body paints. Dubbed the "lipstick tree," this small evergreen bears beautiful pink flowers and then red spiky seedpods, which open when ripe to reveal dozens of red, pebble-shaped seeds.

Annatto is now a common color additive in cheeses—like cheddar, which is naturally paler without the annatto—as well as in butter, margarine, and chorizo sausage. In large quantities, annatto also offers a subtle, lightly peppery flavor to a variety of dishes from Central and South America, the Caribbean, and the Philippines.

HEALTH BENEFITS

Annatto seeds are rich in the antioxidants vitamin C and beta-carotene, both of which help slow down or prevent symptoms of aging. But even more remarkable is annatto's high levels of tocotrienol, a vitamin E compound that's believed to offer fantastic benefits for cardiovascular health. Studies have shown tocotrienol's ability to lower cholesterol, which may reduce the risk of clogged arteries and heart attack.

In the Garden

The small annatto tree (or shrub) will grow in tropical and subtropical climates where there is no threat of frost. It can be grown successfully in a large container and brought indoors during the winter months in temperate climates.

Size: 6 to 20 feet tall

Container: Any large size, or about 15 gallons; transplant to larger containers as necessary
Light: Full sun to partial shade
Soil: Rich, well drained
Plant: Seeds or cuttings
Water: Regularly, to keep the soil consistently moist
Harvest: After 3 to 4 years, once the seed heads are ripe and dry, snip off into a paper bag to catch all the seeds.
Care: Trim occasionally to control size and remove dead flowers when necessary. Prune in late winter or early spring to promote new growth.

> **SUBSTITUTIONS**
> • Paprika
> • Turmeric
> • Saffron
> *Note: These ingredients offer distinct flavors that are stronger than annatto seeds, but they offer similar coloring effects.

PAIRINGS

Vegetables: cabbage, carrots, okra, onions, peppers, plantains, potatoes, squash, sweet potatoes, tomatoes
Proteins: beans, beef, cheeses, chicken, eggs, fish and seafood, peanuts, pork, turkey
Seasonings: allspice, chili peppers, cilantro, cloves, coriander seeds, culantro, cumin, epazote, garlic, oregano, paprika, pepper

In the Kitchen

Dishes: Curries, soups, rice, marinades, moles
Prep: Whole seeds can be very difficult to grind, even in a food processor, so look for ground powder, paste, or oil instead. If you have seeds, you can easily make a liquid dye or cooking oil: To make dye for veggies or rice, soak the seeds in hot water for several minutes, until the liquid reaches your desired orange-y color. For an oil to use in soups, curries, or meat dishes, fry the seeds in oil over low heat until the color turns golden or orange. Strain out the seeds before using.
Serve: The flavor of annatto is very subtle, so use plenty of it to get a real taste in any dish, much more than you'd use for dyeing. Mexican cooks combine annatto powder with oregano, cumin, peppercorns, allspice, and garlic to prepare a paste (*recado rojo*, or achiote paste, see page 251), used to flavor chicken, fish, and pork. It's often used to color paella rice. Swap in annatto for the ultra-expensive saffron to get a similar color effect, but none of the flavor.

ASAFETIDA

Ferula asafoetida

Flavors: pungent, bitter, unpleasant raw but onion-like when cooked

With nicknames like "food of the gods" and "devil's dung," asafetida clearly has a divisive reputation in the culinary world. Culled from the taproot of a giant fennel plant, asafetida is a dried resinous gum that has a foul odor and, to most people, an equally foul taste when eaten on its own. Used in very small quantities in cooked dishes, however, it offers a garlic- or onion-like flavor, as well as powerful anti-flatulence effects in the legume-heavy Indian diet.

Fresh-from-the-plant asafetida is a white creamy sap, but it browns and hardens with age and exposure to air. It's sold at Indian markets in solid chunks and as a powder, often under the name "hing." In order to make the powder, the solid resin is ground with rice or wheat flour and gum arabic; sometimes turmeric is added to the mix, resulting in a yellow asafetida with a milder flavor.

HEALTH BENEFITS

Asafetida is considered a medicinal spice in India, thanks to its beneficial effects on the digestive system. It's a common addition to bean dishes for this very reason: The spice helps prevent gas, stomach cramps, and digestive upset. It's also used to treat respiratory problems stemming from mucous buildup in the chest and throat, including coughs, croup, bronchitis, and asthma.

In the Garden

A perennial native to the dry climates of Afghanistan and Iran, asafetida grows thick, pulpy roots and won't transplant well after seedling stage. It can be very difficult to find seeds at a nursery or garden center in the West, but it's worth checking online to find some in stock. Seeds must be fresh in order to germinate.

Size: 3 to 6 feet tall and 5 feet wide

Container: Deep and wide from seedling stage; do not transplant
Light: Full sun
Soil: Dry to somewhat moist, well drained
Plant: Fresh seeds or young plants
Water: Occasionally and lightly, when the soil dries out completely; do not overwater.
Harvest: After 4 to 5 years of growth, before the plant flowers in early spring, the stems and roots should be cut open to let the sap ooze out. The sap is collected and dried in the sun until solid.
Care: Protect from cold weather; try padding the soil with a thick layer of mulch to retain heat.

> **SUBSTITUTIONS**
> • Garlic powder
> • Onion powder

PAIRINGS

Vegetables: cabbage, cauliflower, cucumbers, mushrooms, okra, onions, peppers, potatoes, squash, tomatoes, zucchini
Proteins: beans, chickpeas, fish and seafood, lentils
Seasonings: ajwain, amchoor powder, caraway, cardamom, cayenne, chili peppers, cilantro, cinnamon, cloves, coriander seeds, cumin, curry leaf, fennel seeds, fenugreek seeds, garlic, ginger, lemon juice, mint, mustard, paprika, pepper, saffron, turmeric

Keep It Fresh

Store in an airtight container to keep the flavor intact and prevent its fragrance from escaping into the house.

In the Kitchen

Dishes: soups, stews, curries, pickles, chutneys
Prep: Always cook asafetida in hot oil or ghee to mellow the stinky flavor and bring out its garlicky-onion essence. If using a chunk or lump of resin, crush it up before frying. Asafetida is used as a tempering spice in Indian cooking: It's first fried in fat to tone down the flavor, then joined by other spices (like cumin or mustard) for more frying; the spiced oil is then added either at the start of cooking or at the very end.
Serve: Stir a small amount of asafetida (¼ teaspoon or less) into lentils and dals, curries with veggies or fish, cooked green beans, or any meat dish. It's used in chaat masala and sambar masala (see page 251), a tasty spice blend used in vegetarian sambar soup.

BARBERRY

Berberis vulgaris

Flavors: sweet, tart, tangy

Known as *zereshk* in Iran, these ruby-colored berries bring a sweet-sour zest to many dishes in Middle Eastern cuisine. The barberry shrub has many varieties, with leaves that vary in color from pink to red to violet. The fresh berries appear plump and bright red; they're dried for use in cooking, where they resemble dried currants or cranberries. Their acidic, lip-puckering flavor is best enjoyed in cooked dishes and sauces to accompany meats; raw berries can be too tart on their own. Dried barberries are sold at Middle Eastern and Iranian markets, and barberry plants can be found at nurseries in the West.

HEALTH BENEFITS
Barberry has been used medicinally for 2,500 years. The plant's roots and stems contain the chemical berberine, believed to have anti-inflammatory, antibacterial, and immune-boosting powers. Barberry has been used to treat infection and inflammation in the digestive system, especially cases of food poisoning and diarrhea, and may be helpful in relieving urinary tract infections, too.

In the Garden
Barberry bushes are adaptable and easy to grow in temperate climates. They come in hundreds of varieties, including some that are poisonous and some with thorns, so check your plant's specific growing instructions to prepare accordingly (i.e., you might need protective gloves!).

Size: Up to 13 feet tall and 7 feet wide
Container: At least 5 gallons
Light: Full sun to partial shade
Soil: Dry to moist, loose, well drained; adaptable to various well-draining soils. Mix

compost into the soil and place a layer of mulch around the plant to retain moisture and add nutrients.

Plant: Seeds or cuttings

Water: Regularly, to keep the soil somewhat moist; about 1 inch per week

Harvest: When berries are plump and bright red, they're ready for harvest. Pick individually by hand to avoid getting pricked by thorns.

Care: Prune occasionally to control shape and remove dead branches and flowers.

PAIRINGS

Fruits and Vegetables: apples, bananas, cherries, lemons, onions, oranges, raisins, raspberries, strawberries

Proteins: almonds, beef, cheeses, chicken, duck, game, lamb, pistachios, pork, veal, venison

Seasonings: allspice, bay leaf, cardamom, cinnamon, cloves, coriander seeds, cumin, dill, garlic, lemon juice and zest, mint, parsley, saffron, vanilla

Drying Barberries

Barberries are usually dried in the sun, but an oven or dehydrator will also do the trick. To oven-dry, spread the berries onto a baking sheet and heat in the oven on the lowest temperature setting until completely dry; prop open the oven door to prevent cooking.

In the Kitchen

Dishes: Rice, stews, sauces, preserves, syrups

Prep: Use dried barberries whole or crush them using a mortar and pestle. Plump up dried berries with a quick, light fry over the stove.

Serve: Toss berries into rice pilafs and couscous, stuffings, and stews. Crushed, they can be added to ground beef, meat rubs, or marinades, serving as a sweet-tart counterpoint to beef, lamb, chicken, or game meats. Naturally, barberries make wonderful desserts, jams, and jellies; they give a sour punch to fruity pie fillings and muffins.

FENUGREEK SEEDS

Trigonella foenum-graecum

Flavors: pungent, bitter when raw; nutty, bittersweet, burnt-sugar when roasted

The fenugreek plant plays a major role in Indian and Middle Eastern cuisines for both its tasty leaves and pungent seeds.

The seeds have a strong fragrance that reminds many people of curry powder—that's because the spice is often used heavy-handedly in curry powder blends. They're a crucial component of several other spice blends too: Ethiopian berbere and Yemeni hilbeh (see pages 250–251). Fenugreek seeds offer an undercurrent of sweetness, which is extracted to make imitation maple syrup.

In the Garden

Fenugreek, an annual, grows success-fully in containers if treated to plenty of sun. In cooler climates, bring potted fen-ugreek indoors during the winter months. They don't transplant easily, so choose a suitable container and stick with it. The seeds grow in long, slender pods that can be easily opened and removed.

Size: Up to 2 feet tall
Container: Any size
Light: Full sun

HEALTH BENEFITS

Fenugreek seeds contain a significant amount of soluble fiber, which has been shown to slow digestion and possibly lower blood sugar, a sign that it may be helpful in treating diabetes. Studies have suggested that it may also help regulate cholesterol levels, reducing the bad (LDL) cholesterol, while increasing the healthy (HDL) cholesterol. A tea made of fenugreek seeds is said to stimulate the production of milk in breastfeeding moms, and it's been used to relieve symptoms of PMS and menopause, including erratic mood and hot flashes.

Soil: Moist, fertile, well drained. Mix compost into the soil for added nutrients.

Plant: Seeds, presoaked in warm water for 24 hours

Water: Moderately, only when soil feels dry to the touch

Harvest: To harvest seeds, wait until fall, when the plant has died and the seedpods are mature; let them dry completely before picking.

PAIRINGS

Fruits and Vegetables: carrots, cauliflower, eggplant, green beans, okra, onions, peppers, potatoes, spinach, tomatoes

Protein: beans, beef, chicken, fish and seafood, lamb, lentils

Seasonings: allspice, amchoor powder, anise, bay leaf, cardamom, cayenne, chili peppers, cilantro, cinnamon, cloves, coriander seeds, cumin, fennel seeds, fenugreek leaves, galangal, garlic, ginger, lemon juice, lime juice, mustard, nigella, nutmeg, paprika, pepper, sesame seeds, star anise, tamarind, turmeric

In the Kitchen

Dishes: Curries, breads, sauces, chutneys, pickles, pastes

Prep: Seeds should be dry-roasted or fried before cooking to reduce their bitterness and bring out their nutty-sweet flavor (see pages 149–150); but cook for too long, and they'll just get *bitterer*. For optimal flavor, grind seeds using a spice grinder or coffee grinder when ready to use, and use sparingly.

Serve: Add seeds early in long-cooked dishes, and also use them in chutneys, curry powders, and pickling spices. Ground seeds can be used in meat rubs. You can also bake the seeds and leaves into tasty savory breads, like the traditional naan, paratha, and chapati.

GALANGAL

Alpinia galangal

Flavors: pungent, sharp, and hot, with tart lemon, pepper, ginger, and cardamom

At first sight, you might take galangal for its more popular cousin, ginger. Galangal is plumper and harder with shiny, striped, orange- or pink-tinted skin. Its flavor is distinct, too, with citrus, pepper, pine, and cardamom in the mix. Also known as Thai ginger, galangal is used similarly to its Chinese counterpart and is a common ingredient in Thai curry powders and pastes.

In the Garden

The tropical, perennial galangal loves warm, humid climates and grows to be quite large aboveground with long, lance-shaped leaves. In temperate regions, plants should be grown in a greenhouse or in a suitable container indoors to provide optimal conditions.

HEALTH BENEFITS
Like ginger, galangal has powerful stomach-calming effects and can be used to treat indigestion, relieve constipation, and quell nausea due to morning sickness and motion sickness. Its anti-inflammatory properties can help ease stomach cramps and arthritis pain, and it's often used to clear up respiratory congestion caused by the common cold.

Size: Up to 6 feet tall

Container: At least 15 inches in diameter

Light: Partial shade

Soil: Moist, rich, well drained. If growing outdoors in a garden, add plenty of mulch, which retains water, adds nutrients, and prevents weeds.

Plant: Whole rhizomes, plant divisions, or 3-inch sections with at least one bud. Soak in water overnight before planting. Sow with bud-end up, just under the surface of the soil.

Water: Regularly, to keep the soil consistently moist. Mist with water to simulate the humidity in the tropics.

Harvest: After 4 to 6 years, the rhizomes are ready for harvest in late summer. Simply dig up the soil and lift them out. If you're not harvesting everything for the year, break off the parts you need and replant.

Keep It Fresh

Wrap fresh galangal rhizome in paper towels and store in a plastic bag in the refrigerator's crisper, where it should keep for up to 2 weeks. For longer freshness, store in the freezer for 2 to 3 months.

Dried galangal will be usable for about a year. Fresh rhizomes can be peeled and dried in the sun. For quicker drying, slice the rhizome into thin rounds (less then ¼ inch thick). Spread onto a baking sheet and bake on your oven's lowest temperature setting, 130° to 150°F. Keep the oven door open to ensure the lowest amount of heat. Dried slices can be grated to a powder, which will stay fresh for about 2 months.

In the Kitchen

Dishes: Curries, stews, soups, stir-fries, rice, sauces, pastes

Prep: To infuse galangal flavor into soups, stews, and rice, slice into ¼-inch rounds, cook, and remove before serving. Shred or julienne and add to stir-fries and salads. Peel and grate finely, or crush using a mortar and pestle or food processor, and add to sauces, pastes, and curries. Dried slices should be reconstituted before cooking.

Serve: In Thai cooking, galangal is often paired with fish to help balance out strong fishy odors. It's a common partner for classic Asian flavors like lemongrass, garlic, chili peppers, and lime juice.

SUBSTITUTIONS
• Ginger
• ½-inch piece fresh galangal = 1 teaspoon galangal powder

PAIRINGS

Fruits and Vegetables: bean sprouts, cabbage, carrots, cucumber, eggplant, green beans, mushrooms, pineapple, onions, shallots, tomatoes

Proteins: almonds, beef, chicken, fish and seafood, lamb, peanuts, pork

Seasonings: allspice, cardamom, cassia, chili peppers, cilantro, cinnamon, cloves, coriander seeds, cumin, curry leaf, fennel, fenugreek, fish sauce, garlic, ginger, lemongrass, lemon juice and zest, lime juice and zest, makrut lime, mint, mustard, nigella, paprika, soy sauce, tamarind, Thai basil, turmeric,

GRAINS OF PARADISE

Amomum melegueta

Flavors: pungent, hot, peppery, earthy, with citrus

Exotic to most modern-day Western cuisines, this West African spice was used abundantly during the Middle Ages as an alternative for costly black pepper. However, in contrast to pepper's straightforward heat, grains of paradise are more complex—earthy with a hint of citrus and, of course, that peppery bite.

Also called melegueta pepper or alligator pepper, grains of paradise are actually related to cardamom and ginger. Grown from a rhizome, the shrub bears pretty yellow-pink flowers and red fig-sized fruits, or seedpods, containing the tiny "grains."

Traditionally, grains of paradise was used to flavor beer and wine, and it's still used in the Scandinavian spirit akvavit. The spice serves similarly to black pepper in the kitchen, but with added zesty flavor. It's an important ingredient in the Tunisian five-spice blend qâlat daqqa, as well as in Moroccan ras el hanout (see page 250).

HEALTH BENEFITS
In addition to their zesty flavors, grains of paradise are enjoyed for their digestive properties, known to prevent and relieve flatulence, diarrhea, and heartburn. The spice also contains healthy compounds such as gingerols, which can reduce inflammation and lower blood sugar, suggesting it might be useful in treating conditions like diabetes and heart disease.

In the Garden
This tropical perennial plant thrives on the warm, humid, swampy coast of Ghana, where the average low temperature is around 75°F. It's not often grown in the temperate climates of the West, but can be started indoors during the cooler months and transplanted outside in warm spring weather. Seeds need humidity, sun, and

warmth in order to germinate, and the growing plants need consistently warm, wet conditions to thrive.

Size: 4 to 5 feet tall

Container: Start seedlings in 4-inch pots, and increase size as the rhizomes grow; up to 10-gallon containers or half barrels

Light: Full sun to partial shade

Soil: Moist, rich, well drained. Mix compost into the soil for added nutrients and improved drainage.

Plant: Seeds or divided rhizomes

PAIRINGS

Vegetables: carrots, celery, eggplant, mushrooms, okra, onions, potatoes, pumpkin, shallots, spinach, tomatoes

Proteins: beans, beef, cheeses, chicken, eggs, fish and seafood, game, lamb, lentils, nuts, pork

Seasonings: allspice, cardamom, chili peppers, cinnamon, cloves, coriander seeds, cumin, garlic, ginger, lemon juice and zest, mustard, nutmeg, oregano, parsley, pepper, rosemary, sage, thyme

> ## SUBSTITUTIONS
> - Black pepper
> - Cardamom

Water: Regularly, to keep soil consistently moist. Mist regularly with water using a spray bottle to simulate the humidity in the tropics.

Harvest: Once the seedpods turn from green to red-brown, about 9 to 11 months after planting, they are ready for harvest. Dry in the sun until the pods are hard, wrinkled, and brown; then open and dry the seeds before storing.

In the Kitchen

Dishes: Stews, sauces, marinades, dressings, rice, beer, mulled wine

Prep: Grind seeds to unleash their flavors and add to any dish toward the end of cooking or just before serving.

Serve: Grains of paradise can be used with any foods normally seasoned with black pepper—and that's just about everything! Add them to marinades and sauces for meats like lamb, beef, and chicken, as well as for fish and shellfish and fleshy veggies like squash, pumpkin, potatoes, and eggplant.

JUNIPER BERRY

Juniperus communis

Flavors: pungent, piney and clean, spicy, lightly sweet

Juniper berries are the signature flavoring in gin, whose name is derived from the French or Dutch word for "juniper," *genévrier* or *jenever*. That refreshing pine flavor actually comes from the small, juicy cones of a coniferous evergreen—they're not technically "berries," as the name would suggest. These blueberry lookalikes can be eaten fresh or dried, but should be crushed to release their flavor into prepared dishes.

In the Garden

Juniper is a cool-weather shrub or tree that is easy to grow in most well-draining soils and, if necessary, in suitable containers. There are around 50 species of varying sizes (from short shrubs to 40-foot trees), including some whose berries are not edible, so it's important to choose the right species for planting and cooking. *Juniperus communis* is the shrub most often used for its berries; they take 2 to 3 years to ripen. These plants are dioecious, or single-sexed, so you'll need both a male and female plant if you want to grow the tasty berries. When harvesting, wear protective gloves to prevent pricks from the leaves.

Size: 5 to 6 feet tall
Container: Half barrel, or about 15 gallons, for most evergreen trees; smaller or larger depending on tree size
Light: Full sun

HEALTH BENEFITS
Juniper berries contain an essential oil that supports kidney function and serves as an effective diuretic, helping to disinfect the urinary tract and, in the process, prevent and treat infection. The spice has also been shown to have antiviral properties, believed to be helpful against viruses like herpes and the flu, as well as anti-inflammatory effects: Prepared as an ointment or infusion, juniper extract can be applied topically via compress to reduce joint inflammation caused by arthritis and gout.

Soil: Moist, rich, well drained; adaptable to various well-draining soils. Mix compost into the soil to prevent weeds, and weed regularly.

Plant: Seeds, cuttings, or young plants; cuttings and young plants are preferred as seeds need to be stratified in order to germinate (see page 14).

Water: Occasionally; more frequently within the first month of planting, about twice per week; afterward, only when the soil dries out; drought tolerant

Harvest: In the fall of its second or third year, once the berries are blue-black, they're ready for harvest. Handpick carefully and wear gloves.

Care: Junipers don't like to be pruned, so make sure the growing site is suitable for the plant's mature size; trim only the tips when they're in need of shaping, preferably in the fall.

SUBSTITUTIONS

- Gin: 1 teaspoon = 2 juniper berries
- Bay leaf + caraway seeds
- Rosemary + lemon juice

PAIRINGS

Fruits and Vegetables: apples, beets, berries, cabbage, carrots, celery, cranberries, currants, grapes, leeks, mushrooms, onions, oranges, potatoes, shallots, tomatoes

Proteins: beans, beef, boar, cheeses, chicken, duck, game, goose, lamb, pork, sausage, turkey, venison

Seasonings: allspice, bay leaf, caraway, celery leaf, chili peppers, cinnamon, cloves, coriander seeds, dill, fennel, garlic, honey, horseradish, lemon juice and zest, lime juice and zest, marjoram, mustard, nutmeg, oregano, parsley, pepper, rosemary, sage, savory, tarragon, thyme, vinegar

Drying Juniper Berries

Spread fresh berries onto a flat surface and let dry at room temperature for up to 3 weeks. Discard brown berries and any with holes, which are a sign of bugs. Dried berries will keep for 1 to 2 years in a sealed jar.

In the Kitchen

Dishes: Stews, braises, marinades, sauces, rubs

Prep: Crush whole berries using a mortar and pestle or grind to a powder just before using.

Serve: The clean, vibrant flavor of juniper berries enlivens hearty stews and rich meats. Crushed berries combined with salt and garlic make a tasty rub for any meat. The subtle sweetness of the berries also complements a variety of fruits and creamy desserts. Place juniper leaves on a grill to flavor grilled meats.

LICORICE

Glycyrrhiza glabra

Flavors: sweet, bitter aftertaste, with strong anise

Most foods with "licorice" flavor don't actually contain any licorice at all.

Black jellybeans, twists, and Jujubes? Those are flavored with anise, not licorice. Fennel, tarragon, and anise? They're completely different plants.

In fact, true licorice is much more frequently used in medicine than in cooking, and it's exponentially healthier than the sugar-loaded candy that bears its name. Ironically, the chemical that gives licorice its sweet flavor, glycyrrhizin, is more than 50 times sweeter than sugar.

Licorice root extract is commonly used to flavor tobacco products, sodas, beer, and cough medicines, as well as candies, baked goods, and other food products. Specialty markets and spice shops sell licorice in various forms: the woody dried roots, molded extract (often in sticks or disks), or a fine powder.

HEALTH BENEFITS

Considered a medicinal herb since ancient times, licorice is currently one of the most frequently used herbs in modern medicine. It offers powerful anti-inflammatory properties, and it's widely used to relieve inflammation in the respiratory system, digestive tract, and on the skin. Licorice is a common ingredient in cough medicines and throat lozenges for its ability to clear out phlegm; the root itself can be chewed for this effect. It's also believed to help heal stomach ulcers and heartburn.

In the Garden

The perennial licorice plant grows one very deep taproot with additional rhizomes branching out horizontally from the central root. They'll reach at least 3 feet deep into the soil and spread at least 3 feet wide. However, some roots can grow up to 25 feet long, so make sure your planting site offers plenty of space underground. Licorice will also grow indoors in large containers, which will help control the spread of the roots. Roots and rhizomes need to mature for at least 3 years before they develop optimal flavor.

Size: Aboveground, up to 7 feet tall; taproot, 3 to 4 feet deep and at least 3 feet wide

Container: At least 10 to 12 inches deep for seedlings; transplant to larger containers as the roots develop

Light: Full sun to partial shade

Soil: Moist, loose, fertile, well drained; soil should be deep to make room for the long taproot. Mix compost or manure into the soil for added nutrients and improved drainage.

Plant: Seeds or rhizome divisions. Rhizomes are preferred, as seeds are difficult to germinate and must be stratified before sowing (see page 14).

Water: Regularly, to keep the soil consistently moist

Harvest: After 3 to 5 years, once the plant has died back in the fall, dig up the roots. Harvest the whole plant, or split off only the top segments and leave the deeper roots to regrow.

Care: Pick flowers regularly so the plant focuses all its energy on its roots. Protect from slugs.

PAIRINGS

Fruits and Vegetables: apples, carrots, celery, lemons, mushrooms, onions, oranges, peas, peppers, tomatoes

Proteins: almonds, cashews, cheeses, chicken, peanuts, sausage, walnuts

Seasonings: allspice, anise, cardamom, cassia, cinnamon, cloves, coriander seeds, fennel, garlic, ginger, honey, lemon juice and zest, nutmeg, Sichuan pepper, star anise, tarragon, thyme, vanilla

SUBSTITUTION
- Anise

Keep It Fresh

Licorice root can be used fresh, but it's usually dried in the shade over a period of 6 months. To yield the extract, the root is boiled and filtered out, leaving a black liquid that forms a "cake" when dried.

In the Kitchen

Dishes: Candies, chews, teas, beverages, soup stocks, marinades, rubs

Serve: Use root segments to infuse licorice flavor into teas, cooked fruit, syrups, and sauces, and remove before serving. Licorice is often used in Chinese stocks, marinades, soy sauce, and five-spice powder. Roots can also add flavor to sugar; store a few segments in a sugar container and use the licorice sugar for baking or for sweetening coffee and tea.

Powdered licorice can be added to batters, puddings, marinades, and meat rubs for a sweet kick. Use this spice sparingly, as it has a bitter aftertaste.

MAHLAB

Prunus mahaleb

Flavors: nutty, fruity, and floral, with almonds, cherry, and rose, and a bitter aftertaste

Mahlab is a delicious but somewhat obscure spice that comes from the seed of a cherry tree. A member of the peach and almond family, mahlab or St. Lucie cherries are harvested for their pits, which are cracked open to reveal small light-brown kernels. These kernels are then sold whole and ground to form the spice.

Mahlab flavors baked sweets from the Middle East and southern European countries like Greece and Turkey. Its cherry-almond fragrance is reminiscent of marzipan, and its flavor is similarly sweet with a trace of bitterness. Whole mahlab kernels may be harder to find than the powdered spice, which loses flavor quickly; buy the powder only in small amounts and use it as soon as possible.

HEALTH BENEFITS
Mahlab does not have any specific benefits attributed to it, and, in fact, it has raised a few alarms because it contains the mild toxin coumarin that can affect the liver and kidneys. In small quantities, it poses no real danger to humans, but its toxic effects show up more readily in rodents.

In the Garden
Mahlab cherry trees are native to dry woodland climates; they grow wide canopies suitable for a spacious yard. Cherries appear green at first, then turn red and finally black when ripe and ready for harvest.

Size: 6 to 40 feet tall; trunk, 1 to 2 feet in diameter
Container: 20 gallons for a full-size tree
Light: Full sun
Soil: Moist, poor, well drained; adaptable to various well-draining soils

Plant: Seeds, cuttings, or grafted trees
Water: Occasionally; somewhat drought tolerant
Harvest: The tree flowers in spring, and its fruits ripen in summer.

In the Kitchen

Dishes: Baked sweets, breads, puddings, cheeses
Prep: Grind whole kernels in a mortar and pestle, spice grinder, or coffee grinder just before using.
Serve: With its range of nutty-sweet flavors, mahlab is a perfect match for any sweet dessert, especially when baked into cookies, cakes, breads, and other pastries. It's also suited for dairy-based treats like pudding, cheesecake, crème brûlée, and ice cream. Dried fruit, honey, nuts, and cinnamon are natural complements. Use mahlab sparingly, as it can be bitter: 1 teaspoon per cup of sugar.

PAIRINGS

Vegetables: apples, apricots, dates, peaches, plums, raisins, rhubarb, strawberries
Proteins: almonds, cashews, cream cheese, mascarpone, pistachios, walnuts
Seasonings: allspice, anise, cassia, cinnamon, cloves, honey, lemon juice and zest, mastic, nigella, nutmeg, poppy seeds, sesame seeds, rose, vanilla

MAKRUT LIME

Citrus hystrix

Flavors: **leaves** *zesty, bright citrus, with lemon, lime, and mandarin;* **rind** *pungent citrus with subtle bitterness*

Formerly known as kaffir lime, a term that has been abandoned due to racist connotations, makrut lime trees are prized in Thai and Southeast Asian cuisines for the bright-citrus flavor of their leaves and their fruits' grated rind—but only rarely for their lime juice, which is very sour. The trees are a common sight in backyards and home gardens throughout rural Thailand.

The leaves are sturdy, leathery, and glossy green. They're attached in pairs by a vein running through their center. The fruit itself is small (about 3 inches long) and has a thick, crinkled, bumpy green skin. Both the leaves and rind offer citrus tang reminiscent of lime, lemon, and mandarin, but it's not distinctly like any one of them. The leaves are deliciously fragrant when crushed or torn, and these aromatics are indispensible in Thai curries, stir-fries, and soups like the popular tom yum.

HEALTH BENEFITS
Makrut limes and leaves contain fragrant essential oils that are used for their cleansing properties in shampoos, soaps, and detergents. One traditional Southeast Asian home remedy involves using the leaves and juice to clean the teeth and gums. The fresh scent of makrut lime is believed to stimulate the mind and improve mood, while the rind is infused into tonics that aid in digestion.

In the Garden

The makrut lime tree loves warm and humid subtropical climates, but it also makes a great container plant indoors if given optimal growing conditions. The branches contain sharp thorns, so be careful when pruning and harvesting.

Size: Up to 5 feet tall in a container; up to 20 feet tall in the ground

Container: Up to 25 or 30 gallons when mature. Start small to fit the size of your plant and re-pot as the tree grows.

Light: Full sun

Soil: Moist, sandy, well drained. Mix compost into the soil to improve drainage.

Plant: Seeds, cuttings, or young plants; grafted trees are easiest to grow.

Water: Regularly, when the soil feels dry beneath the surface. Mist with water from a spray bottle to simulate the humidity of the tropics.

Harvest: Snip off leaves as you need them, and harvest fruits when plump and ripe.

Care: Prune to encourage new leaf growth and healthy fruit production. Protect from winds and frosts. Trees grown indoors will need to be hand-pollinated in order to bear fruit.

PAIRINGS

Fruits and Vegetables: bamboo shoots, cabbage, carrots, celery, eggplant, green beans, mushrooms, onions, peas, potatoes, shallots, tomatoes

Proteins: beans, beef, cashews, chicken, duck, fish and seafood, lamb, peanuts, pork

Seasonings: cardamom, chili peppers, coriander seeds, cumin, curry leaf, fish sauce, galangal, garlic, ginger, holy basil, lemongrass, lime juice and zest, mint, pepper, rau răm, sesame seeds, soy sauce, star anise, tamarind, Thai basil, turmeric

Keep It Fresh

Store fresh leaves in a zip-tight plastic bag in the freezer for up to a year. Leaves can be dried for future use, but will lose some of their potent flavor (see drying tips on page 21). Only use dried leaves in cooked, liquid-based dishes like soups and curries; if slicing, reconstitute them first by soaking in warm water.

In the Kitchen

Dishes: Curries, soups, salads, pastes

Prep: Bruise whole leaves and add to curries, soups, and marinades to infuse their flavor; remove before serving. If the leaves will be eaten, slice or shred very finely, as the rubbery texture is difficult to chew, and discard the vein at the center of each leaf. For efficient and safe slicing, stack a few same-size leaves on top of one another and hold securely with one hand; then slice through the stack with a sharp kitchen knife. Grate the rind before adding to a dish, taking care not to include the bitter pith. Or, use the rind whole to infuse flavor and remove before serving.

Serve: The zesty flavor of makrut lime pairs harmoniously with other Asian seasonings, especially lemongrass, garlic, cilantro, and ginger. The grated rind, or zest, is often added to fried fish cakes, spicy soups, and curry pastes.

MASTIC

Pistacia lentiscus

Flavors: somewhat piney, anise-like, slightly bitter, and freshening

Mastic was history's first chewing gum, used in ancient times to aid in digestion and freshen breath. In fact, the word "mastic" is derived from the Greek *mastichon*, meaning "to chew."

True mastic is culled from trees grown on the Greek Island of Chios. When the trunk is sliced open, the sap seeps out and gradually hardens with exposure to air. This hardened resin forms into small transparent chunks or "tears," ranging from ⅛ inch to 3 inches in size.

Mastic tears are quite costly and should only be purchased and used in small quantities. They offer freshening flavor and chewy texture to many Greek, Turkish, and Middle Eastern sweets, from pastries to creamy puddings to gummy candies like Turkish delight.

HEALTH BENEFITS
Mastic has long been prized as a stimulant for the digestive system and a breath freshener. Chewing mastic triggers the production of saliva, which, in turn, jumpstarts healthy digestion. It's also been shown to possess antibacterial powers that can help prevent cavities and tooth decay, as well as ulcers in the stomach and intestines—which explains its use in many toothpastes and mouthwashes.

In the Garden

The mastic tree thrives in warm, dry locations similar to its native Mediterranean climate. It grows slowly and compactly (wide, like a shrub), and will be healthy in a container outdoors or indoors if provided with plenty of sunlight. The tree only begins producing mastic after 5 or 6 years. It won't reach peak production until it's 15 years old, but will continue for another 60 years more.

Size: 6 to 25 feet tall, proportionate width

Container: At least 15 gallons for most evergreen trees; larger depending on tree size

Light: Full sun

Soil: Well drained; adaptable to various well-draining soils. Mix mulch or compost into the soil for added nutrients and improved drainage.

Plant: Grafter trees

Water: Occasionally, once or twice per month; somewhat drought tolerant

Harvest: After 6 years or longer, harvest takes place from June through September: The trunk is sliced shallowly, just through the bark, to release the slow-oozing sap. Over the next 2 weeks, the sap continues to ooze out of the trunk and hardens into tears, which are collected, cleaned, and sorted by size.

Care: Prune lightly to maintain shape.

PAIRINGS

Fruits and Vegetables: apples, apricots, dates, figs, lemons, oranges, peaches, pears, plums, raisins

Proteins: almonds, cheeses, pine nuts, pistachios, walnuts

Seasonings: allspice, anise, cardamom, cinnamon, cloves, lemon juice and zest, mahlab, nigella, poppy seeds, rose, sesame seeds, vanilla

Keep It Fresh

Store mastic in a cool spot for up to 3 years; heat will cause its flavor and color to deteriorate. Fresh mastic should be an almost transparent yellow gold.

In the Kitchen

Dishes: Baked sweets, liqueurs, cordials, candies, puddings, preserves, syrups, ice cream

Prep: Grind to a powder with a mortar and pestle just before using. If it's too soft and sticky for grinding, chill in the freezer so it hardens.

Serve: Mastic gives texture and subtle fresh flavor to a variety of sweet dishes. It pairs well with dried fruit, nuts, and cheeses, making it a natural addition to pastry fillings, preserves, and chewy candies like Turkish delight. It's also a common ingredient in spirits, like the classic Greek ouzo, and an increasingly popular spice for ice cream.

NIGELLA

Nigella sativa

Flavors: sharp, peppery, nutty, bitter, and dry

A common seasoning in Indian cooking, nigella is sometimes confusingly called "black cumin," even though the two are unrelated. The plant is *actually* related to the ornamental love-in-a-mist (*Nigella damascene*), but that bright-bloomed species has no use in the kitchen.

Nigella sativa might be less attractive than its pretty cousin, but its small peppery seeds make up for it in flavor. It's found in many Indian and Middle Eastern dishes, dotting savory breads and spicing up curries, rice, and pickles. Also called black caraway, black onion seed, *charnushka*, and *kalonji* in Hindi, nigella can be found in many Indian and Middle Eastern markets.

HEALTH BENEFITS
Nigella has been known to benefit various systems in the human body: It can help prevent and relieve gas, indigestion, diarrhea, and constipation. It's also used for its positive effects on respiratory health, improving conditions like bronchitis, asthma, and sore throat.

In the Garden
Nigella plants have a short lifespan and may produce a few harvests throughout the growing season if seeded regularly. To grow a full stock of the spice for use in cooking, you'll need several plants. They'll grow healthily in containers indoors with plenty of light; make sure the container is deep enough to fit the long taproot. Maturing nigella plants don't transplant easily, so it's best to sow seeds directly into their permanent spots. They flower and produce strange-looking seedpods within a couple months.

Size: 8 to 12 inches tall

Container: At least 12 inches deep

Light: Full sun

Soil: Dry to average, light, well drained. Mix compost into the soil for added nutrients and improved drainage.

Plant: Seeds

Water: Regularly, to keep the soil consistently moist but not waterlogged; about one inch per week

Harvest: When the seedpods ripen, turn brown, and start to dry, they are ready for harvest. Snip the stems from their base or pull up the entire plant, then place in a paper bag and hang to dry. Break or crush the seedpods to release the seeds, and let them dry completely.

Care: If you'd like more plants, let the seeds fall to the ground and wait for a new batch of seedlings. You can also sow fresh seeds yourself every month through early summer to ensure a steady supply of nigella.

PAIRINGS

Fruits and Vegetables: beets, carrots, cauliflower, eggplant, green beans, leeks, lemons, onions, oranges, peas, potatoes, pumpkin, spinach, squash, sweet potatoes, tomatoes, zucchini

Proteins: almonds, beans, beef, cheeses, chicken, eggs, fish and seafood, lamb, nuts, pistachios, pork, sausage

Seasonings: ajwain, allspice, caraway, cardamom, chili peppers, cilantro, cinnamon, coriander seeds, cumin, dill, fennel, fenugreek, garlic, ginger, honey, horseradish, lemon juice and zest, lime juice and zest, mint, mustard, paprika, parsley, pepper, rosemary, sage, savory, sesame seeds, thyme, turmeric

In the Kitchen

Dishes: Breads, rice, curries, braises, pickles, chutneys

Prep: Dry-roast or lightly fry nigella seeds to bring out their nutty flavor. Use them whole or grind in a mortar and pestle (see pages 149–150).

Serve: Nigella is often paired with lamb, beans, potatoes, and other root vegetables. Like sesame, poppy, and caraway seeds, nigella makes a delicious spice for savory breads, and it's a common addition to Turkish varieties and Indian naan. In *panch phoron*, an Indian spice blend, nigella is lightly fried with mustard seeds, cumin, fennel, and fenugreek then added to lentil, veggie, and fish curries.

ROSE

Rosa

Flavors: sweet and floral, with fruit, mint, or spice, depending on variety

Treasured for their elegant appearance and fragrance, roses are concentrated into perfumes, lotions, and cosmetics around the world. In Middle Eastern and Indian cuisines, rose is also an important seasoning, adding delicate floral flavor to everything from pastries to marinades to rice. The petals and hips (their fruit) are often distilled to make rose water, which itself is sold as a spice in many specialty markets, along with rose oil and rose preserves.

All roses are edible, but for the best flavor, opt for varieties with the strongest fragrance. Those most frequently used in the kitchen are the damask rose (*Rosa damascena*), rugosa rose (*Rosa rugosa*), and cabbage rose (*Rosa centifolia*). Note that flower shop roses contain dangerous pesticides and are intended for ornamental use only.

> **HEALTH BENEFITS**
> Rose hips are loaded with vitamin C, the powerful antioxidant prized for its effects on the immune system. Prepared as a tea, both petals and hips can help protect against cold and flu. Roses lose some of their nutritional value when dried, so use fresh if you're looking for optimal health benefits.

In the Garden

There are more than 100 species of rose. Some grow into bushy shrubs, while others climb around fences and trellises. Shrub roses will grow successfully in containers; choose a deep pot to make room for the lengthy roots. Healthy roses largely depend on climate. Choose flowers that will grow easily in your region while also providing optimal fragrance and flavor in the kitchen. Always wear protective gloves when handling prickly roses, and invest in safety goggles for protection while pruning.

Size: Shrubs, up to 8 feet tall and 3 feet wide; climbing roses, up to 20 feet tall and 6 feet wide

Container: Half barrel, about 15 gallons; smaller or larger depending on variety

Light: Full sun

Soil: Moist, rich, loose, well drained. Mix compost or mulch into the soil around the roses to retain moisture, prevent weeds, and add nutrients.

Plant: Cuttings

Water: Regularly and thoroughly, to keep the soil and deep roots consistently moist but not soaking; at least two waterings per week in hot summers

Harvest: Rose petals are ready for harvest when just freshly opened. If growing for the hips, let the flowers die away so the hips can develop. Harvest hips when they are bright red or orange and become soft and slightly wrinkled. Wait until after the first frost in fall for the best flavor.

Care: Prune in springtime. If growing for the petals, snip dead flowers regularly to promote new growth. To prepare for a cold winter season, stop pruning in the fall.

PAIRINGS

Fruits and Vegetables: apples, apricots, carrots, cherries, lemons, oranges, raspberries, rhubarb, strawberries, tomatoes

Proteins: almonds, cheeses, chicken, lamb, pecans, pistachios, walnuts

Seasonings: basil, cardamom, chili peppers, cinnamon, cloves, coriander seeds, cumin, ginger, honey, lavender, lemon juice and zest, lime juice and zest, mint, nutmeg, pepper, rose geranium, saffron, turmeric, vanilla

Keep It Fresh

Don't wash fresh-picked rose petals, as the water will cause them to brown. To dry petals and hips, spread them over a flat surface and dry in a shady spot with good air circulation; you can also use an oven or dehydrator.

To remove the prickly hairs inside the rose hips, grind them coarsely in a food processor and pour through a sieve to filter out the hairs. Store dried petals and hips in a cool, dark, dry location.

In the Kitchen

Dishes: baked sweets, preserves, syrups, ice cream, sorbet, pudding, marinades, sauces, teas

Prep: Petals and hips can be used fresh, dried, whole, or ground in any dish. Infuse petals in boiling water to make rose water.

Serve: Store rose petals in a sugar container to make a delicious rose sugar for baking. Or infuse them into cream or milk for use in custards, puddings, and ice cream. Rose-infused honey is a delicious addition to teas, jams, and fruity desserts. Candied petals make beautiful edible cake decorations, while crushed petals can be sprinkled over yogurt, salads, and soups. Add ground petals to savory spice blends.

SAFFRON

Crocus sativus

Flavors: rich, warm, earthy, slightly bitter

Saffron is as coveted for its flavor as it is for its deep red-orange color, historically used to dye the robes of Buddhist monks. Today, the spice is revered for its role in authentic Italian risotto, Spanish paella, and, of course, saffron rice. It's also the most expensive spice in the world, thanks to the painstaking manual labor involved in its production.

Native to Turkey, most saffron is produced in Iran, India, Spain, and Greece. Saffron "threads" are the stigmas of the saffron crocus, a purple flower that remains dormant all summer, only to bloom for about two weeks in the fall. The stigmas are carefully removed by hand. It takes between 70,000 and 80,000 flowers to yield only one pound of dried saffron.

To avoid wasting money on imposter saffron, look for threads that are uniform in shape and color: a very deep red with one yellowish end and one fluted end. A great rule of thumb is to check the price tag. If it sounds like you're getting a good deal, it's probably not saffron.

HEALTH BENEFITS

Historically, saffron has been used to treat digestive problems, insomnia, anxiety, and skin irritation. The spice contains carotenoids such as crocin, the chemical responsible for its golden-red hue, which offer antioxidant effects that can help stave off disease and boost immunity.

In the Garden

Grown from a bulb, or "corm," the saffron crocus is actually fairly easy to care for; it's the harvest that requires work. In its first year, each corm will yield just one flower with three stigmas, but your harvest will get larger each year. The saffron crocus, a perennial, grows healthily in temperate climates. It needs a moist spring and a dry, dormant summer, after which it finally sends up its flower in fall.

Size: 4 to 6 inches tall

Container: 10 inches deep

Light: Full sun

Soil: Rich, well drained. Mix compost into the soil and add mulch to improve drainage and provide added nutrients.

Plant: Bulbs or "corms," 3 to 5 inches deep, with point facing upward

Water: Soak thoroughly after planting the corms. Water regularly in spring, about 1 inch per week; don't water in summer when the plants are dormant.

Harvest: Flowers typically bloom 6 to 8 weeks after planting, in fall, and last for 1 to 2 weeks. (However, sometimes they'll take a full year to flower.) To harvest, pick the flower and gently pluck the 3 stigmas.

Care: In cold climates, dig up the corms after the first light frosts and bring them indoors for the winter; you can also sow them in containers to make this easier. Store them in a cool, dark spot, like a basement or garage, and bring them back outside in spring. After 4 to 6 years, dig up the corms, divide them into smaller batches, and replant.

> ### SUBSTITUTIONS
> - Marigold petals
> - Annatto seeds
> - Turmeric

PAIRINGS

Fruits and Vegetables: apples, artichoke, carrots, cauliflower, celery, fennel bulb, leeks, lemons, onions, oranges, peas, peppers, potatoes, shallots, tomatoes

Proteins: almonds, beans, cashews, cheeses, chicken, fish and seafood, lamb, pistachios, sausage

Seasonings: basil, bay leaf, cardamom, cilantro, cinnamon, cloves, coriander seeds, cumin, garlic, ginger, honey, lemon juice, paprika, parsley, rosemary, thyme, turmeric

Keep It Fresh

The drying process is crucial in developing saffron's signature flavor and color. Dry saffron threads completely in a dark, dry location for several days. They should feel brittle and crumble easily.

In the Kitchen

Dishes: rice, soups, stews

Prep: A pinch of saffron (between 10 to 20 threads) adds plenty of flavor to any dish. To activate saffron's color and flavor for cooking, infuse the threads in a small amount of hot water for at least 10 minutes. Bright-yellow color will seep into the liquid. If adding saffron to a pan of cooking liquids, just use the dry threads, and their essence will permeate into the pan as they heat up. For dishes without liquids, dry-roast the threads briefly beforehand and grind them.

Serve: Saffron is added to many European stews and soups. It also brings earthy complexity to sweet dishes. Use very sparingly; too much will ruin a dish with bitterness.

SICHUAN PEPPER

Zanthoxylum simulans

Flavors: peppery, woody, tangy, with slight citrus

These reddish-brown berries are unrelated to the common black pepper (*Piper nigrum*) and chili pepper (*Capsicum*), and they offer a flavor all their own. With subtle lemon and a light tongue-tingling effect, Sichuan pepper adds complexity and mild heat to many dishes from its namesake region of China, which is famous for its fiery spices.

Grown on prickly ash trees, the berries open when dried and their bitter, sandy seeds are removed; only the husks are ground and used in cooking. Sichuan pepper—*hua jiao*, or "flower pepper," in Mandarin and *faa jiu* in Cantonese—is an integral ingredient in Chinese five-spice powder (see page 250), frequently used in traditional "red-cooked," or braised, dishes.

The leaves of another prickly ash, *Zanthoxylym piperitem*, are also harvested. Called *kinome*, these leaves are dried and powdered to create *sancho*, a spice used in Japanese cooking that's essential to shichimi togarashi, or Japanese seven-spice powder (see page 250).

HEALTH BENEFITS

Like other hot spices, Sichuan pepper stimulates digestion starting from the moment it enters your mouth, triggering the release of saliva and other gastric juices. It's also known to prevent and relieve gas and cramps. The bark of the prickly ash tree was used historically to soothe toothaches, thanks to its signature numbing effect; this earned it the nickname "toothache tree."

In the Garden

As perennials grown in temperate climates in China, Japan, and the Himalayas, prickly ash trees are dioecious, or single-sexed, meaning they need both male and female specimens in order to bear fruit. However, a couple trees will produce tasty peppercorns for many years. Handle them with care: The trunk, branches, and twigs are lined with spines or thorns. They're not called "prickly" for nothing!

Size: 6 to 20 feet tall, about 15 feet wide

Container: At least 15 gallons

Light: Full sun to partial shade

Soil: Moist, well drained; adaptable to various well-draining soils. Add mulch to the site to prevent the growth of weeds.

Plant: Cuttings or young plants; seeds require stratification, and sometimes scarification to germinate, as well as several years to mature into fruit-bearing trees

Water: Regularly, to keep the soil consistently moist

Harvest: Berries are ready for harvest in the fall, usually in October, when they're reddish-brown. Snip off bunches from the stems.

PAIRINGS

Vegetables: eggplant, green beans, mushrooms, onions

Proteins: beans, beef, chicken, duck, eggs, pork

Seasonings: allspice, bay leaf, chili peppers, cloves, coriander seeds, fennel seeds, garlic, ginger, juniper berries, lemon juice, paprika, parsley, pepper, poppy seeds, rosemary, sage, scallions, sesame seeds, sesame oil, soy sauce, star anise, thyme

Keep It Fresh

Dry fresh berries in the sun or in any dry location for a couple days. They should split open while drying. If the berries are still closed, open them by lightly crushing the husks using a mortar and pestle, and remove the seeds. A rolling pin gently worked over the closed berries will also do the trick. Store the split husks in an airtight container.

In the Kitchen

Dishes: Stir-fries, braises, marinades, sauces, rubs, noodles, rice

Prep: Inspect dried berries for stray seeds, stems, and thorns, and discard any you find. They should be dry-roasted before cooking to release their flavor (see page 150). Grind using a mortar and pestle or an electric spice grinder, and sift out any remaining stems and husks. Berries begin losing flavor after they're ground, so grind only small batches at a time.

Serve: In Chinese cooking, Sichuan pepper is most frequently partnered with chili peppers, star anise, and ginger. The Sichuan pepper–chili pepper combo is beloved for its own distinct flavor, called *ma la*, or "numbing spicy." *Ma* is the numbing Sichuan pepper and *la* is the spicy chili. Ground Sichuan pepper is also often combined with salt and black pepper to make a dry rub for beef or chicken. It's a natural complement to fatty meats like pork and duck.

STAR ANISE

Illicium verum

Flavors: pungent, sweet, intensely anise-like, with cloves and cassia

This beautiful, star-shaped spice is the fruit of an evergreen magnolia tree native to China and Vietnam. While it looks like a delicate sculpted ornament—a star with eight points cradling glossy, brown seeds—star anise offers pungent, warm flavor.

Its strong anise essence ties it to similarly flavored spices, like anise and fennel, but it's related to neither. Star anise does, however, share a chemical with other anise seasonings: anethole, which is used to flavor candy, gum, and liqueurs like ouzo and pastis. In addition to its intense licorice flavor, star anise also leaves a slightly numb feeling on the tongue, and its seeds are edible and somewhat nutty, though less flavorful than the woody star itself.

In the Garden

Star anise, a perennial, grows in tropical and subtropical climates, so a greenhouse or a warm spot indoors will be necessary in cooler regions. The trees often begin fruiting after 6 years, but might take even longer. Once they're in the fruiting stage, however, it's believed they can continue producing for 100 years. The unripe star anise fruits are harvested while still green and fleshy, and then dried in the sun, where they harden, develop their flavor, and turn a dark, woody brown.

Size: 25 to 45 feet tall

Container: 3 to 5 gallons for seedlings; transplant to a larger container (at least 15 gallons) after 3 years

HEALTH BENEFITS

Star anise has been used traditionally to aid digestion and relieve gas, its shiny seeds chewed to stimulate gastric juices and freshen breath. It also contains powerful antibacterial and antifungal compounds, and is being researched for its antioxidant properties. Star anise is a rich source of shikimic acid, an important chemical used in the anti-flu medication Tamiflu. The spice is also believed to relieve respiratory conditions like cough, bronchitis, and congestion. Chinese star anise should not be confused with the variety from Japan, *Illicium anisatum,* which is highly toxic.

Light: Full sun
Soil: Moist, rich, well drained
Plant: Cuttings or seeds. Seeds must be fresh in order to germinate, within a few days of harvesting.
Water: Regularly, to keep the soil consistently moist
Harvest: Seedlings take about 3 years to develop into larger trees, at which point they should be transplanted to their permanent site. After at least 6 years, when the fruits appear and grow to about 1 inch in size, they should be ready for harvest, still green and unripe.
Care: Weed regularly and add mulch for nutrients. After the first harvest, healthy trees usually fruit 3 times per year, providing spice all year long.

> **SUBSTITUTIONS**
> • Anise seed + a pinch of allspice
> • 1 star anise fruit = ½ teaspoon anise seed
> • Chinese five-spice powder

PAIRINGS

Fruits and Vegetables: carrots, leeks, lemons, onions, oranges, pears, pumpkin, shallots, tomatoes
Proteins: almonds, beef, chicken, duck, fish and seafood, pork
Seasonings: allspice, basil, cardamom, cassia, chili peppers, cilantro, cinnamon, cloves, coriander seeds, cumin, fennel, fish sauce, garlic, ginger, honey, lemon juice and zest, nutmeg, pepper, sesame seeds, Sichuan pepper, soy sauce, vanilla

Keep It Fresh

Fresh-picked star anise is dried in the sun until brown and hard. The seeds sometimes pop out during drying.

Store whole or broken fruits in an airtight container in a cool, dark, dry location, where it will stay fresh for about a year. Ground star anise should be stored the same way for up to 3 months. To check freshness, smell the spice for its trademark licorice fragrance.

In the Kitchen

Dishes: soups, stocks, stir-fries, marinades, braises, rice, curries, liqueurs, syrups, fruit compotes
Prep: Use fruits whole or break into chunks; remove before serving. Though hard, star anise can be ground (with seeds) using a mortar and pestle or an electric grinder. For the ground spice, consider buying small amounts from a shop.
Serve: In Chinese cuisine, star anise is a staple spice for soups, fatty meats, and traditional "red-cooking" or braising. It's also essential in Vietnamese pho. Its warm licorice flavor also naturally lends itself to sweet dishes, as it's most commonly used in the West. Use very sparingly; a couple star anise fruits will flavor an entire dish.

SUMAC

Rhus coriaria

Flavors: tart, fruity, tangy, with citrus

While many are familiar with poison sumac (*Toxicodendron vernix*), which grows wild in regions throughout North America, sumac the spice is completely safe and completely delicious. Grown from a shrub native to Iran, deep-red sumac berries emerge upright in beautiful, jewel-like clusters. When ripe, each berry is covered with fine red hairs; they're sun-dried and ground to a reddish-brown powder for use in cooking. The berries of poison sumac are white and bear little resemblance to the spice.

With its citrus-like acidity, sumac is used in Middle Eastern dishes much like lemon juice is used in Western cooking— to add sour, tangy flavor to a wide variety of savory dishes, from salads to meats to breads. It's an integral spice in traditional za'atar (see page 251) and in the classic Lebanese salad known as *fattoush*.

> **HEALTH BENEFITS**
> Considered a medicinal spice throughout history, sumac has been used to treat a range of conditions, including digestive upset and cold, cough, and flu. More recent research has implied an even greater role in human health: Sumac is remarkably high in antioxidants, which can help prevent or postpone symptoms of aging, including age-related degenerative conditions as well as heart disease and cancer.

In the Garden

There are around 250 species of sumac, with only a handful that bear edible berries. Common edible varieties seen in the United States are the staghorn sumac (*Rhus typhina*), smooth sumac (*Rhus glabra*), and the shorter fragrant sumac (*Rhus aromatica*), which grows low to the ground. In addition to their white flowers and scarlet berries, deciduous shrubs and trees often showcase dazzling leaf color in the fall. They're easy to grow in the garden and in containers, and adaptable to various climate conditions. However, sumac plants are dioecious, or single-sexed, meaning they need both male and female specimens in order to bear fruit.

Size: Varies according to species; common varieties range from 6 to 15 feet tall

Container: Depends on species size
Light: Full sun to partial shade
Soil: Dry to medium, well drained; adaptable to various well-draining soils
Plant: Root suckers or young plants; seeds require stratification and scarification in order to germinate.
Water: Occasionally and moderately, more frequently in hot summer weather and during drought; somewhat drought tolerant
Harvest: In the fall, when berries are bright and covered with fine hairs, they're ready for harvest. Snip off clusters at the base of the stem.

SUBSTITUTIONS
- Lemon juice
- Lemon zest + salt
- Vinegar

PAIRINGS
Vegetables: avocado, carrots, cucumber, eggplant, lettuce, onions, peppers, potatoes, tomatoes, zucchini
Proteins: beans, beef, chicken, chickpeas, fish and seafood, lamb, lentils, pine nuts, walnuts
Seasonings: allspice, chili peppers, coriander seeds, cumin, garlic, ginger, lemon juice and zest, mint, oregano, paprika, parsley, pepper, rosemary, sesame seeds, thyme

Keep It Fresh

Dry fresh berries in the sun or in the oven for several days. Store whole dried berries in an airtight container for up to a year. Ground sumac will stay fresh for a few months.

To extract juice from the berries and store it for future use, infuse fresh berries in water for several hours or overnight.

In the Kitchen

Dishes: Marinades, rubs, dressings, salads, breads, stews, stuffings, beverages
Prep: To infuse sumac flavor into marinades, dressings, and beverages, lightly crush or crack open the berries, then soak in water for up to 30 minutes. Strain and squeeze any remaining juice out of the berries, then use as needed. Or, grind whole berries to a powder using a food processor. The goal is to separate the dried red flesh and skin from the berries' seeds and stems, so use the processor on low power until the red sumac detaches from the yellow seeds. Run the powder through a sieve to remove any hard bits. Include as much flesh and skin as possible for the best sumac flavor.

Serve: Sumac can be used in place of lemon juice; it's the perfect dry alternative when less liquid is needed. Sprinkle it over salads, hummus, and yogurt dips. Sumac makes a tasty rub for grilled meats. It's a common seasoning for lamb kebabs and pairs just as well with chicken and fish.

TAMARIND

Tamarindus indica

Flavors: tart, acidic, fruity, sweet

Tamarind is a brown, sticky pulp found inside the seedpods of a large evergreen tree. Also known as "date of India," or *tamr-al-hindi* in Arabic, it is native to eastern Africa, grows wild in India, and is cultivated in tropical climates across the globe.

A common ingredient in Indian and Southeast Asian cuisines, tamarind brings acidity and sour flavor to the signature spicy dishes of those regions. When ripe, the pulp is removed from its brittle pod and molded into blocks or slabs, sometimes with its fibers and seeds still included. It's also sold as tamarind paste and concentrate—a thick syrup without the fibers and seeds—as well as dried powder. Tamarind extract is a key ingredient in Worcestershire sauce.

HEALTH BENEFITS

Tamarind may help boost the digestive system and offer mild laxative effects, thanks to its dietary fiber content. This fiber is also known to help lower blood sugar and regulate appetite, making tamarind a healthy substitute for refined sugar. Believed to lower cholesterol levels and improve liver function, tamarind also contains vitamin C and beta-carotene, two powerful antioxidants that can help stave off signs of aging and boost immunity.

In the Garden

The tamarind tree thrives in tropical and subtropical climates. Grown from seed, a tree can take 8 years to bear fruit, while a grafted tree will fruit in a fraction of that.

Size: 40 to 60 feet tall (rarely, up to 100 feet), 25 to 30 feet wide

Container: 1 to 2 feet in diameter and 20 inches deep, depending on tree size

Light: Full sun to filtered sun

Soil: Dry to moist, well drained; adaptable to various well-draining soils

Plant: Seeds, cuttings, or grafted trees; grafted trees are quickest to fruit.

Water: Regularly and thoroughly after sowing and for the first few years, when the soil feels dry 1 inch deep; decrease during seedling stage, then water only occasionally or not at all when mature; drought tolerant.

Harvest: After at least 1 year for grafted trees or 6 years for seedlings, the ripe seedpods are ready for harvest in spring or summer. They can be harvested while still green and unripe, but the unripe fruit is intensely tart rather than sweet. If left on the tree for several months, the seedpods will dry out and develop sweeter flavor. They should be brown, brittle, and sound hollow when knocked with a finger.

Care: Protect from winds and cold temperatures. Prune occasionally to discard decaying or damaged branches.

SUBSTITUTIONS
- Lime juice + brown sugar
- Amchoor powder
- Sumac

PAIRINGS

Fruits and Vegetables: apples, cabbage, carrots, coconut, cucumber, dates, lemons, mangoes, mushrooms, onions, peas, peppers, pineapple, potatoes, raisins, shallots, tomatoes

Proteins: beans, beef, cashews, chicken, duck, fish and seafood, lamb, lentils, nuts, pork

Seasonings: asafetida, chili peppers, cilantro, cinnamon, cloves, coriander seeds, cumin, curry powder, fennel, fenugreek, fish sauce, galangal, garam masala, garlic, ginger, honey, lemon juice and zest, lemongrass, lime juice and zest, mint, mustard, paprika, saffron, sesame seeds, soy sauce, Thai basil, turmeric

In the Kitchen

Dishes: curries, stews, marinades, sauces, dressings, preserves, chutneys

Prep: If using whole dried pods, crack open the hard shell, separate the stringy fibers from the pulp, and remove the seeds. If using a block of tamarind, cut off a 1-inch piece (or less) for any one dish. To make tamarind liquid for use in cooking, soak the pulp in hot water; stir and press with a spoon to soften it, and let sit for 20 minutes. Strain, squeeze the pulp to wring out any remaining liquid, and discard seeds, fibers, and dried pulp. If using tamarind concentrate, dilute with about 2 teaspoons of water before adding to a dish.

Serve: Tamarind will swap in for lemon juice or zest in any recipe. It's a natural addition to jams, syrups, and candies, thanks to its dried-fruit texture and sweet-tart flavor. But it shines most often in hot dishes with other Asian flavors. Its acidity is particularly useful in marinades for beef, where it tenderizes the meat while adding flavor. Tamarind adds tang to chutneys and pickles, and puts the "sour" in classic hot-and-sour soup.

TURMERIC

Curcuma longa

Flavors: **fresh** *warm, earthy, with citrus;* **dried** *pungent, warm, earthy, musky, slightly bitter*

Peel away the drab brown skin of the turmeric rhizome, and its glowing, golden-yellow flesh reveals a versatile spice that's invaluable in every Indian kitchen. Related to that other famous rhizome, ginger, turmeric is used for both its color and its flavor, which tends to fuse and enhance other flavors in a dish. Turmeric's bright hue is used to dye many foods sold in the West, including mustards, cheeses, dressings, and soups.

Most often sold as a dried powder, the spice can be used in both fresh and dried forms. Only buy powdered turmeric in small quantities, as the flavor dissipates quickly after grinding.

> ## HEALTH BENEFITS
> Turmeric is believed to be one of the healthiest spices in the world, thanks to its remarkable antiseptic, anti-inflammatory, and antioxidant properties. It's often prescribed to help treat inflammatory conditions like arthritis, Crohn's disease, and ulcerative colitis. One of its main compounds, curcumin, is a powerful antioxidant; turmeric and curcumin are being studied for their potential in preventing degenerative conditions like heart disease, Alzheimer's, and various cancers.

In the Garden
Turmeric rhizomes need 8 to 10 months of growth in a warm, humid environment before they're ready for harvest. In cooler climates, they can be grown in containers and brought indoors in winter, when they're dormant. A perennial in hot climates, turmeric can survive the winter outdoors and will start growing again the following spring.

Size: Up to 3 feet tall

Container: At least 12 inches deep and wide

Light: Full sun to partial shade

Soil: Moist, rich, well drained. Mix compost into the soil for added nutrients.

Plant: Whole rhizomes or smaller sections with at least one bud. Soak in water overnight before planting. Sow with bud-end up, just under the surface of the soil.

Water: Regularly, to keep the soil consistently moist, especially in hot climates; less frequently in cooler climates. Mist with water using a spray bottle to simulate the humidity in the tropics.

Harvest: After 8 to 10 months, the rhizomes are ready for harvest. Simply dig up the soil and lift them out. If you're not harvesting everything for the year, break off the parts you need and replant the rest.

Care: Place a thick layer of mulch over the site for protection from cold weather. In regions that experience hard freezes, they should be dug up and moved indoors for the season.

SUBSTITUTIONS
- Curry powder
- Mustard powder
- Saffron or annatto (for color)

PAIRINGS

Vegetables: carrots, cauliflower, onions, peas, peppers, potatoes, shallots, tomatoes

Proteins: almonds, beans, cashews, chicken, eggs, fish and seafood, lamb, lentils

Seasonings: cardamom, chili peppers, cilantro, cinnamon, cloves, coriander seeds, cumin, dill, fenugreek, galangal, garam masala, garlic, ginger, lemongrass, lemon juice, makrut lime, mustard, paprika, parsley, pepper, tamarind

Keep It Fresh

Wrap fresh turmeric rhizome in paper towels and store in a plastic bag in the refrigerator's crisper for up to 2 weeks. For longer freshness, slice, chop, or mince and store in the freezer.

To dry, fresh rhizomes should be boiled for one hour, then peeled and sliced into smaller sections, and dried in the sun for 15 days. For quicker drying, slice the rhizome into thin coins (less then ¼ inch thick). Spread onto a baking sheet and bake on your oven's lowest temperature setting, 130° to 150°F. Keep the oven door open to ensure the lowest amount of heat.

In the Kitchen

Dishes: Curries, lentils, stews, braises, sautés, stir-fries, rice

Prep: Whenever handling, wear gloves and an apron to protect your skin and clothes from pesky stains. Grated or powdered dried turmeric is often used in cooking, but fresh is also simple to prepare: Peel the fresh rhizome, then chop, slice, or grate.

Serve: Turmeric is an essential spice in curries and stews, where it's paired with virtually any kind of meat as well as classic Indian flavors like cumin, coriander seeds, and ginger.

HERB & SPICE BLENDS

AFRICA

Berbere (Ethiopia): dried hot chili peppers, peppercorns, fenugreek seeds, cardamom, coriander seeds, ajwain, nigella, cumin, allspice, cloves, ground ginger, cinnamon

Qâlat Daqqa, or Tunisian Five-Spice Blend: peppercorns, cloves, grains of paradise, cinnamon, nutmeg

Ras el Hanout (Morocco): can contain more than 20 spices, typically including cardamom, cumin, cloves, cassia, cinnamon, allspice, nutmeg, chili peppers, coriander seeds, peppercorns, grains of paradise, paprika, fenugreek seeds, turmeric, ground ginger

ASIA

Chinese Five-Spice Powder: star anise, Sichuan peppers, fennel seeds, cloves, cassia or cinnamon

Shichimi Togarashi, or Japanese Seven-Spice Powder: white sesame seeds, black sesame seeds, hemp seeds (or poppy seeds), powdered dried tangerine peel, nori flakes, hot chili flakes, sansho, ginger

EUROPE

Bouquet Garni: fresh or dried herbs tied into bundles or sachets; parsley, thyme, marjoram, bay leaves; sometimes oregano, savory, sage, rosemary, and tarragon

Fines Herbes: fresh chervil, parsley, tarragon, chives, marjoram

Herbes de Provence: fresh or dried basil, bay leaf, hyssop, chervil, marjoram, fennel seeds, lavender flowers, oregano, rosemary, sage, summer savory, tarragon, thyme

Italian Seasoning: dried basil, oregano, rosemary, thyme, garlic powder or flakes

Quatre Épices: black or white peppercorns, cloves, nutmeg, ground ginger

INDIA

Chaat Masala: amchoor, asafetida, cumin, black peppercorns, ajwain, dried mint, chili powder, coriander seeds

Curry Powder: cumin, fenugreek seeds, coriander seeds, hot chili peppers, turmeric, mustard seeds, black peppercorns, ground ginger, cinnamon, cloves, cardamom, dried red chili peppers

Garam Masala: black cardamom, cinnamon, coriander seeds, cumin, black peppercorns; sometimes sesame seeds, fennel seeds, ajwain, hot chili peppers, green cardamom, mace, and ginger

THE MIDDLE EAST

Zhug (Yemeni paste): fresh green or red chili peppers (seeds removed to reduce heat), garlic, coriander seeds, cardamom, cilantro, cumin, black peppercorns

Hilbeh (Yemeni dip): fenugreek seeds, cilantro, garlic, ground black pepper, cardamom, caraway seeds, green chili peppers (seeds removed), lemon juice

Za'atar: dried ground oregano, thyme, marjoram, dry-roasted sesame seeds, ground sumac

---

TIP

Za'atar is both an herb blend and an individual herb on its own: *Origanum syriacum*. Za'atar the herb can be used in place of oregano, thyme, and marjoram in the blend. Combine the blend with olive oil to form a paste.

LATIN AMERICA AND THE CARIBBEAN

Adobo: oregano, garlic, black peppercorns, turmeric

Jerk Seasoning (Jamaica): allspice, cinnamon, brown sugar, red chili flakes, cloves, cumin, black peppercorns, thyme, dried parsley, garlic powder

Recado Rojo (Mexico and Belize): annatto seeds, coriander seeds, cumin, black peppercorns, cloves, Mexican oregano, crushed garlic; sometimes cinnamon, allspice

NORTH AMERICA

BBQ Seasoning: garlic powder (or finely chopped garlic), paprika, black peppercorns, cumin, thyme, cayenne, mustard powder, brown sugar

Cajun Seasoning: paprika, black peppercorns, cayenne, fennel seeds, cumin, garlic powder (or crushed garlic), onion flakes, oregano, thyme

BIBLIOGRAPHY

BOOKS

Balick, Michael J., PhD. *Rodale's 21st Century Herbal: A Practical Guide for Healthy Living Using Nature's Most Powerful Plants*. New York: Rodale, 2014.

Bharadwaj, Monisha. *The Indian Spice Kitchen: A Book of Essential Ingredients with Over 200 Easy and Authentic Recipes*. New York: Hippocrene Books, 2000.

Boning, Charles. *Florida's Best Herbs & Spices: Native and Exotic Plants Grown for Scent and Flavor*. Sarasota, Florida: Pineapple Press, Inc., 2010.

Brickell, Christopher, ed. *American Horticultural Society Encyclopedia of Plants & Flowers*. London: DK Publishing, 2011.

Castleman, Michael. *The New Healing Herbs: The Essential Guide to More Than 125 of Nature's Most Potent Herbal Remedies*. New York: Rodale, 2010.

Farooqi, Azhar Ali, B. S. Sreeramu, and K. N. Srinivasappa. *Cultivation of Spice Crops*. India: Universities Press India Private Limited. Orient Blackswan [Distributor], 2005.

Grieve, Maud. *A Modern Herbal: The Medicinal, Culinary, Cosmetic, and Economic Properties, Cultivation and Folk-lore of Herbs, Grasses, Fungi, Shrubs, and Trees with All Their Modern Scientific Uses*. Mineola, New York: Dover Publications, 1931, 1971. Electronic version.

Guerra, Michael. *The Edible Container Garden: Growing Fresh Food in Small Spaces*. New York: Fireside/Simon & Schuster, 2000.

Hawkins, Kathryn and Marcus A. Webb. *The Herb and Spice Companion: A Connoisseur's Guide*. Philadelphia: Running Press, 2007.

Hemphill, Ian and Kate Hemphill. *The Spice and Herb Bible*, 3rd Edition. Toronto: Robert Rose, Inc., 2014.

Hsiung, Deh-Ta and Ken Hom. *The Chinese Kitchen: A Book of Essential Ingredients with Over 200 Easy and Authentic Recipes*. New York: St. Martin's Press, 2002.

Lim, T. K. *Edible Medicinal and Non-Medicinal Plants*, Vol. 5, Fruits. Netherlands: Springer Science & Business Media, 2013. Google ebook: books.google.com/books?id=_ZZEAAAAQBAJ

McVicar, Jekka. *Grow Herbs: An Inspiring Guide to Growing and Using Herbs*. London: DK Publishing, 2010. Google ebook: books.google.com/books?id=HIrL5qtBUtgC

Miloradovich, Milo. *Growing and Using Herbs and Spices*. Mineola, NY: Dover Publications, 1986, 2012. Google ebook: books.google.com/books?id=mARfLt03NRYC

Murray, Michael T., N.D., Joseph Pizzorno, N.D., and Lara Pizzorno. *The Encyclopedia of Healing Foods*. New York: Atria Books, 2005.

Norman, Jill. *Herbs & Spices: The Cook's Reference*. London: DK Publishing, 2002.

Peter, K. V., ed. *Handbook of Herbs & Spices*, 2nd Edition. Cambridge, UK: Woodhead Publishing, 2012. Google ebook: books.google.com/books?id=2I9wAgAAQBAJ

Pleasant, Barbara. *The Whole Herb: For Cooking, Crafts, Gardening, Health, and Other Joys of Life*. Garden City Park, New York: Square One Publishers, 2004.

Raghavan, Susheela. *Handbook of Spices, Seasonings, and Flavorings*, 2nd Edition. Boca Raton, Florida: CRC Press/Taylor & Francis, 2006. Google ebook: books.google.com/books?id=m4vvs87XiucC

Ravindran, P. N., K. Nirmal-Babu, and M. Shylaja, eds. *Cinnamon and Cassia: The Genus Cinnamomum*. Boca Raton, Florida: CRC Press/Taylor & Francis, 2005. Google ebook: books.google.com/books?id=KZa8aPxR_-wC

Schafer, Peg. *The Chinese Medicinal Herb Farm: A Cultivator's Guide to Small-Scale Organic Herb Production*. White River Junction, Vermont: Chelsea Green Publishing, 2011.

Singh, Dueep J., and John Davidson. *The Magic of Asafetida for Cooking and Healing*. Mendon, Utah: JD-Biz Publishing, 2014. Google ebook: books.google.com/books?id=QhoABQAAQBAJ

Small, Ernest. *Culinary Herbs*, 2nd edition. Ottawa: National Research Council of Canada, NRC Research Press, 2006.

Smith, Edward C. *The Vegetable Gardener's Container Bible*. North Adams, Massachusetts: Storey Publishing, 2009. Google ebook: books.google.com/books?id=Uayl-LiU93AC

Sterling, David. Yucatán: *Recipes from a Culinary Expedition*. Austin: University of Texas Press, 2014.

Tucker, Arthur O., and Thomas DeBaggio. *The Encyclopedia of Herbs: A Comprehensive Reference to Herbs of Flavor and Fragrance*. Portland, Oregon: Timber Press, 2009.

van Wyk, Ben-Erik. *Culinary Herbs and Spices of the World*. Chicago: University of Chicago Press, 2013. Google ebook: books.google.com/books?id=WEPbAwAAQBAJ

Weiss, E. A. *Spice Crops*. New York: CABI Publishing, 2002.

ARTICLES

National Center for Home Food Preservation. "How Do I Dry Herbs?" From *So Easy to Preserve*, 5th edition. 2006. Bulletin 989, Cooperative Extension Service, The University of Georgia, Athens. Revised by Elizabeth L. Andress, PhD, and Judy A. Harrison, PhD, Extension Foods Specialists. http://nchfp.uga.edu/how/dry/herbs.html

Schmidt, James C., and Dianne Noland. "Harvesting and Drying Herbs." Department of Natural Resources and Environmental Sciences, Cooperative Extension Service, University of Illinois at Urbana-Champaign College of Agricultural, Consumer, and Environmental Sciences. PDF publication. http://web.aces.uiuc.edu/vista/pdf_pubs/DRYHERBS.PDF

WEBSITES

Adventures in Spice: AdventuresInSpice.com
BBC Food: BBC.co.uk/food
Botanical Growers Network: BotanicalGrowersNetwork.net
California Rare Fruit Growers: CRFG.org
Container Gardens 101: ContainerGardens101.com
The Epicentre: TheEpicentre.com
Gardening Know How: GardeningKnowHow.com
Gourmet Sleuth: GourmetSleuth.com
GrowVeg: GrowVeg.com
Guide to Houseplants: Guide-To-Houseplants.com
The Herb Society of America: HerbSociety.org
Home Gardening Resource, Cornell University Cooperative Extension and Department of Horticulture: gardening.cce.cornell.edu
The Kitchn: TheKitchn.com

My Garden Life: MyGardenLife.com/Plant-Library
National Gardening Association (NGA): garden.org
Serious Eats, Spice Hunting: seriouseats.com/spice_hunting

ONLINE RESOURCES

SEED CATALOGS FOR HOMEGROWN HERBS

Bountiful Gardens: BountifulGardens.org
Burpee: Burpee.com
Edible Landscaping (does not ship to Canada): EdibleLandscaping.com
Fedco Seeds: FedcoSeeds.com
Horizon Herbs: HorizonHerbs.com
Johnny's Selected Seeds: JohnnySeeds.com
Mountain Valley Growers: MountainValleyGrowers.com
Nichols Garden Nursery: NicholsGardenNursery.com
Peaceful Valley Farm & Garden Supply: GrowOrganic.com
Pinetree Garden Seeds: SuperSeeds.com
R. H. Shumway's: RHShumway.com
Richters (Canada): Richters.com
Seed Savers Exchange: SeedSavers.org
Sustainable Seed Company: SustainableSeedCo.com
Territorial Seed Company: TerritorialSeed.com
Urban Farmer: UFSeeds.com

HELPFUL WEBSITES

Frontier Co-op: FrontierCoop.com
The Great American Spice Company: AmericanSpice.com
Monterey Bay Spice Company: HerbCo.com
Mountain Rose Herbs: MountainRoseHerbs.com
Penzey's, various locations in 29 states: Penzeys.com
Savory Spice Shop: SavorySpiceShop.com
Seasoned Pioneers (UK): SeasonedPioneers.com
Spiceologist: Spiceologist.com
Whole Spice: WholeSpice.com

INDEX

IMAGE CREDITS